Functional Programming in Sc

Functional Programming in Scala

PAUL CHIUSANO
RÚNAR BJARNASON

MANNING

SHELTER ISLAND

For online information and ordering of this and other Manning books, please visit
www.manning.com. The publisher offers discounts on this book when ordered in quantity.
For more information, please contact

> Special Sales Department
> Manning Publications Co.
> 20 Baldwin Road
> PO Box 761
> Shelter Island, NY 11964
> Email: orders@manning.com

Manning Publications Co.
20 Baldwin Road
PO Box 261
Shelter Island, NY 11964

Development editor:	Jeff Bleiel
Copyeditor:	Benjamin Berg
Proofreader:	Katie Tennant
Project editor:	Janet Vail
Typesetter:	Dottie Marsico
Illustrator:	Chuck Larson
Cover designer:	Irene Scala

ISBN 9781617290657
Printed in the United States of America
7 8 9 10 – EBM – 19 18 17

brief contents

v

contents

vii

foreword

Functional Programming in Scala is an intriguing title. After all, Scala is generally called a functional programming language and there are dozens of books about Scala on the market. Are all these other books missing the functional aspects of the language? To answer the question it's instructive to dig a bit deeper. What is *functional programming*? For me, it's simply an alias for "programming with functions," that is, a programming style that puts the focus on the functions in a program. What are *functions*? Here, we find a larger spectrum of definitions. While one definition often admits functions that may have side effects in addition to returning a result, pure functional programming restricts functions to be as they are in mathematics: binary relations that map arguments to results.

Scala is an impure functional programming language in that it admits impure as well as pure functions, and in that it does not try to distinguish between these categories by using different syntax or giving them different types. It shares this property with most other functional languages. It would be nice if we could distinguish pure and impure functions in Scala, but I believe we have not yet found a way to do so that is lightweight and flexible enough to be added to Scala without hesitation.

To be sure, Scala programmers are generally encouraged to use pure functions. Side effects such as mutation, I/O, or use of exceptions are not ruled out, and they can indeed come in quite handy sometimes, be it for reasons of interoperability, efficiency, or convenience. But overusing side effects is generally not considered good style by experts. Nevertheless, since impure programs are possible and even convenient to write in Scala, there is a temptation for programmers coming from a more imperative background to keep their style and not make the necessary effort to adapt to the functional mindset. In fact, it's quite possible to write Scala as if it were Java without the semicolons.

So to properly learn functional programming in Scala, should one make a detour via a pure functional language such as Haskell? Any argument in favor of this approach has been severely weakened by the appearance of *Functional Programming in Scala*.

What Paul and Rúnar do, put simply, is treat Scala as a pure functional programming language. Mutable variables, exceptions, classical input/output, and all other traces of impurity are eliminated. If you wonder how one can write useful programs without any of these conveniences, you need to read the book. Building up from first principles and extending all the way to incremental input and output, they demonstrate that, indeed, one can express every concept using only pure functions. And they show that it is not only possible, but that it also leads to beautiful code and deep insights into the nature of computation.

The book is challenging, both because it demands attention to detail and because it might challenge the way you think about programming. By reading the book and doing the recommended exercises, you will develop a better appreciation of what pure functional programming is, what it can express, and what its benefits are.

What I particularly liked about the book is that it is self-contained. It starts with the simplest possible expressions and every abstraction is explained in detail before further abstractions are built on them in turn. In a sense, the book develops an alternative Scala universe, where mutable state does not exist and all functions are pure. Commonly used Scala libraries tend to deviate a bit from this ideal; often they are based on a partly imperative implementation with a (mostly) functional interface. That Scala allows the encapsulation of mutable state in a functional interface is, in my opinion, one of its strengths. But it is a capability that is also often misused. If you find yourself using it too often, *Functional Programming in Scala* is a powerful antidote.

MARTIN ODERSKY
CREATOR OF SCALA

preface

Writing good software is hard. After years of struggling with other approaches, both of us discovered and fell in love with functional programming (FP). Though the FP approach is different, we came to appreciate how the discipline leads to a coherent, composable, and beautiful way of writing programs.

Both of us participated in the Boston Area Scala Enthusiasts, a group that met regularly in Cambridge. When the group first started, it mainly consisted of Java programmers who were looking for something better. Many expressed frustration that there wasn't a clear way to learn how to take advantage of FP in Scala. We could empathize—we had both learned FP somewhat haphazardly, by writing lots of functional code, talking to and learning from other Scala and Haskell programmers, and reading a patchwork of different articles, blog posts, and books. It felt like there should be an easier way. In April 2010 one of the group's organizers, Nermin Šerifović, suggested that we write a book specifically on the topic of FP in Scala. Based on our learning experiences, we had a clear idea of the kind of book we wanted to write, and we thought it would be quick and easy. More than four years later, we think we have created a good book. It's the book we wish had existed when we were learning functional programming.

We hope to convey in this book some of the excitement that we felt when we were first discovering FP.

acknowledgments

We would like to thank the many people who participated in the creation of this book. To Nermin Šerifović, our friend from the Boston Scala group, thank you for first planting the seed of this book in our minds.

To the amazing team at Capital IQ, thank you for your support and for bravely helping beta test the first version of the book's curriculum.

We would like to especially acknowledge Tony Morris for embarking on this journey with us. His work on the early stages of the book remains invaluable, as does his larger contribution to the practice of functional programming in Scala.

Martin, thank you for your wonderful foreword, and of course for creating this powerful language that is helping to reshape our industry.

During the book-writing process, we were grateful for the encouragement from the enthusiastic community of Scala users interested in functional programming. To our reviewers, MEAP readers, and everyone else who provided feedback or submitted bug reports and pull requests, thank you! This book would not be what it is today without your help.

Special thanks to our development editor Jeff Bleiel, our graphics editor Ben Kovitz, our technical proofreader Tom Lockney, and everyone else at Manning who helped make this a better book, including the following reviewers who read the manuscript at various stages of its development: Ashton Hepburn, Bennett Andrews, Chris Marshall, Chris Nauroth, Cody Koeninger, Dave Cleaver, Douglas Alan, Eric Torreborre, Erich W. Schreiner, Fernando Dobladez, Ionuţ G. Stan, Jeton Bacaj, Kai Gellien, Luc Duponcheel, Mark Janssen, Michael Smolyak, Ravindra Jaju, Rintcius Blok, Rod Hilton, Sebastien Nichele, Sukant Hajra, Thad Meyer, Will Hayworth, and William E. Wheeler.

Lastly, Sunita and Allison, thank you so much for your support throughout our multi-year odyssey to make this book a reality.

about this book

This is not a book about Scala. This book is an introduction to *functional programming* (FP), a radical, principled approach to writing software. We use Scala as the vehicle to get there, but you can apply the lessons herein to programming in any language. As you work through this book, our goal is for you to gain a firm grasp of functional programming concepts, become comfortable writing purely functional programs, and be able to absorb new material on the subject, beyond what we cover here.

How this book is structured

The book is organized into four parts. In part 1, we talk about exactly what functional programming is and introduce some core concepts. The chapters in part 1 give an overview of fundamental techniques like how to organize small functional programs, define purely functional data structures, handle errors, and deal with state.

Building on this foundation, part 2 is a series of tutorials on *functional design*. We work through some examples of practical functional libraries, laying bare the thought process that goes into designing them.

While working through the libraries in part 2, it will become clear to you that these libraries follow certain patterns and contain some duplication. This will highlight the need for new and higher abstractions for writing more generalized libraries, and we introduce those abstractions in part 3. These are very powerful tools for reasoning about your code. Once you master them, they hold the promise of making you extraordinarily productive as a programmer.

Part 4 then bridges the remainder of the gap towards writing real-world applications that perform I/O (like working with databases, files, or video displays) and make use of mutable state, all in a purely functional way.

Throughout the book, we rely heavily on programming exercises, carefully sequenced to help you internalize the material. To understand functional programming, it's not enough to learn the theory abstractly. You have to fire up your text editor and write some code. You have to take the theory that you have learned and put it into practice in your work.

We've also provided online notes for all the chapters. Each chapter has a section with discussion related to that chapter, along with links to further material. These chapter notes are meant to be expanded by the community of readers, and are available as an editable wiki at https://github.com/fpinscala/fpinscala/wiki.

Audience

This book is intended for readers with at least some programming experience. We had a particular kind of reader in mind while writing the book—an intermediate-level Java or C programmer who is curious about functional programming. But we believe this book is well suited for programmers coming from any language, at any level of experience.

Prior expertise is not as important as motivation and curiosity. Functional programming is a lot of fun, but it's a challenging topic. It may be especially challenging for the most experienced programmers, because it requires such a different way of thinking than they might be used to. No matter how long you have been programming, you must come prepared to be a beginner once again.

This book does not require any prior experience with Scala, but we won't spend a lot of time and space discussing Scala's syntax and language features. Instead we will introduce them as we go, with minimal ceremony, mostly as a consequence of covering other material. These introductions to Scala should be enough to get you started with the exercises. If you have further questions about the Scala language, you should supplement your reading with another book on Scala (http://scala-lang.org/documentation/books.html) or look up specific questions in the Scala language documentation (http://scala-lang.org/documentation/).

How to read this book

Although the book can be read sequentially straight through, the sequencing of the four parts is designed so that you can comfortably break between them, apply what you have learned to your own work, and then come back later for the next part. For example, the material in part 4 will make the most sense after you have a strong familiarity with the functional style of programming developed in parts 1, 2, and 3. After part 3, it may be a good idea to take a break and try getting more practice writing functional programs beyond the exercises we work on in the chapters. Of course, this is ultimately up to you.

Most chapters in this book have a similar structure. We introduce some new idea or technique, explain it with an example, and then work through a number of exercises. We *strongly* suggest that you download the exercise source code and do the exercises as you go through each chapter. Exercises, hints, and answers are all available at https://github.com/fpinscala/fpinscla. We also encourage you to visit the scala-functional

Google group (https://groups.google.com/forum/#!topic/scala-functional/) and the #fp-in-scala IRC channel on irc.freenode.net for questions and discussion.

Exercises are marked for both their difficulty and importance. We will mark exercises that we think are *hard* or that we consider to be *optional* to understanding the material. The *hard* designation is our effort to give you some idea of what to expect— it is only our guess and you may find some unmarked questions difficult and some questions marked *hard* to be quite easy. The *optional* designation is for exercises that are informative but can be skipped without impeding your ability to follow further material. The exercises have the following icons in front of them to denote whether or not they are optional:

EXERCISE 1

A filled-in square next to an exercise means the exercise is critical.

EXERCISE 2

An open square means the exercise is optional.

Examples are presented throughout the book, and they are meant to be *tried* rather than just read. Before you begin, you should have the Scala interpreter running and ready. We encourage you to experiment on your own with variations of what you see in the examples. A good way to understand something is to change it slightly and see how the change affects the outcome.

Sometimes we will show a Scala interpreter session to demonstrate the result of running or evaluating some code. This will be marked by lines beginning with the scala> prompt of the interpreter. Code that follows this prompt is to be typed or pasted into the interpreter, and the line just below will show the interpreter's response, like this:

```
scala> println("Hello, World!")
Hello, World!
```

Code conventions and downloads

All source code in listings or in text is in a fixed-width font like this to separate it from ordinary text. Keywords in Scala are set in **bold fixed-width font like this**. Code annotations accompany many of the listings, highlighting important concepts.

To download the source code for the examples in the book, the exercise code, and the chapter notes, please go to https://github.com/fpinscala/fpinscala or to the publisher's website at www.manning.com/FunctionalProgramminginScala.

Setting expectations

Although functional programming has a profound impact on the way we write software at every level, it takes time to build up to that. It's an incremental process. Don't expect to be blown away by how amazing functional programming is right in the first chapter. The principles laid out in the beginning are quite subtle, and may even seem like they're just common sense. If you think to yourself "that's something I can already do without knowing FP," then that's great! That's exactly the point. Most programmers are already doing FP to some extent, without even knowing it. Many things that most people consider to be best practices (like making a function have only a single responsibility, or making data immutable) are implied by accepting the premise of functional programming. We are simply taking the principles underlying those best practices and carrying them all the way to their logical conclusion.

It's highly likely that in reading this book, you will simultaneously learn both Scala syntax and functional programming. As a result, at first it may seem to you that the code looks very alien, the techniques are unnatural, and the exercises are brain-bending. That is perfectly normal. Do not be deterred. If you get stuck, look at the hints and answers,[1] or take your questions to the Google Group (https://groups .google.com/forum/#!topic/scala-functional/) or the IRC channel (#fp-in-scala on irc.freenode.net).

Above all, we hope that this book will be a fun and rewarding experience for you, and that functional programming makes your work easier and more enjoyable as it has done for us. This book's purpose, when all is said and done, is to help you be more productive in your work. It should make you feel less like the software you are writing is a collection of dirty hacks, and more like you are creating a thing of beauty and utility.

Author Online

Purchase of *Functional Programming in Scala* includes free access to a private web forum run by Manning Publications where you can make comments about the book, ask technical questions, and receive help from the authors and other users. To access the forum and subscribe to it, point your web browser to www.manning.com/Functional ProgramminginScala. This Author Online page provides information on how to get on the forum once you're registered, what kind of help is available, and the rules of conduct on the forum.

Manning's commitment to our readers is to provide a venue where a meaningful dialog among individual readers and between readers and the authors can take place. It's not a commitment to any specific amount of participation on the part of the authors, whose contribution to the forum remains voluntary (and unpaid).

The Author Online forum and the archives of previous discussions will be accessible from the publisher's website as long as the book is in print.

---

[1] https://github.com/fpinscala/fpinscala.

Part 1

Introduction to functional programming

We begin this book with a radical premise—that we will restrict ourselves to constructing programs using only pure functions with no side effects such as reading from files or mutating memory. This idea, of functional programming, leads to a very different way of writing programs than you may be used to. We therefore start from the very beginning, relearning how to write the simplest of programs in a functional way.

In the first chapter, we'll explain exactly what functional programming means and give you some idea of its benefits. The rest of the chapters in part 1 introduce the basic techniques for functional programming in Scala. Chapter 2 introduces Scala the language and covers fundamentals like how to write loops functionally and manipulate functions as ordinary values. Chapter 3 deals with in-memory data structures that may change over time. Chapter 4 talks about handling errors in pure functions, and chapter 5 introduces the notion of nonstrictness, which can be used to improve the efficiency and modularity of functional code. Finally, chapter 6 introduces modeling stateful programs using pure functions.

The intent of this first part of the book is to get you thinking about programs purely in terms of functions from inputs to outputs, and to teach you the techniques you'll need in part 2, when we start writing some practical code.

What is functional programming?

Functional programming (FP) is based on a simple premise with far-reaching implications: we construct our programs using only *pure functions*—in other words, functions that have no *side effects*. What are side effects? A function has a side effect if it does something other than simply return a result, for example:

- Modifying a variable
- Modifying a data structure in place
- Setting a field on an object
- Throwing an exception or halting with an error
- Printing to the console or reading user input
- Reading from or writing to a file
- Drawing on the screen

We'll provide a more precise definition of side effects later in this chapter, but consider what programming would be like without the ability to do these things, or with significant restrictions on when and how these actions can occur. It may be difficult to imagine. How is it even possible to write useful programs at all? If we can't reassign variables, how do we write simple programs like loops? What about working with data that changes, or handling errors without throwing exceptions? How can we write programs that must perform I/O, like drawing to the screen or reading from a file?

The answer is that functional programming is a restriction on *how* we write programs, but not on *what* programs we can express. Over the course of this book, we'll learn how to express *all* of our programs without side effects, and that includes programs that perform I/O, handle errors, and modify data. We'll learn how following the discipline of FP is tremendously beneficial because of the increase in *modularity* that we gain from programming with pure functions. Because of their modularity, pure functions are easier to test, reuse, parallelize, generalize, and reason about. Furthermore, pure functions are much less prone to bugs.

In this chapter, we'll look at a simple program with side effects and demonstrate some of the benefits of FP by removing these side effects. We'll also discuss the benefits of FP more generally and define two important concepts—*referential transparency* and the *substitution model.*

1.1 The benefits of FP: a simple example

Let's look at an example that demonstrates some of the benefits of programming with pure functions. The point here is just to illustrate some basic ideas that we'll return to throughout this book. This will also be your first exposure to Scala's syntax. We'll talk through Scala's syntax much more in the next chapter, so don't worry too much about following every detail. As long as you have a basic idea of what the code is doing, that's what's important.

1.1.1 A program with side effects

Suppose we're implementing a program to handle purchases at a coffee shop. We'll begin with a Scala program that uses side effects in its implementation (also called an *impure* program).

Listing 1.1   A Scala program with side effects

The `class` keyword introduces a class, much like in Java. Its body is contained in curly braces, { and }.

```
class Cafe {

    def buyCoffee(cc: CreditCard): Coffee = {

        val cup = new Coffee()

        cc.charge(cup.price)

        cup

    }
}
```

A method of a class is introduced by the `def` keyword.
`cc: CreditCard` defines a parameter named `cc` of type `CreditCard`. The `Coffee` return type of the `buyCoffee` method is given after the parameter list, and the method body consists of a block within curly braces after an = sign.

Side effect. Actually charges the credit card.

No semicolons are necessary. Newlines delimit statements in a block.

We don't need to say `return`. Since `cup` is the last statement in the block, it is automatically returned.

The line `cc.charge(cup.price)` is an example of a side effect. Charging a credit card involves some interaction with the outside world—suppose it requires contacting the credit card company via some web service, authorizing the transaction, charging the card, and (if successful) persisting some record of the transaction for later reference. But our function merely returns a Coffee and these other actions are happening *on the side*, hence the term "side effect." (Again, we'll define side effects more formally later in this chapter.)

As a result of this side effect, the code is difficult to test. We don't want our tests to actually contact the credit card company and charge the card! This lack of testability is suggesting a design change: arguably, CreditCard shouldn't have any knowledge baked into it about how to contact the credit card company to actually execute a charge, nor should it have knowledge of how to persist a record of this charge in our internal systems. We can make the code more modular and testable by letting Credit-Card be ignorant of these concerns and passing a Payments object into buyCoffee.

Listing 1.2   Adding a payments object

```
class Cafe {
  def buyCoffee(cc: CreditCard, p: Payments): Coffee = {
    val cup = new Coffee()
    p.charge(cc, cup.price)
    cup
  }
}
```

Though side effects still occur when we call p.charge(cc, cup.price), we have at least regained some testability. Payments can be an interface, and we can write a mock implementation of this interface that is suitable for testing. But that isn't ideal either. We're forced to make Payments an interface, when a concrete class may have been fine otherwise, and any mock implementation will be awkward to use. For example, it might contain some internal state that we'll have to inspect after the call to buy-Coffee, and our test will have to make sure this state has been appropriately modified (*mutated*) by the call to charge. We can use a *mock framework* or similar to handle this detail for us, but this all feels like overkill if we just want to test that buyCoffee creates a charge equal to the price of a cup of coffee.

Separate from the concern of testing, there's another problem: it's difficult to reuse buyCoffee. Suppose a customer, Alice, would like to order 12 cups of coffee. Ideally we could just reuse buyCoffee for this, perhaps calling it 12 times in a loop. But as it is currently implemented, that will involve contacting the payment system 12 times, authorizing 12 separate charges to Alice's credit card! That adds more processing fees and isn't good for Alice or the coffee shop.

What can we do about this? As the figure at the top of page 6 illustrates, we could write a whole new function, buyCoffees, with special logic for batching up the charges.[1] Here, that might not be such a big deal, since the logic of buyCoffee is so

---

[1] We could also write a specialized BatchingPayments implementation of the Payments interface, that some-how attempts to batch successive charges to the same credit card. This gets complicated though. How many charges should it try to batch up, and how long should it wait? Do we force buyCoffee to indicate that the batch is finished, perhaps by calling closeBatch? And how would it know when it's appropriate to do that, anyway?

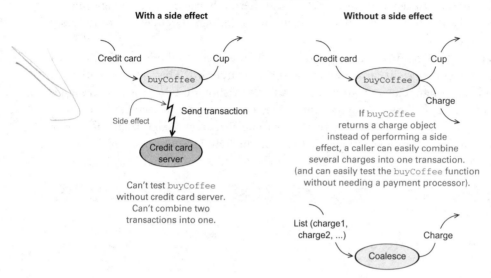

A call to buyCoffee

With a side effect

Credit card   Cup

buyCoffee

Side effect   Send transaction

Credit card
server

Can't test buyCoffee
without credit card server.
Can't combine two
transactions into one.

Without a side effect

Credit card   Cup

buyCoffee

Charge

If buyCoffee
returns a charge object
instead of performing a side
effect, a caller can easily combine
several charges into one transaction.
(and can easily test the buyCoffee function
without needing a payment processor).

List (charge1,
charge2, ...)   Charge

Coalesce

simple, but in other cases the logic we need to duplicate may be nontrivial, and we should mourn the loss of code reuse and composition!

1.1.2   *A functional solution: removing the side effects*

The functional solution is to eliminate side effects and have buyCoffee *return the charge as a value* in addition to returning the Coffee. The concerns of processing the charge by sending it off to the credit card company, persisting a record of it, and so on, will be handled elsewhere. Again, we'll cover Scala's syntax more in later chapters, but here's what a functional solution might look like:

```
class Cafe {
  def buyCoffee(cc: CreditCard): (Coffee, Charge) = {
    val cup = new Coffee()
    (cup, Charge(cc, cup.price))
  }
}
```

> buyCoffee now returns a pair of a Coffee and a Charge, indicated with the type (Coffee, Charge). Whatever system processes payments is not involved at all here.

> To create a pair, we put the cup and Charge in parentheses separated by a comma.

Here we've separated the concern of *creating* a charge from the *processing* or *interpretation* of that charge. The buyCoffee function now returns a Charge as a value along with the Coffee. We'll see shortly how this lets us reuse it more easily to purchase multiple coffees with a single transaction. But what is Charge? It's a data type we just invented containing a CreditCard and an amount, equipped with a handy function, combine, for combining charges with the same CreditCard:

A case class has one primary constructor whose argument list comes after the class name (here, `Charge`). The parameters in this list become public, unmodifiable (immutable) fields of the `class` and can be accessed using the usual object-oriented dot notation, as in `other.cc`.

```
case class Charge(cc: CreditCard, amount: Double) {

    def combine(other: Charge): Charge =

      if (cc == other.cc)

        Charge(cc, amount + other.amount)

      else

        throw new Exception("Can't combine charges to different cards")

}
```

An `if` expression has the same syntax as in Java, but it also returns a value equal to the result of whichever branch is taken. If `cc == other.cc`, then `combine` will return `Charge(..)`; otherwise the exception in the `else` branch will be thrown.

The syntax for throwing exceptions is the same as in Java and many other languages. We'll discuss more functional ways of handling error conditions in a later chapter.

A `case class` can be created without the keyword `new`. We just use the class name followed by the list of arguments for its primary constructor.

Now let's look at `buyCoffees`, to implement the purchase of n cups of coffee. Unlike before, this can now be implemented in terms of `buyCoffee`, as we had hoped.

Listing 1.3 Buying multiple cups with `buyCoffees`

```
class Cafe {

    def buyCoffee(cc: CreditCard): (Coffee, Charge) = ...

    def buyCoffees(cc: CreditCard, n: Int): (List[Coffee], Charge) = {
      val purchases: List[(Coffee, Charge)] = List.fill(n)(buyCoffee(cc))
      val (coffees, charges) = purchases.unzip
      (coffees, charges.reduce((c1,c2) => c1.combine(c2)))
    }
}
```

`List.fill(n)(x)` creates a `List` with n copies of `x`. We'll explain this funny function call syntax in a later chapter.

`List[Coffee]` is an immutable singly linked list of `Coffee` values. We'll discuss this data type more in chapter 3.

`charges.reduce` reduces the entire list of charges to a single charge, using `combine` to combine charges two at a time. `reduce` is an example of a *higher-order function*, which we'll properly introduce in the next chapter.

`unzip` splits a list of pairs into a pair of lists. Here we're destructuring this pair to declare two values (`coffees` and `charges`) on one line.

Overall, this solution is a marked improvement—we're now able to reuse `buyCoffee` directly to define the `buyCoffees` function, and both functions are trivially testable without having to define complicated mock implementations of some `Payments` interface! In fact, the `Cafe` is now completely ignorant of how the `Charge` values will be processed. We can still have a `Payments` class for actually processing charges, of course, but `Cafe` doesn't need to know about it.

Making `Charge` into a first-class value has other benefits we might not have anticipated: we can more easily assemble business logic for working with these charges. For instance, Alice may bring her laptop to the coffee shop and work there for a few hours, making occasional purchases. It might be nice if the coffee shop could combine these purchases Alice makes into a single charge, again saving on credit card processing fees. Since `Charge` is first-class, we can write the following function to coalesce any same-card charges in a `List[Charge]`:

```
def coalesce(charges: List[Charge]): List[Charge] =
  charges.groupBy(_.cc).values.map(_.reduce(_ combine _)).toList
```

We're passing functions as values to the `groupBy`, `map`, and `reduce` methods. You'll learn to read and write one-liners like this over the next several chapters. The `_.cc` and `_ combine _` are syntax for *anonymous functions*, which we'll introduce in the next chapter.

You may find this kind of code difficult to read because the notation is very compact. But as you work through this book, reading and writing Scala code like this will become second nature to you very quickly. This function takes a list of charges, groups them by the credit card used, and then combines them into a single charge per card. It's perfectly reusable and testable without any additional mock objects or interfaces. Imagine trying to implement the same logic with our first implementation of `buyCoffee`!

This is just a taste of why functional programming has the benefits claimed, and this example is intentionally simple. If the series of refactorings used here seems natural, obvious, unremarkable, or standard practice, that's *good*. FP is merely a discipline that takes what many consider a good idea to its logical endpoint, applying the discipline even in situations where its applicability is less obvious. As you'll learn over the course of this book, the consequences of consistently following the discipline of FP are profound and the benefits enormous. FP is a truly radical shift in how programs are organized at every level—from the simplest of loops to high-level program architecture. The style that emerges is quite different, but it's a beautiful and cohesive approach to programming that we hope you come to appreciate.

What about the real world?

We saw in the case of `buyCoffee` how we could separate the creation of the `Charge` from the interpretation or processing of that `Charge`. In general, we'll learn how this sort of transformation can be applied to *any* function with side effects to push these effects to the outer layers of the program. Functional programmers often speak of implementing programs with a pure core and a thin layer on the outside that handles effects.

But even so, surely at some point we must actually have an effect on the world and submit the `Charge` for processing by some external system. And aren't there other useful programs that necessitate side effects or mutation? How do we write such programs? As we work through this book, we'll discover how many programs that seem to necessitate side effects have some functional analogue. In other cases we'll find ways to structure code so that effects occur but aren't *observable*. (For example, we can mutate data that's declared locally in the body of some function if we ensure that it can't be referenced outside that function, or we can write to a file as long as no enclosing function can observe this occurring.)

1.2   *Exactly what is a (pure) function?*

We said earlier that FP means programming with pure functions, and a pure function is one that lacks side effects. In our discussion of the coffee shop example, we worked off an informal notion of side effects and purity. Here we'll formalize this notion, to pinpoint more precisely what it means to program functionally. This will also give us additional insight into one of the benefits of functional programming: pure functions are easier to reason about.

A function f with input type A and output type B (written in Scala as a single type: A => B, pronounced "A to B" or "A arrow B") is a computation that relates every value a of type A to exactly one value b of type B such that b is determined solely by the value of a. Any changing state of an internal or external process is irrelevant to computing the result f(a). For example, a function intToString having type Int => String will take every integer to a corresponding string. Furthermore, if it really is a *function*, it will do nothing else.

In other words, a function has no observable effect on the execution of the program other than to compute a result given its inputs; we say that it has no side effects. We sometimes qualify such functions as *pure* functions to make this more explicit, but this is somewhat redundant. Unless we state otherwise, we'll often use *function* to imply no side effects.[2]

You should be familiar with a lot of pure functions already. Consider the addition (+) function on integers. It takes two integer values and returns an integer value. For any two given integer values, it will *always return the same integer value*. Another example is the length function of a String in Java, Scala, and many other languages where strings can't be modified (are immutable). For any given string, the same length is always returned and nothing else occurs.

We can formalize this idea of pure functions using the concept of *referential transparency (RT)*. This is a property of *expressions* in general and not just functions. For the purposes of our discussion, consider an expression to be any part of a program that can be evaluated to a result—anything that you could type into the Scala interpreter

---

[2]   *Procedure* is often used to refer to some parameterized chunk of code that may have side effects.

and get an answer. For example, 2 + 3 is an expression that applies the pure function + to the values 2 and 3 (which are also expressions). This has no side effect. The evaluation of this expression results in the same value 5 every time. In fact, if we saw 2 + 3 in a program we could simply replace it with the value 5 and it wouldn't change a thing about the meaning of our program.

This is all it means for an expression to be referentially transparent—in any program, the expression can be replaced by its result without changing the meaning of the program. And we say that a function is *pure* if calling it with RT arguments is also RT. We'll look at some examples next.

Referential transparency and purity

An expression e is *referentially transparent* if, for all programs p, all occurrences of e in p can be replaced by the result of evaluating e without affecting the meaning of p. A function f is *pure* if the expression f(x) is referentially transparent for all referentially transparent x.[3]

1.3   *Referential transparency, purity, and the substitution model*

Let's see how the definition of RT applies to our original buyCoffee example:

```
def buyCoffee(cc: CreditCard): Coffee = {
  val cup = new Coffee()
  cc.charge(cup.price)
  cup
}
```

Whatever the return type of cc.charge(cup.price) (perhaps it's Unit, Scala's equivalent of void in other languages), it's discarded by buyCoffee. Thus, the result of evaluating buyCoffee(aliceCreditCard) will be merely cup, which is equivalent to a new Coffee(). For buyCoffee to be pure, by our definition of RT, it must be the case that p(buyCoffee(aliceCreditCard)) behaves the same as p(new Coffee()), for *any* p. This clearly doesn't hold—the program new Coffee() doesn't do anything, whereas buyCoffee(aliceCreditCard) will contact the credit card company and authorize a charge. Already we have an observable difference between the two programs.

Referential transparency forces the invariant that everything a function *does* is represented by the *value* that it returns, according to the result type of the function. This constraint enables a simple and natural mode of reasoning about program evaluation called the *substitution model*. When expressions are referentially transparent, we can imagine that computation proceeds much like we'd solve an algebraic equation. We fully expand every part of an expression, replacing all variables with their referents, and then reduce it to its simplest form. At each step we replace a term with an

---

[3] There are some subtleties to this definition, and we'll refine it later in this book. See the chapter notes at our GitHub site (https://github.com/pchiusano/fpinscala; see the preface) for more discussion.

equivalent one; computation proceeds by substituting *equals for equals*. In other words, RT enables *equational reasoning* about programs.

Let's look at two more examples—one where all expressions are RT and can be reasoned about using the substitution model, and one where some expressions violate RT. There's nothing complicated here; we're just formalizing something you likely already understand.

Let's try the following in the Scala interpreter (also known as the Read-Eval-Print-Loop or REPL, pronounced like "ripple," but with an *e* instead of an *i*). Note that in Java and in Scala, strings are immutable. A "modified" string is really a new string and the old string remains intact:

```
scala> val x = "Hello, World"
x: java.lang.String = Hello, World

scala> val r1 = x.reverse
r1: String = dlroW ,olleH

scala> val r2 = x.reverse          ←——— r1 and r2 are the same.
r2: String = dlroW ,olleH
```

Suppose we replace all occurrences of the term x with the expression referenced by x (its *definition*), as follows:

```
scala> val r1 = "Hello, World".reverse
r1: String = dlroW ,olleH

scala> val r2 = "Hello, World".reverse     ←——— r1 and r2 are still the same.
r2: String = dlroW ,olleH
```

This transformation doesn't affect the outcome. The values of r1 and r2 are the same as before, so x was referentially transparent. What's more, r1 and r2 are referentially transparent as well, so if they appeared in some other part of a larger program, they could in turn be replaced with their values throughout and it would have no effect on the program.

Now let's look at a function that is *not* referentially transparent. Consider the append function on the java.lang.StringBuilder class. This function operates on the StringBuilder in place. The previous state of the StringBuilder is destroyed after a call to append. Let's try this out:

```
scala> val x = new StringBuilder("Hello")
x: java.lang.StringBuilder = Hello

scala> val y = x.append(", World")
y: java.lang.StringBuilder = Hello, World

scala> val r1 = y.toString
r1: java.lang.String = Hello, World

scala> val r2 = y.toString
r2: java.lang.String = Hello, World     ←——— r1 and r2 are the same.
```

So far so good. Now let's see how this side effect breaks RT. Suppose we substitute the call to append like we did earlier, replacing all occurrences of y with the expression referenced by y:

```scala
scala> val x = new StringBuilder("Hello")
x: java.lang.StringBuilder = Hello

scala> val r1 = x.append(", World").toString
r1: java.lang.String = Hello, World

scala> val r2 = x.append(", World").toString
r2: java.lang.String = Hello, World, World   ←——— r1 and r2 are no longer the same.
```

This transformation of the program results in a different outcome. We therefore conclude that StringBuilder.append is *not* a pure function. What's going on here is that although r1 and r2 look like they're the same expression, they are in fact referencing two different values of the same StringBuilder. By the time r2 calls x.append, r1 will have already mutated the object referenced by x. If this seems difficult to think about, that's because it is. Side effects make reasoning about program behavior more difficult.

Conversely, the substitution model is simple to reason about since effects of evaluation are purely local (they affect only the expression being evaluated) and we need not mentally simulate sequences of state updates to understand a block of code. Understanding requires only *local reasoning*. We need not mentally track all the state changes that may occur before or after our function's execution to understand what our function will do; we simply look at the function's definition and substitute the arguments into its body. Even if you haven't used the name "substitution model," you have certainly used this mode of reasoning when thinking about your code.[4]

Formalizing the notion of purity this way gives insight into why functional programs are often more modular. Modular programs consist of components that can be understood and reused independently of the whole, such that the meaning of the whole depends only on the meaning of the components and the rules governing their composition; that is, they are *composable*. A pure function is modular and composable because it separates the logic of the computation itself from "what to do with the result" and "how to obtain the input"; it's a black box. Input is obtained in exactly one way: via the argument(s) to the function. And the output is simply computed and returned. By keeping each of these concerns separate, the logic of the computation is more reusable; we may reuse the logic wherever we want without worrying about whether the side effect being done with the result or the side effect requesting the input are appropriate in all contexts. We saw this in the buyCoffee example—by eliminating the side effect of payment processing being done with the output, we were more easily able to reuse the logic of the function, both for purposes of testing and for purposes of further composition (like when we wrote buyCoffees and coalesce).

---

[4] In practice, programmers don't spend time mechanically applying substitution to determine if code is pure—it will usually be obvious.

1.4 *Summary*

In this chapter, we introduced functional programming and explained exactly what FP is and why you might use it. Though the full benefits of the functional style will become more clear over the course of this book, we illustrated some of the benefits of FP using a simple example. We also discussed referential transparency and the substitution model and talked about how FP enables simpler reasoning about programs and greater modularity.

In this book, you'll learn the concepts and principles of FP as they apply to every level of programming, starting from the simplest of tasks and building on that foundation. In subsequent chapters, we'll cover some of the fundamentals—how do we write loops in FP? Or implement data structures? How do we deal with errors and exceptions? We need to learn how to do these things and get comfortable with the low-level idioms of FP. We'll build on this understanding when we explore functional design techniques in parts 2, 3, and 4.

Getting started with functional programming in Scala

Now that we have committed to using only pure functions, a question naturally emerges: how do we write even the simplest of programs? Most of us are used to thinking of programs as sequences of instructions that are executed in order, where each instruction has some kind of effect. In this chapter, we'll begin learning how to write programs in the Scala language just by combining pure functions.

This chapter is mainly intended for those readers who are new to Scala, to functional programming, or both. Immersion is an effective method for learning a foreign language, so we'll just dive in. The only way for Scala code to look familiar and not foreign is if we look at a lot of Scala code. We've already seen some in the first chapter. In this chapter, we'll start by looking at a small but complete program. We'll then break it down piece by piece to examine what it does in some detail, in order to understand the basics of the Scala language and its syntax. Our goal in this book is to teach functional programming, but we'll use Scala as our vehicle, and need to know enough of the Scala language and its syntax to get going.

Once we've covered some of the basic elements of the Scala language, we'll then introduce some of the basic techniques for how to write functional programs. We'll discuss how to write loops using *tail recursive functions*, and we'll introduce *higher-order functions (HOFs)*. HOFs are functions that take other functions as arguments and may themselves return functions as their output. We'll also look at some examples of *polymorphic* HOFs where we use types to guide us toward an implementation.

There's a lot of new material in this chapter. Some of the material related to HOFs may be brain-bending if you have a lot of experience programming in a language *without* the ability to pass functions around like that. Remember, it's not crucial that you internalize every single concept in this chapter, or solve every exercise.

14

We'll come back to these concepts again from different angles throughout the book, and our goal here is just to give you some initial exposure.

2.1 *Introducing Scala the language: an example*

The following is a complete program listing in Scala, which we'll talk through. We aren't introducing any new concepts of functional programming here. Our goal is just to introduce the Scala language and its syntax.

Listing 2.1 A simple Scala program

```
// A comment!
/* Another comment */
/** A documentation comment */
object MyModule {
  def abs(n: Int): Int =
    if (n < 0) -n
    else n

  private def formatAbs(x: Int) = {
    val msg = "The absolute value of %d is %d"
    msg.format(x, abs(x))
  }

  def main(args: Array[String]): Unit =
    println(formatAbs(-42))
}
```

Declares a singleton object, which simultaneously declares a class and its only instance.

abs takes an integer and returns an integer.

A private method can only be called by other members of `MyModule`.

Returns the negation of n if it's less than zero.

A string with two placeholders for numbers marked as %d.

Replaces the two %d placeholders in the string with x and abs(x) respectively.

`Unit` serves the same purpose as `void` in languages like Java or C.

We declare an object (also known as a *module*) named `MyModule`. This is simply to give our code a place to live and a name so we can refer to it later. Scala code has to be in an `object` or a `class`, and we use an `object` here because it's simpler. We put our code inside the object, between curly braces. We'll discuss objects and classes in more detail shortly. For now, we'll just look at this particular object.

The `MyModule` object has three *methods*, introduced with the `def` keyword: `abs`, `formatAbs`, and `main`. We'll use the term *method* to refer to some function or field defined within an object or class using the `def` keyword. Let's now go through the methods of `MyModule` one by one.

The object keyword

The `object` keyword creates a new *singleton type*, which is like a `class` that only has a single named instance. If you're familiar with Java, declaring an `object` in Scala is a lot like creating a new instance of an anonymous class.

Scala has no equivalent to Java's `static` keyword, and an `object` is often used in Scala where you might use a class with static members in Java.

The abs method is a pure function that takes an integer and returns its absolute value:

```
def abs(n: Int): Int =
  if (n < 0) -n
  else n
```

The def keyword is followed by the name of the method, which is followed by the parameter list in parentheses. In this case, abs takes only one argument, n of type Int. Following the closing parenthesis of the argument list, an optional type annotation (the : Int) indicates that the type of the result is Int (the colon is pronounced "has type").

The body of the method itself comes after a single equals sign (=). We'll sometimes refer to the part of a declaration that goes before the equals sign as the *left-hand side* or *signature*, and the code that comes after the equals sign as the *right-hand side* or *definition*. Note the absence of an explicit return keyword. The value returned from a method is simply whatever value results from evaluating the right-hand side. All expressions, including if expressions, produce a result. Here, the right-hand side is a single expression whose value is either -n or n, depending on whether n < 0.

The formatAbs method is another pure function:

```
private def formatAbs(x: Int) = {
  val msg = "The absolute value of %d is %d."
  msg.format(x, abs(x))        ←————  format is a standard
}                                      library method defined
                                       on String
```

Here we're calling the format method on the msg object, passing in the value of x along with the value of abs applied to x. This results in a new string with the occurrences of %d in msg replaced with the evaluated results of x and abs(x), respectively.

This method is declared private, which means that it can't be called from any code outside of the MyModule object. This function takes an Int and returns a String, but note that the return type is not declared. Scala is usually able to infer the return types of methods, so they can be omitted, but it's generally considered good style to explicitly declare the return types of methods that you expect others to use. This method is private to our module, so we can omit the type annotation.

The body of the method contains more than one statement, so we put them inside curly braces. A pair of braces containing statements is called a *block*. Statements are separated by newlines or by semicolons. In this case, we're using a newline to separate our statements, so a semicolon isn't necessary.

The first statement in the block declares a String named msg using the val keyword. It's simply there to give a name to the string value so we can refer to it again. A val is an immutable variable, so inside the body of the formatAbs method the name msg will always refer to the same String value. The Scala compiler will complain if you try to reassign msg to a different value in the same block.

Remember, a method simply returns the value of its right-hand side, so we don't need a return keyword. In this case, the right-hand side is a block. In Scala, the value of a multistatement block inside curly braces is the same as the value returned by the last expression in the block. Therefore, the result of the formatAbs method is just the value returned by the call to msg.format(x, abs(x)).

Finally, our main method is an outer shell that calls into our purely functional core and prints the answer to the console. We'll sometimes call such methods *procedures* (or *impure functions*) rather than functions, to emphasize the fact that they have side effects:

```
def main(args: Array[String]): Unit =
  println(formatAbs(-42))
```

The name main is special because when you run a program, Scala will look for a method named main with a specific signature. It has to take an Array of Strings as its argument, and its return type must be Unit.

The args array will contain the arguments that were given at the command line that ran the program. We're not using them here.

Unit serves a similar purpose to void in programming languages like C and Java. In Scala, every method has to return some value as long as it doesn't crash or hang. But main doesn't return anything meaningful, so there's a special type Unit that is the return type of such methods. There's only one value of this type and the literal syntax for it is (), a pair of empty parentheses, pronounced "unit" just like the type. Usually a return type of Unit is a hint that the method has a side effect.

The body of our main method prints to the console the String returned by the call to formatAbs. Note that the return type of println is Unit, which happens to be what we need to return from main.

2.2   *Running our program*

This section discusses the simplest possible way of running your Scala programs, suitable for short examples. More typically, you'll build and run your Scala code using sbt, the build tool for Scala, and/or an IDE like IntelliJ or Eclipse. See the book's source code repo on GitHub (https://github.com/fpinscala/fpinscala) for more information on getting set up with sbt.

The simplest way we can run this Scala program (MyModule) is from the command line, by invoking the Scala compiler directly ourselves. We start by putting the code in a file called MyModule.scala or something similar. We can then compile it to Java bytecode using the scalac compiler:

```
> scalac MyModule.scala
```

This will generate some files ending with the .class suffix. These files contain compiled code that can be run with the Java Virtual Machine (JVM). The code can be executed using the scala command-line tool:

```
> scala MyModule
The absolute value of -42 is 42.
```

Actually, it's not strictly necessary to compile the code first with `scalac`. A simple program like the one we've written here can be run using just the Scala interpreter by passing it to the `scala` command-line tool directly:

```
> scala MyModule.scala
The absolute value of -42 is 42.
```

This can be handy when using Scala for scripting. The interpreter will look for any object within the file `MyModule.scala` that has a `main` method with the appropriate signature, and will then call it.

Lastly, an alternative way is to start the Scala interpreter's interactive mode, the REPL (which stands for read-evaluate-print loop). It's a great idea to have a REPL window open so you can try things out while you're programming in Scala.

We can load our source file into the REPL and try things out (your actual console output may differ slightly):

```
> scala
Welcome to Scala.
Type in expressions to have them evaluated.
Type :help for more information.

scala> :load MyModule.scala
Loading MyModule.scala...
defined module MyModule

scala> MyModule.abs(-42)
res0: Int = 42
```

> **We can type Scala expressions at the prompt.**

> **:load is a command to the REPL to interpret a Scala source file. (Note that unfortunately this won't work for Scala files with package declarations.)**

> **The REPL evaluates our Scala expression and prints the answer. It also gives the answer a name, res0, that we can refer to later, and shows its type, which in this case is Int.**

It's also possible to copy and paste individual lines of code into the REPL. It even has a paste mode (accessed with the `:paste` command) designed to paste code that spans multiple lines. It's a good idea to get familiar with the REPL and its features because it's a tool that you'll use a lot as a Scala programmer.

2.3   *Modules, objects, and namespaces*

In this section, we'll discuss some additional aspects of Scala's syntax related to modules, objects, and namespaces. In the preceding REPL session, note that in order to refer to our `abs` method, we had to say `MyModule.abs` because `abs` was defined in the `MyModule` object. We say that `MyModule` is its *namespace*. Aside from some technicalities, every value in Scala is what's called an *object*,[1] and each object may have zero or more *members*. An object whose primary purpose is giving its members a namespace is sometimes called a *module*. A member can be a method declared with the `def` keyword, or it can be another object declared with `val` or `object`. Objects can also have other kinds of members that we'll ignore for now.

We access the members of objects with the typical object-oriented dot notation, which is a namespace (the name that refers to the object) followed by a dot (the period

---

[1]   Unlike Java, values of primitive types like `Int` are also considered objects for the purposes of this discussion.

character), followed by the name of the member, as in `MyModule.abs(-42)`. To use the `toString` member on the object 42, we'd use `42.toString`. The implementations of members within an object can refer to each other unqualified (without prefixing the object name), but if needed they have access to their enclosing object using a special name: `this`.[2]

Note that even an expression like `2 + 1` is just calling a member of an object. In that case, what we're calling is the + member of the object 2. It's really syntactic sugar for the expression `2.+(1)`, which passes 1 as an argument to the method + on the object 2. Scala has no special notion of *operators*. It's simply the case that + is a valid method name in Scala. Any method name can be used infix like that (omitting the dot and parentheses) when calling it with a single argument. For example, instead of `MyModule.abs(42)` we can say `MyModule abs 42` and get the same result. You can use whichever you find more pleasing in any given case.

We can bring an object's member into scope by *importing* it, which allows us to call it unqualified from then on:

```
scala> import MyModule.abs
import MyModule.abs

scala> abs(-42)
res0: 42
```

We can bring *all* of an object's (nonprivate) members into scope by using the underscore syntax:

```
import MyModule._
```

2.4 *Higher-order functions: passing functions to functions*

Now that we've covered the basics of Scala's syntax, we'll move on to covering some of the basics of writing functional programs. The first new idea is this: *functions are values*. And just like values of other types—such as integers, strings, and lists—functions can be assigned to variables, stored in data structures, and passed as arguments to functions.

When writing purely functional programs, we'll often find it useful to write a function that accepts other functions as arguments. This is called a *higher-order function (HOF)*, and we'll look next at some simple examples to illustrate. In later chapters, we'll see how useful this capability really is, and how it permeates the functional programming style. But to start, suppose we wanted to adapt our program to print out both the absolute value of a number *and* the factorial of another number. Here's a sample run of such a program:

```
The absolute value of -42 is 42
The factorial of 7 is 5040
```

---

[2] Note that in this book, we'll use the term *function* to refer more generally to either so-called standalone functions like sqrt or abs, or members of some class, including methods. When it's clear from the context, we'll also use the terms *method* and *function* interchangeably, since what matters is not the syntax of invocation (`obj.method(12)` vs. `method(obj, 12)`, but the fact that we're talking about some parameterized block of code.

2.4.1 A short detour: writing loops functionally

First, let's write `factorial`:

```scala
def factorial(n: Int): Int = {
  def go(n: Int, acc: Int): Int =
    if (n <= 0) acc
    else go(n-1, n*acc)

  go(n, 1)
}
```

> An inner function, or *local definition*. It's common in Scala to write functions that are local to the body of another function. In functional programming, we shouldn't consider this a bigger deal than local integers or strings.

The way we write loops functionally, without mutating a loop variable, is with a recursive function. Here we're defining a recursive helper function inside the body of the `factorial` function. Such a helper function is often called `go` or `loop` by convention. In Scala, we can define functions inside any block, including within another function definition. Since it's local, the `go` function can only be referred to from within the body of the `factorial` function, just like a local variable would. The definition of `factorial` finally just consists of a call to `go` with the initial conditions for the loop.

The arguments to `go` are the state for the loop. In this case, they're the remaining value n, and the current accumulated factorial acc. To advance to the next iteration, we simply call `go` recursively with the new loop state (here, `go(n-1, n*acc)`), and to exit from the loop, we return a value without a recursive call (here, we return acc in the case that `n <= 0`). Scala detects this sort of *self-recursion* and compiles it to the same sort of bytecode as would be emitted for a `while` loop,[3] so long as the recursive call is in *tail position*. See the sidebar for the technical details on this, but the basic idea is that this optimization[4] (called *tail call elimination*) is applied when there's no additional work left to do after the recursive call returns.

Tail calls in Scala

A call is said to be in *tail position* if the caller does nothing other than return the value of the recursive call. For example, the recursive call to `go(n-1,n*acc)` we discussed earlier is in tail position, since the method returns the value of this recursive call directly and does nothing else with it. On the other hand, if we said `1 + go(n-1,n*acc)`, `go` would no longer be in tail position, since the method would still have work to do when `go` returned its result (namely, adding `1` to it).

If all recursive calls made by a function are in tail position, Scala automatically compiles the recursion to iterative loops that don't consume call stack frames for each iteration. By default, Scala doesn't tell us if tail call elimination was successful, but if we're expecting this to occur for a recursive function we write, we can tell the Scala

---

[3] We can write `while` loops by hand in Scala, but it's rarely necessary and considered bad form since it hinders good compositional style.

[4] The term *optimization* is not really appropriate here. An optimization usually connotes some nonessential performance improvement, but when we use tail calls to write loops, we generally rely on their being compiled as iterative loops that don't consume a call stack frame for each iteration (which would result in a `StackOverflowError` for large inputs).

compiler about this assumption using the `tailrec` annotation (http://mng.bz/ bWT5), so it can give us a compile error if it's unable to eliminate the tail calls of the function. Here's the syntax for this:

```
def factorial(n: Int): Int = {
  @annotation.tailrec
  def go(n: Int, acc: Int): Int =
    if (n <= 0) acc
    else go(n-1, n*acc)
  go(n, 1)
}
```

We won't talk much more about annotations in this book (you'll find more information at http://mng.bz/GK8T), but we'll use `@annotation.tailrec` extensively.

NOTE   See the preface for information on the exercises.

EXERCISE 2.1

Write a recursive function to get the *n*th Fibonacci number (http://mng.bz/C29s). The first two Fibonacci numbers are 0 and 1. The *n*th number is always the sum of the previous two—the sequence begins 0, 1, 1, 2, 3, 5. Your definition should use a local tail-recursive function.

```
def fib(n: Int): Int
```

2.4.2   *Writing our first higher-order function*

Now that we have `factorial`, let's edit our program from before to include it.

Listing 2.2   A simple program including the factorial function

```
object MyModule {
  ...
  private def formatAbs(x: Int) = {          Definitions of abs and
    val msg = "The absolute value of %d is %d."   factorial go here.
    msg.format(x, abs(x))
  }

  private def formatFactorial(n: Int) = {
    val msg = "The factorial of %d is %d."
    msg.format(n, factorial(n))
  }

  def main(args: Array[String]): Unit = {
    println(formatAbs(-42))
    println(formatFactorial(7))
  }
}
```

The two functions, `formatAbs` and `formatFactorial`, are almost identical. If we like, we can generalize these to a single function, `formatResult`, which accepts as an argument the *function* to apply to its argument:

```
def formatResult(name: String, n: Int, f: Int => Int) = {     ⟵  f is required to be
  val msg = "The %s of %d is %d."                                  a function from
  msg.format(name, n, f(n))                                        Int to Int.
}
```

Our `formatResult` function is a higher-order function (HOF) that takes another function, called `f` (see sidebar on variable-naming conventions). We give a type to `f`, as we would for any other parameter. Its type is `Int => Int` (pronounced "int to int" or "int arrow int"), which indicates that `f` expects an integer argument and will also return an integer.

Our function `abs` from before matches that type. It accepts an `Int` and returns an `Int`. And likewise, `factorial` accepts an `Int` and returns an `Int`, which also matches the `Int => Int` type. We can therefore pass `abs` or `factorial` as the `f` argument to `formatResult`:

```
scala> formatResult("absolute value", -42, abs)
res0: String = "The absolute value of -42 is 42."

scala> formatResult("factorial", 7, factorial)
res1: String = "The factorial of 7 is 5040."
```

Variable-naming conventions

It's a common convention to use names like `f`, `g`, and `h` for parameters to a higher-order function. In functional programming, we tend to use very short variable names, even one-letter names. This is usually because HOFs are so general that they have no opinion on what the argument should actually *do*. All they know about the argument is its type. Many functional programmers feel that short names make code easier to read, since it makes the structure of the code easier to see at a glance.

2.5   *Polymorphic functions: abstracting over types*

So far we've defined only *monomorphic* functions, or functions that operate on only one type of data. For example, `abs` and `factorial` are specific to arguments of type `Int`, and the higher-order function `formatResult` is also fixed to operate on functions that take arguments of type `Int`. Often, and especially when writing HOFs, we want to write code that works for *any* type it's given. These are called *polymorphic functions*,[5] and in the chapters ahead, you'll get plenty of experience writing such functions. Here we'll just introduce the idea.

---

[5] We're using the term *polymorphism* in a slightly different way than you might be used to if you're familiar with object-oriented programming, where that term usually connotes some form of subtyping or inheritance relationship. There are no interfaces or subtyping here in this example. The kind of polymorphism we're using here is sometimes called *parametric polymorphism.*

2.5.1 An example of a polymorphic function

We can often discover polymorphic functions by observing that several monomorphic functions all share a similar structure. For example, the following monomorphic function, `findFirst`, returns the first index in an array where the key occurs, or `-1` if it's not found. It's specialized for searching for a `String` in an `Array` of `String` values.

> **Listing 2.3 Monomorphic function to find a `String` in an array**

Otherwise, increment n and keep looking.

```
def findFirst(ss: Array[String], key: String): Int = {
  @annotation.tailrec
  def loop(n: Int): Int =
    if (n >= ss.length) -1
    else if (ss(n) == key) n
    else loop(n + 1)

  loop(0)
}
```

If n is past the end of the array, return –1, indicating the key doesn't exist in the array.

`ss(n)` extracts the nth element of the array `ss`. If the element at n is equal to the key, return n, indicating that the element appears in the array at that index.

Start the loop at the first element of the array.

The details of the code aren't too important here. What's important is that the code for `findFirst` will look almost identical if we're searching for a `String` in an `Array[String]`, an `Int` in an `Array[Int]`, or an `A` in an `Array[A]` for any given type `A`. We can write `findFirst` more generally for any type `A` by accepting a function to use for testing a particular `A` value.

> **Listing 2.4 Polymorphic function to find an element in an array**

```
def findFirst[A](as: Array[A], p: A => Boolean): Int = {
  @annotation.tailrec
  def loop(n: Int): Int =
    if (n >= as.length) -1
    else if (p(as(n))) n
    else loop(n + 1)

  loop(0)
}
```

Instead of hardcoding `String`, take a type `A` as a parameter. And instead of hardcoding an equality check for a given key, take a function with which to test each element of the array.

If the function p matches the current element, we've found a match and we return its index in the array.

This is an example of a polymorphic function, sometimes called a *generic* function. We're *abstracting over the type* of the array and the function used for searching it. To write a polymorphic function as a method, we introduce a comma-separated list of *type parameters*, surrounded by square brackets (here, just a single `[A]`), following the name of the function, in this case `findFirst`. We can call the type parameters anything we want—`[Foo, Bar, Baz]` and `[TheParameter, another_good_one]` are valid type parameter declarations—though by convention we typically use short, one-letter, uppercase type parameter names like `[A,B,C]`.

The type parameter list introduces *type variables* that can be referenced in the rest of the type signature (exactly analogous to how variables introduced in the parameter list to a function can be referenced in the body of the function). In findFirst, the type variable A is referenced in two places: the elements of the array are required to have the type A (since it's an Array[A]), and the p function must accept a value of type A (since it's a function of type A => Boolean). The fact that the same type variable is referenced in both places in the type signature implies that the type must be the same for both arguments, and the compiler will enforce this fact anywhere we try to call findFirst. If we try to search for a String in an Array[Int], for instance, we'll get a type mismatch error.

■ **EXERCISE 2.2**

Implement isSorted, which checks whether an Array[A] is sorted according to a given comparison function:

```
def isSorted[A](as: Array[A], ordered: (A,A) => Boolean): Boolean
```

2.5.2   *Calling HOFs with anonymous functions*

When using HOFs, it's often convenient to be able to call these functions with *anonymous functions* or *function literals*, rather than having to supply some existing named function. For instance, we can test the findFirst function in the REPL as follows:

```
scala> findFirst(Array(7, 9, 13), (x: Int) => x == 9)
res2: Int = 1
```

There is some new syntax here. The expression Array(7, 9, 13) is an *array literal*. It constructs a new array with three integers in it. Note the lack of a keyword like new to construct the array.

The syntax (x: Int) => x == 9 is a *function literal* or *anonymous function*. Instead of defining this function as a method with a name, we can define it inline using this convenient syntax. This particular function takes one argument called x of type Int, and it returns a Boolean indicating whether x is equal to 9.

In general, the arguments to the function are declared to the left of the => arrow, and we can then use them in the body of the function to the right of the arrow. For example, if we want to write an equality function that takes two integers and checks if they're equal to each other, we could write that like this:

```
scala> (x: Int, y: Int) => x == y
res3: (Int, Int) => Boolean = <function2>
```

The <function2> notation given by the REPL indicates that the value of res3 is a function that takes two arguments. When the type of the function's inputs can be inferred by Scala from the context, the type annotations on the function's arguments may be elided, for example, `(x,y) => x < y`. We'll see an example of this in the next section, and lots more examples throughout this book.

Functions as values in Scala

When we define a function literal, what is actually being defined in Scala is an object with a method called `apply`. Scala has a special rule for this method name, so that objects that have an `apply` method can be called as if they were themselves methods. When we define a function literal like `(a, b) => a < b`, this is really syntactic sugar for object creation:

```scala
val lessThan = new Function2[Int, Int, Boolean] {
  def apply(a: Int, b: Int) = a < b
}
```

`lessThan` has type `Function2[Int,Int,Boolean]`, which is usually written `(Int,Int) => Boolean`. Note that the `Function2` interface (known in Scala as a *trait*) has an `apply` method. And when we call the `lessThan` function with `lessThan(10, 20)`, it's really syntactic sugar for calling its `apply` method:

```scala
scala> val b = lessThan.apply(10, 20)
b: Boolean = true
```

`Function2` is just an ordinary trait (an interface) provided by the standard Scala library (API docs link: http://mng.bz/qFMr) to represent function objects that take two arguments. Also provided are `Function1`, `Function3`, and others, taking a number of arguments indicated by the name. Because functions are just ordinary Scala objects, we say that they're *first-class* values. We'll often use "function" to refer to either such a first-class function or a method, depending on context.

2.6 *Following types to implementations*

As you might have seen when writing `isSorted`, the universe of possible implementations is significantly reduced when implementing a polymorphic function. If a function is polymorphic in some type `A`, the only operations that can be performed on that `A` are those passed into the function as arguments (or that can be defined in terms of these given operations).[6] In some cases, you'll find that the universe of possibilities for a given polymorphic type is constrained such that only one implementation is possible!

Let's look at an example of a function signature that can only be implemented in one way. It's a higher-order function for performing what's called *partial application*. This function, `partial1`, takes a value and a function of two arguments, and returns a function of one argument as its result. The name comes from the fact that the function is being applied to some but not all of the arguments it requires:

```scala
def partial1[A,B,C](a: A, f: (A,B) => C): B => C
```

---

[6] Technically, all values in Scala can be compared for equality (using `==`), and turned into strings with `toString` and integers with `hashCode`. But this is something of a wart inherited from Java.

The `partial1` function has three type parameters: A, B, and C. It then takes two arguments. The argument f is itself a function that takes two arguments of types A and B, respectively, and returns a value of type C. The value returned by `partial1` will also be a function, of type B => C.

How would we go about implementing this higher-order function? It turns out that there's only one implementation that compiles, and it follows logically from the type signature. It's like a fun little logic puzzle.[7]

Let's start by looking at the type of thing that we have to return. The return type of `partial1` is B => C, so we know that we have to return a function of that type. We can just begin writing a function literal that takes an argument of type B:

```
def partial1[A,B,C](a: A, f: (A,B) => C): B => C =
  (b: B) => ???
```

This can be weird at first if you're not used to writing anonymous functions. Where did that B come from? Well, we've just written, "Return a function that takes a value b of type B." On the right-hand-side of the => arrow (where the question marks are now) comes the body of that anonymous function. We're free to refer to the value b in there for the same reason that we're allowed to refer to the value a in the body of `partial1`.[8]

Let's keep going. Now that we've asked for a value of type B, what do we want to return from our anonymous function? The type signature says that it has to be a value of type C. And there's only one way to get such a value. According to the signature, C is the return type of the function f. So the only way to get that C is to pass an A and a B to f. That's easy:

```
def partial1[A,B,C](a: A, f: (A,B) => C): B => C =
  (b: B) => f(a, b)
```

And we're done! The result is a higher-order function that takes a function of two arguments and partially applies it. That is, if we have an A and a function that needs both A and B to produce C, we can get a function that just needs B to produce C (since we already have the A). It's like saying, "If I can give you a carrot for an apple and a banana, and you already gave me an apple, you just have to give me a banana and I'll give you a carrot."

Note that the type annotation on b isn't needed here. Since we told Scala the return type would be B => C, Scala knows the type of b from the context and we could just write b => f(a,b) as the implementation. Generally speaking, we'll omit the type annotation on a function literal if it can be inferred by Scala.

---

[7] Even though it's a fun puzzle, this isn't a purely academic exercise. Functional programming in practice involves a lot of fitting building blocks together in the only way that makes sense. The purpose of this exercise is to get practice using higher-order functions, and using Scala's type system to guide your programming.

[8] Within the body of this inner function, the outer a is still in scope. We sometimes say that the inner function *closes over* its environment, which includes a.

■ **EXERCISE 2.3**

Let's look at another example, *currying*,[9] which converts a function f of two arguments into a function of one argument that partially applies f. Here again there's only one implementation that compiles. Write this implementation.

```
def curry[A,B,C](f: (A, B) => C): A => (B => C)
```

□ **EXERCISE 2.4**

Implement uncurry, which reverses the transformation of curry. Note that since => associates to the right, A => (B => C) can be written as A => B => C.

```
def uncurry[A,B,C](f: A => B => C): (A, B) => C
```

Let's look at a final example, *function composition*, which feeds the output of one function to the input of another function. Again, the implementation of this function is fully determined by its type signature.

■ **EXERCISE 2.5**

Implement the higher-order function that composes two functions.

```
def compose[A,B,C](f: B => C, g: A => B): A => C
```

This is such a common thing to want to do that Scala's standard library provides compose as a method on Function1 (the interface for functions that take one argument). To compose two functions f and g, we simply say f compose g.[10] It also provides an andThen method. f andThen g is the same as g compose f:

```
scala> val f = (x: Double) => math.Pi / 2 - x
f: Double => Double = <function1>

scala> val cos = f andThen math.sin
cos: Double => Double = <function1>
```

It's all well and good to puzzle together little one-liners like this, but what about programming with a large real-world code base? In functional programming, it turns out to be exactly the same. Higher-order functions like compose don't care whether

---

[9] This is named after the mathematician Haskell Curry, who discovered the principle. It was independently discovered earlier by Moses Schoenfinkel, but *Schoenfinkelization* didn't catch on.

[10] Solving the compose exercise by using this library function is considered cheating.

they're operating on huge functions backed by millions of lines of code or functions that are simple one-liners. Polymorphic, higher-order functions often end up being extremely widely applicable, precisely because they say nothing about any particular domain and are simply abstracting over a common pattern that occurs in many contexts. For this reason, programming in the large has much the same flavor as programming in the small. We'll write a lot of widely applicable functions over the course of this book, and the exercises in this chapter are a taste of the style of reasoning you'll employ when writing such functions.

2.7   *Summary*

In this chapter, we learned enough of the Scala language to get going, and some preliminary functional programming concepts. We learned how to define simple functions and programs, including how we can express loops using recursion; then we introduced the idea of higher-order functions, and we got some practice writing polymorphic functions in Scala. We saw how the implementations of polymorphic functions are often significantly constrained, such that we can often simply "follow the types" to the correct implementation. This is something we'll see a lot of in the chapters ahead.

Although we haven't yet written any large or complex programs, the principles we've discussed here are scalable and apply equally well to programming in the large as they do to programming in the small.

Next we'll look at using pure functions to manipulate data.

Functional data structures

3

We said in the introduction that functional programs don't update variables or modify mutable data structures. This raises pressing questions: what sort of data structures *can* we use in functional programming, how do we define them in Scala, and how do we operate on them? In this chapter, we'll learn the concept of *functional data structures* and how to work with them. We'll use this as an opportunity to introduce how data types are defined in functional programming, learn about the related technique of *pattern matching*, and get practice writing and generalizing pure functions.

This chapter has a lot of exercises, particularly to help with this last point—writing and generalizing pure functions. Some of these exercises may be challenging. As always, consult the hints or the answers at our GitHub site (https://github.com/fpinscala/fpinscala; see the preface), or ask for help online if you need to.

3.1 Defining functional data structures

A functional data structure is (not surprisingly) operated on using only pure functions. Remember, a pure function must not change data in place or perform other side effects. *Therefore, functional data structures are by definition immutable.* For example, the empty list (written `List()` or `Nil` in Scala) is as eternal and immutable as the integer values 3 or 4. And just as evaluating 3 + 4 results in a new number 7 without modifying either 3 or 4, concatenating two lists together (the syntax for this is a ++ b for two lists a and b) yields a new list and leaves the two inputs unmodified.

Doesn't this mean we end up doing a lot of extra copying of the data? Perhaps surprisingly, the answer is no, and we'll talk about exactly why that is. But first let's examine what's probably the most ubiquitous functional data structure, the singly linked list. The definition here is identical in spirit to (though simpler than) the

List data type defined in Scala's standard library. This code listing introduces a lot of new syntax and concepts that we'll talk through in detail.

Listing 3.1   Singly linked lists

List companion object. Contains functions for creating and working with lists.

List data type, parameterized on a type, A.

A List data constructor representing the empty list.

```
package fpinscala.datastructures

sealed trait List[+A]
case object Nil extends List[Nothing]
case class Cons[+A](head: A, tail: List[A]) extends List[A]

object List {
  def sum(ints: List[Int]): Int = ints match {
    case Nil => 0
    case Cons(x,xs) => x + sum(xs)
  }

  def product(ds: List[Double]): Double = ds match {
    case Nil => 1.0
    case Cons(0.0, _) => 0.0
    case Cons(x,xs) => x * product(xs)
  }

  def apply[A](as: A*): List[A] =
    if (as.isEmpty) Nil
    else Cons(as.head, apply(as.tail: _*))
}
```

Another data constructor, representing nonempty lists. Note that `tail` is another `List[A]`, which may be `Nil` or another `Cons`.

The sum of a list starting with `x` is `x` plus the sum of the rest of the list.

The sum of the empty list is 0.

A function that uses pattern matching to add up a list of integers.

Variadic function syntax.

Let's look first at the definition of the data type, which begins with the keywords `sealed trait`. In general, we introduce a data type with the `trait` keyword. A `trait` is an abstract interface that may optionally contain implementations of some methods. Here we're declaring a `trait`, called `List`, with no methods on it. Adding `sealed` in front means that all implementations of the `trait` must be declared in this file.[1]

There are two such implementations, or *data constructors*, of `List` (each introduced with the keyword `case`) declared next, to represent the two possible forms a `List` can take. As the figure at the top of page 31 shows, a `List` can be empty, denoted by the data constructor `Nil`, or it can be nonempty, denoted by the data constructor `Cons` (traditionally short for *construct*). A nonempty list consists of an initial element, head, followed by a `List` (possibly empty) of remaining elements (the `tail`):

```
case object Nil extends List[Nothing]
case class Cons[+A](head: A, tail: List[A]) extends List[A]
```

---

[1] We could also say `abstract class` here instead of `trait`. The distinction between the two is not at all significant for our purposes right now. See section 5.3 in the Scala Language Specification (http://mng.bz/R75t) for more on the distinction.

Singly linked lists

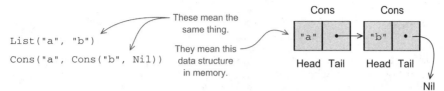

List("a", "b")

Cons("a", Cons("b", Nil))

Just as functions can be polymorphic, data types can be as well, and by adding the type parameter [+A] after sealed trait List and then using that A parameter inside of the Cons data constructor, we declare the List data type to be polymorphic in the type of elements it contains, which means we can use this same definition for a list of Int elements (denoted List[Int]), Double elements (denoted List[Double]), String elements (List[String]), and so on (the + indicates that the type parameter A is *covariant*—see sidebar "More about variance" for more information).

A data constructor declaration gives us a function to construct that form of the data type. Here are a few examples:

```
val ex1: List[Double] = Nil
val ex2: List[Int] = Cons(1, Nil)
val ex3: List[String] = Cons("a", Cons("b", Nil))
```

The case object Nil lets us write Nil to construct an empty List, and the case class Cons lets us write Cons(1, Nil), Cons("a", Cons("b", Nil)) and so on to build singly linked lists of arbitrary lengths.[2] Note that because List is parameterized on a type, A, these are polymorphic functions that can be instantiated with different types for A. Here, ex2 instantiates the A type parameter to Int, while ex3 instantiates it to String. The ex1 example is interesting—Nil is being instantiated with type List[Double], which is allowed because the empty list contains no elements and can be considered a list of whatever type we want!

Each data constructor also introduces a *pattern* that can be used for *pattern matching*, as in the functions sum and product. We'll examine pattern matching in more detail next.

More about variance

In the declaration trait List[+A], the + in front of the type parameter A is a *variance annotation* that signals that A is a *covariant* or "positive" parameter of List. This means that, for instance, List[Dog] is considered a subtype of List[Animal], assuming Dog is a subtype of Animal. (More generally, for all types X and Y, if X is a

---

2   Scala generates a default def toString: String method for any case class or case object, which can be convenient for debugging. You can see the output of this default toString implementation if you experiment with List values in the REPL, which uses toString to render the result of each expression. Cons(1,Nil) will be printed as the string "Cons(1, Nil)", for instance. But note that the generated toString will be naively recursive and will cause stack overflow when printing long lists, so you may wish to provide a different implementation.

(continued)

subtype of Y, then List[X] is a subtype of List[Y]). We could leave out the + in front of the A, which would make List *invariant* in that type parameter.

But notice now that Nil extends List[Nothing]. Nothing is a subtype of all types, which means that in conjunction with the *variance annotation*, Nil can be considered a List[Int], a List[Double], and so on, exactly as we want.

These concerns about variance aren't very important for the present discussion and are more of an artifact of how Scala encodes data constructors via subtyping, so don't worry if this is not completely clear right now. It's certainly possible to write code without using variance annotations at all, and function signatures are sometimes simpler (whereas type inference often gets worse). We'll use variance annotations throughout this book where it's convenient to do so, but you should feel free to experiment with both approaches.

3.2   *Pattern matching*

Let's look in detail at the functions sum and product, which we place in the object List, sometimes called the *companion object* to List (see sidebar). Both these definitions make use of pattern matching:

```
def sum(ints: List[Int]): Int = ints match {
  case Nil => 0
  case Cons(x,xs) => x + sum(xs)
}

def product(ds: List[Double]): Double = ds match {
  case Nil => 1.0
  case Cons(0.0, _) => 0.0
  case Cons(x,xs) => x * product(xs)
}
```

As you might expect, the sum function states that the sum of an empty list is 0, and the sum of a nonempty list is the first element, x, plus the sum of the remaining elements, xs.[3] Likewise the product definition states that the product of an empty list is 1.0, the product of any list starting with 0.0 is 0.0, and the product of any other nonempty list is the first element multiplied by the product of the remaining elements. Note that these are recursive definitions, which are common when writing functions that operate over recursive data types like List (which refers to itself recursively in its Cons data constructor).

Pattern matching works a bit like a fancy switch statement that may descend into the structure of the expression it examines and extract subexpressions of that

---

[3] We could call x and xs anything there, but it's a common convention to use xs, ys, as, or bs as variable names for a sequence of some sort, and x, y, z, a, or b as the name for a single element of a sequence. Another common naming convention is h for the first element of a list (the *head* of the list), t for the remaining elements (the *tail*), and l for an entire list.

structure. It's introduced with an expression (the *target* or *scrutinee*) like ds, followed by the keyword match, and a {}-wrapped sequence of *cases*. Each case in the match consists of a *pattern* (like Cons(x,xs)) to the left of the => and a *result* (like x * product(xs)) to the right of the =>. If the target *matches* the pattern in a case (discussed next), the result of that case becomes the result of the entire match expression. If multiple patterns match the target, Scala chooses the first matching case.

Companion objects in Scala

We'll often declare a *companion object* in addition to our data type and its data constructors. This is just an object with the same name as the data type (in this case List) where we put various convenience functions for creating or working with values of the data type.

If, for instance, we wanted a function def fill[A](n: Int, a: A): List[A] that created a List with n copies of the element a, the List companion object would be a good place for it. Companion objects are more of a convention in Scala.[4] We could have called this module Foo if we wanted, but calling it List makes it clear that the module contains functions relevant to working with lists.

Let's look at a few more examples of pattern matching:

- List(1,2,3) match { case _ => 42 } results in 42. Here we're using a variable pattern, _, which matches any expression. We could say x or foo instead of _, but we usually use _ to indicate a variable whose value we ignore in the result of the case.[5]
- List(1,2,3) match { case Cons(h,_) => h } results in 1. Here we're using a data constructor pattern in conjunction with variables to *capture* or *bind* a subexpression of the target.
- List(1,2,3) match { case Cons(_,t) => t } results in List(2,3).
- List(1,2,3) match { case Nil => 42 } results in a MatchError at runtime. A MatchError indicates that none of the cases in a match expression matched the target.

Matching a list

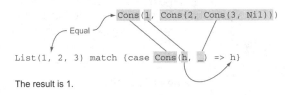

The result is 1.

---

[4] There is some special support for them in the language that isn't really relevant for our purposes.

[5] The _ variable pattern is treated somewhat specially in that it may be mentioned multiple times in the pattern to ignore multiple parts of the target.

What determines if a pattern matches an expression? A pattern may contain *literals* like 3 or "hi"; *variables* like x and xs, which match anything, indicated by an identifier starting with a lowercase letter or underscore; and data constructors like Cons(x,xs) and Nil, which match only values of the corresponding form. (Nil as a pattern matches only the value Nil, and Cons(h,t) or Cons(x,xs) as a pattern only match Cons values.) These components of a pattern may be nested arbitrarily—Cons(x1, Cons(x2, Nil)) and Cons(y1, Cons(y2, Cons(y3, _))) are valid patterns. A pattern *matches* the target if there exists an assignment of variables in the pattern to subexpressions of the target that make it *structurally equivalent* to the target. The resulting expression for a matching case will then have access to these variable assignments in its local scope.

■ EXERCISE 3.1

What will be the result of the following match expression?

```
val x = List(1,2,3,4,5) match {
  case Cons(x, Cons(2, Cons(4, _))) => x
  case Nil => 42
  case Cons(x, Cons(y, Cons(3, Cons(4, _)))) => x + y
  case Cons(h, t) => h + sum(t)
  case _ => 101
}
```

You're strongly encouraged to try experimenting with pattern matching in the REPL to get a sense for how it behaves.

Variadic functions in Scala

The function apply in the object List is a *variadic function*, meaning it accepts zero or more arguments of type A:

```
def apply[A](as: A*): List[A] =
  if (as.isEmpty) Nil
  else Cons(as.head, apply(as.tail: _*))
```

For data types, it's a common idiom to have a variadic apply method in the companion object to conveniently construct instances of the data type. By calling this function apply and placing it in the companion object, we can invoke it with syntax like List(1,2,3,4) or List("hi","bye"), with as many values as we want separated by commas (we sometimes call this the *list literal* or just *literal* syntax).

Variadic functions are just providing a little syntactic sugar for creating and passing a Seq of elements explicitly. Seq is the interface in Scala's collections library implemented by sequence-like data structures such as lists, queues, and vectors. Inside apply, the argument as will be bound to a Seq[A] (documentation at http://mng.bz/f4k9), which has the functions head (returns the first element) and tail (returns all elements but the first). The special _* type annotation allows us to pass a Seq to a variadic method.

3.3 *Data sharing in functional data structures*

When data is immutable, how do we write functions that, for example, add or remove elements from a list? The answer is simple. When we add an element 1 to the front of an existing list, say xs, we return a new list, in this case Cons(1,xs). Since lists are immutable, we don't need to actually copy xs; we can just reuse it. This is called *data sharing*. Sharing of immutable data often lets us implement functions more efficiently; we can always return immutable data structures without having to worry about subsequent code modifying our data. There's no need to pessimistically make copies to avoid modification or corruption.[6]

In the same way, to remove an element from the front of a list mylist = Cons(x,xs), we simply return its tail, xs. There's no real removing going on. The original list, mylist, is still available, unharmed. We say that functional data structures are *persistent*, meaning that existing references are never changed by operations on the data structure.

Data sharing

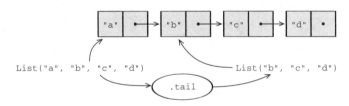

Both lists share the same data in memory. .tail does not modify the
original list, it simply references the tail of the original list.
Defensive copying is not needed, because the list is immutable.

Let's try implementing a few different functions for modifying lists in different ways. You can place this, and other functions that we write, inside the List companion object.

EXERCISE 3.2

Implement the function tail for removing the first element of a List. Note that the function takes constant time. What are different choices you could make in your implementation if the List is Nil? We'll return to this question in the next chapter.

---

[6] Pessimistic copying can become a problem in large programs. When mutable data is passed through a chain of loosely coupled components, each component has to make its own copy of the data because other components might modify it. Immutable data is always safe to share, so we never have to make copies. We find that *in the large*, FP can often achieve greater efficiency than approaches that rely on side effects, due to much greater sharing of data and computation.

■ **EXERCISE 3.3** ──────────────────────────

Using the same idea, implement the function `setHead` for replacing the first element of a `List` with a different value.

3.3.1 *The efficiency of data sharing*

Data sharing often lets us implement operations more efficiently. Let's look at a few examples.

■ **EXERCISE 3.4** ──────────────────────────

Generalize `tail` to the function `drop`, which removes the first n elements from a list. Note that this function takes time proportional only to the number of elements being dropped—we don't need to make a copy of the entire `List`.

```
def drop[A](l: List[A], n: Int): List[A]
```

■ **EXERCISE 3.5** ──────────────────────────

Implement `dropWhile`, which removes elements from the `List` prefix as long as they match a predicate.

```
def dropWhile[A](l: List[A], f: A => Boolean): List[A]
```

A more surprising example of data sharing is this function that adds all the elements of one list to the end of another:

```
def append[A](a1: List[A], a2: List[A]): List[A] =
  a1 match {
    case Nil => a2
    case Cons(h,t) => Cons(h, append(t, a2))
  }
```

Note that this definition only copies values until the first list is exhausted, so its runtime and memory usage are determined only by the length of a1. The remaining list then just points to a2. If we were to implement this same function for two arrays, we'd be forced to copy all the elements in both arrays into the result. In this case, the immutable linked list is much more efficient than an array!

■ **EXERCISE 3.6**

Not everything works out so nicely. Implement a function, `init`, that returns a `List` consisting of all but the last element of a `List`. So, given `List(1,2,3,4)`, `init` will return `List(1,2,3)`. Why can't this function be implemented in constant time like `tail`?

```
def init[A](l: List[A]): List[A]
```

Because of the structure of a singly linked list, any time we want to replace the `tail` of a `Cons`, even if it's the last `Cons` in the list, we must copy all the previous `Cons` objects. Writing purely functional data structures that support different operations efficiently is all about finding clever ways to exploit data sharing. We're not going to cover these data structures here; for now, we're content to use the functional data structures others have written. As an example of what's possible, in the Scala standard library there's a purely functional sequence implementation, `Vector` (documentation at http://mng.bz/Xhl8), with constant-time random access, updates, `head`, `tail`, `init`, and constant-time additions to either the front or rear of the sequence. See the chapter notes for links to further reading about how to design such data structures.

3.3.2 *Improving type inference for higher-order functions*

Higher-order functions like `dropWhile` will often be passed anonymous functions. Let's look at a typical example.

Recall the signature of `dropWhile`:

```
def dropWhile[A](l: List[A], f: A => Boolean): List[A]
```

When we call it with an anonymous function for `f`, we have to specify the type of its argument, here named `x`:

```
val xs: List[Int] = List(1,2,3,4,5)
val ex1 = dropWhile(xs, (x: Int) => x < 4)
```

The value of `ex1` is `List(4,5)`.

It's a little unfortunate that we need to state that the type of `x` is `Int`. The first argument to `dropWhile` is a `List[Int]`, so the function in the second argument must accept an `Int`. Scala can infer this fact if we group `dropWhile` into two argument lists:

```
def dropWhile[A](as: List[A])(f: A => Boolean): List[A] =
  as match {
    case Cons(h,t) if f(h) => dropWhile(t)(f)
    case _ => as
  }
```

The syntax for calling this version of dropWhile looks like dropWhile(xs)(f). That is, dropWhile(xs) is returning a function, which we then call with the argument f (in other words, dropWhile is curried[7]). The main reason for grouping the arguments this way is to assist with type inference. We can now use dropWhile without annotations:

```
val xs: List[Int] = List(1,2,3,4,5)
val ex1 = dropWhile(xs)(x => x < 4)
```

Note that x is not annotated with its type.

More generally, when a function definition contains multiple argument groups, type information flows from left to right across these argument groups. Here, the first argument group fixes the type parameter A of dropWhile to Int, so the annotation on x => x < 4 is not required.[8]

We'll often group and order our function arguments into multiple argument lists to maximize type inference.

3.4   Recursion over lists and generalizing to higher-order functions

Let's look again at the implementations of sum and product. We've simplified the product implementation slightly, so as not to include the "short-circuiting" logic of checking for 0.0:

```
def sum(ints: List[Int]): Int = ints match {
  case Nil => 0
  case Cons(x,xs) => x + sum(xs)
}

def product(ds: List[Double]): Double = ds match {
  case Nil => 1.0
  case Cons(x, xs) => x * product(xs)
}
```

Note how similar these two definitions are. They're operating on different types (List[Int] versus List[Double]), but aside from this, the only differences are the value to return in the case that the list is empty (0 in the case of sum, 1.0 in the case of product), and the operation to combine results (+ in the case of sum, * in the case of product). Whenever you encounter duplication like this, you can generalize it away by pulling subexpressions out into function arguments. If a subexpression refers to any local variables (the + operation refers to the local variables x and xs introduced by the pattern, similarly for product), turn the subexpression into a function that accepts these variables as arguments. Let's do that now. Our function will take as arguments

---

[7]   Recall from the previous chapter that a function of two arguments can be represented as a function that accepts one argument and returns another function of one argument.

[8]   This is an unfortunate restriction of the Scala compiler; other functional languages like Haskell and OCaml provide *complete* inference, meaning type annotations are almost never required. See the notes for this chapter for more information and links to further reading.

the value to return in the case of the empty list, and the function to add an element to the result in the case of a nonempty list.[9]

Listing 3.2   Right folds and simple uses

```
def foldRight[A,B](as: List[A], z: B)(f: (A, B) => B): B =
  as match {
    case Nil => z
    case Cons(x, xs) => f(x, foldRight(xs, z)(f))
  }

def sum2(ns: List[Int]) =
  foldRight(ns, 0)((x,y) => x + y)

def product2(ns: List[Double]) =
  foldRight(ns, 1.0)(_ * _)
```

Again, placing f in its own argument group after as and z lets type inference determine the input types to f.

_ * _ is more concise notation for (x,y) => x * y (see following sidebar).

foldRight is not specific to any one type of element, and we discover while generalizing that the value that's returned doesn't have to be of the same type as the elements of the list! One way of describing what foldRight does is that it replaces the constructors of the list, Nil and Cons, with z and f, illustrated here:

```
Cons(1, Cons(2, Nil))
f   (1, f   (2, z  ))
```

Let's look at a complete example. We'll *trace* the evaluation of foldRight(Cons(1, Cons(2, Cons(3, Nil))), 0)((x,y) => x + y) by repeatedly substituting the definition of foldRight for its usages. We'll use program traces like this throughout this book:

```
foldRight(Cons(1, Cons(2, Cons(3, Nil))), 0)((x,y) => x + y)
1 + foldRight(Cons(2, Cons(3, Nil)), 0)((x,y) => x + y)
1 + (2 + foldRight(Cons(3, Nil), 0)((x,y) => x + y))
1 + (2 + (3 + (foldRight(Nil, 0)((x,y) => x + y))))
1 + (2 + (3 + (0)))
6
```

Replace foldRight with its definition.

Note that foldRight must traverse all the way to the end of the list (pushing frames onto the call stack as it goes) before it can begin collapsing it.

Underscore notation for anonymous functions

The anonymous function (x,y) => x + y can be written as _ + _ in situations where the types of x and y could be inferred by Scala. This is a useful shorthand in cases where the function parameters are mentioned just once in the body of the function. Each underscore in an anonymous function expression like _ + _ introduces a new (unnamed) function parameter and references it. Arguments are introduced in left-to-right order. Here are a few more examples:

---

[9] In the Scala standard library, foldRight is a method on List and its arguments are curried similarly for better type inference.

(continued)

```
_ + _          <———    (x,y) => x + y

_ * 2          <———    x => x * 2

_.head         <———    xs => xs.head

_ drop _       <———
                       (xs,n) => xs.drop(n)
```

Use this syntax judiciously. The meaning of this syntax in expressions like `foo(_, g(List(_ + 1), _))` can be unclear. There are precise rules about scoping of these underscore-based anonymous functions in the Scala language specification, but if you have to think about it, we recommend just using ordinary named function parameters.

EXERCISE 3.7

Can `product`, implemented using `foldRight`, immediately halt the recursion and return `0.0` if it encounters a `0.0`? Why or why not? Consider how any short-circuiting might work if you call `foldRight` with a large list. This is a deeper question that we'll return to in chapter 5.

EXERCISE 3.8

See what happens when you pass `Nil` and `Cons` themselves to `foldRight`, like this: `foldRight(List(1,2,3), Nil:List[Int])(Cons(_,_))`.[10] What do you think this says about the relationship between `foldRight` and the data constructors of `List`?

EXERCISE 3.9

Compute the length of a list using `foldRight`.

```
def length[A](as: List[A]): Int
```

EXERCISE 3.10

Our implementation of `foldRight` is not tail-recursive and will result in a `StackOverflowError` for large lists (we say it's not *stack-safe*). Convince yourself that this is the case, and then write another general list-recursion function, `foldLeft`, that is

---

[10] The type annotation `Nil:List[Int]` is needed here, because otherwise Scala infers the B type parameter in `foldRight` as `List[Nothing]`.

tail-recursive, using the techniques we discussed in the previous chapter. Here is its signature:[11]

```scala
def foldLeft[A,B](as: List[A], z: B)(f: (B, A) => B): B
```

EXERCISE 3.11

Write sum, product, and a function to compute the length of a list using foldLeft.

EXERCISE 3.12

Write a function that returns the reverse of a list (given List(1,2,3) it returns List(3,2,1)). See if you can write it using a fold.

EXERCISE 3.13

Hard: Can you write foldLeft in terms of foldRight? How about the other way around? Implementing foldRight via foldLeft is useful because it lets us implement foldRight tail-recursively, which means it works even for large lists without overflowing the stack.

EXERCISE 3.14

Implement append in terms of either foldLeft or foldRight.

EXERCISE 3.15

Hard: Write a function that concatenates a list of lists into a single list. Its runtime should be linear in the total length of all lists. Try to use functions we have already defined.

3.4.1 More functions for working with lists

There are many more useful functions for working with lists. We'll cover a few more here, to get additional practice with generalizing functions and to get some basic familiarity with common patterns when processing lists. After finishing this section, you're not going to emerge with an automatic sense of when to use each of these functions.

---

[11] Again, foldLeft is defined as a method of List in the Scala standard library, and it is curried similarly for better type inference, so you can write mylist.foldLeft(0.0)(_ + _).

Just get in the habit of looking for possible ways to generalize any explicit recursive functions you write to process lists. If you do this, you'll (re)discover these functions for yourself and develop an instinct for when you'd use each one.

EXERCISE 3.16

Write a function that transforms a list of integers by adding 1 to each element. (Reminder: this should be a pure function that returns a new List!)

EXERCISE 3.17

Write a function that turns each value in a List[Double] into a String. You can use the expression d.toString to convert some d: Double to a String.

EXERCISE 3.18

Write a function map that generalizes modifying each element in a list while maintaining the structure of the list. Here is its signature:[12]

```scala
def map[A,B](as: List[A])(f: A => B): List[B]
```

EXERCISE 3.19

Write a function filter that removes elements from a list unless they satisfy a given predicate. Use it to remove all odd numbers from a List[Int].

```scala
def filter[A](as: List[A])(f: A => Boolean): List[A]
```

EXERCISE 3.20

Write a function flatMap that works like map except that the function given will return a list instead of a single result, and that list should be inserted into the final resulting list. Here is its signature:

```scala
def flatMap[A,B](as: List[A])(f: A => List[B]): List[B]
```

For instance, flatMap(List(1,2,3))(i => List(i,i)) should result in List(1,1,2,2,3,3).

---

[12] In the standard library, map and flatMap are methods of List.

■   **EXERCISE 3.21**

Use `flatMap` to implement `filter`.

■   **EXERCISE 3.22**

Write a function that accepts two lists and constructs a new list by adding corresponding elements. For example, `List(1,2,3)` and `List(4,5,6)` become `List(5,7,9)`.

■   **EXERCISE 3.23**

Generalize the function you just wrote so that it's not specific to integers or addition. Name your generalized function `zipWith`.

LISTS IN THE STANDARD LIBRARY

`List` exists in the Scala standard library (API documentation at http://mng.bz/vu45), and we'll use the standard library version in subsequent chapters. The main difference between the `List` developed here and the standard library version is that `Cons` is called `::`, which associates to the right,[13] so `1 :: 2 :: Nil` is equal to `1 :: (2 :: Nil)`, which is equal to `List(1,2)`. When pattern matching, `case Cons(h,t)` becomes `case h :: t`, which avoids having to nest parentheses if writing a pattern like `case h :: h2 :: t` to extract more than just the first element of the `List`.

There are a number of other useful methods on the standard library lists. You may want to try experimenting with these and other methods in the REPL after reading the API documentation. These are defined as methods on `List[A]`, rather than as stand-alone functions as we've done in this chapter:

- `def take(n: Int): List[A]`—Returns a list consisting of the first n elements of this
- `def takeWhile(f: A => Boolean): List[A]`—Returns a list consisting of the longest valid prefix of this whose elements all pass the predicate f
- `def forall(f: A => Boolean): Boolean`—Returns `true` if and only if all elements of this pass the predicate f
- `def exists(f: A => Boolean): Boolean`—Returns `true` if any element of this passes the predicate f

---

[13] In Scala, all methods whose names end in `:` are right-associative. That is, the expression `x :: xs` is actually the method call `xs.::(x)`, which in turn calls the data constructor `::(x,xs)`. See the Scala language specification for more information.

- scanLeft and scanRight—Like foldLeft and foldRight, but they return the List of partial results rather than just the final accumulated value

We recommend that you look through the Scala API documentation after finishing this chapter, to see what other functions there are. If you find yourself writing an explicit recursive function for doing some sort of list manipulation, check the List API to see if something like the function you need already exists.

3.4.2   *Loss of efficiency when assembling list functions from simpler components*

One of the problems with List is that, although we can often express operations and algorithms in terms of very general-purpose functions, the resulting implementation isn't always efficient—we may end up making multiple passes over the same input, or else have to write explicit recursive loops to allow early termination.

■ **EXERCISE 3.24** ───

Hard: As an example, implement hasSubsequence for checking whether a List contains another List as a subsequence. For instance, List(1,2,3,4) would have List(1,2), List(2,3), and List(4) as subsequences, among others. You may have some difficulty finding a concise purely functional implementation that is also efficient. That's okay. Implement the function however comes most naturally. We'll return to this implementation in chapter 5 and hopefully improve on it. Note: Any two values x and y can be compared for equality in Scala using the expression x == y.

```scala
def hasSubsequence[A](sup: List[A], sub: List[A]): Boolean
```

3.5   *Trees*

List is just one example of what's called an *algebraic data type (ADT)*. (Somewhat confusingly, ADT is sometimes used elsewhere to stand for *abstract data type*.) An ADT is just a data type defined by one or more data constructors, each of which may contain zero or more arguments. We say that the data type is the *sum* or *union* of its data constructors, and each data constructor is the *product* of its arguments, hence the name *algebraic* data type.[14]

---

[14] The naming is not coincidental. There's a deep connection, beyond the scope of this book, between the "addition" and "multiplication" of types to form an ADT and addition and multiplication of numbers.

Algebraic data types can be used to define other data structures. Let's define a simple binary tree data structure:

```
sealed trait Tree[+A]
case class Leaf[A](value: A) extends Tree[A]
case class Branch[A](left: Tree[A], right: Tree[A]) extends Tree[A]
```

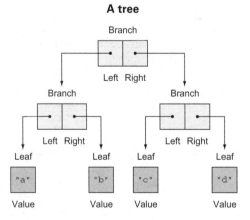

A tree

Pattern matching again provides a convenient way of operating over elements of our ADT. Let's try writing a few functions.

EXERCISE 3.25

Write a function size that counts the number of nodes (leaves and branches) in a tree.

EXERCISE 3.26

Write a function maximum that returns the maximum element in a Tree[Int]. (Note: In Scala, you can use x.max(y) or x max y to compute the maximum of two integers x and y.)

EXERCISE 3.27

Write a function depth that returns the maximum path length from the root of a tree to any leaf.

EXERCISE 3.28

Write a function map, analogous to the method of the same name on List, that modifies each element in a tree with a given function.

ADTs and encapsulation

One might object that algebraic data types violate encapsulation by making public the internal representation of a type. In FP, we approach concerns about encapsulation differently—we don't typically have delicate mutable state which could lead to bugs or violation of invariants if exposed publicly. Exposing the data constructors of a type is often fine, and the decision to do so is approached much like any other decision about what the public API of a data type should be.[15]

We do typically use ADTs for situations where the set of cases is *closed* (known to be fixed). For List and Tree, changing the set of data constructors would significantly change what these data types are. List *is* a singly linked list—that is its nature—and the two cases Nil and Cons form part of its useful public API. We can certainly write code that deals with a more abstract API than List (we'll see examples of this later in the book), but this sort of information hiding can be handled as a separate layer rather than being baked into List directly.

---

[15] It's also possible in Scala to expose patterns like Nil and Cons independent of the actual data constructors of the type.

■ **EXERCISE 3.29**

Generalize `size`, `maximum`, `depth`, and `map`, writing a new function `fold` that abstracts over their similarities. Reimplement them in terms of this more general function. Can you draw an analogy between this `fold` function and the left and right folds for `List`?

3.6 *Summary*

In this chapter, we covered a number of important concepts. We introduced algebraic data types and pattern matching, and showed how to implement purely functional data structures, including the singly linked list. We hope that, through the exercises in this chapter, you got more comfortable writing pure functions and generalizing them. We'll continue to develop these skills in the chapters ahead.

Handling errors
without exceptions

We noted briefly in chapter 1 that throwing exceptions is a side effect. If exceptions aren't used in functional code, what *is* used instead? In this chapter, we'll learn the basic principles for raising and handling errors functionally. The big idea is that we can represent failures and exceptions with ordinary values, and we can write higher-order functions that abstract out common patterns of error handling and recovery. The functional solution, of returning errors as values, is safer and retains referential transparency, and through the use of higher-order functions, we can preserve the primary benefit of exceptions—*consolidation of error-handling logic*. We'll see how this works over the course of this chapter, after we take a closer look at exceptions and discuss some of their problems.

For the same reason that we created our own `List` data type in the previous chapter, we'll re-create in this chapter two Scala standard library types: `Option` and `Either`. The purpose is to enhance your understanding of how these types can be used for handling errors. After completing this chapter, you should feel free to use the Scala standard library version of `Option` and `Either` (though you'll notice that the standard library versions of both types are missing some of the useful functions we define in this chapter).

4.1 The good and bad aspects of exceptions

Why do exceptions break referential transparency, and why is that a problem? Let's look at a simple example. We'll define a function that throws an exception and call it.

Listing 4.1 Throwing and catching an exception

```
def failingFn(i: Int): Int = {
  val y: Int = throw new Exception("fail!")   ◄
  try {
    val x = 42 + 5
    x + y
  }
  catch { case e: Exception => 43 }   ◄
}
```

> **val y: Int = ... declares y as having type Int and sets it equal to the right-hand side of =.**

> **A catch block is just a pattern-matching block like the ones we've seen. case e: Exception is a pattern that matches any Exception, and it binds this value to the identifier e. The match returns the value 43.**

Calling `failingFn` from the REPL gives the expected error:

```
scala> failingFn(12)
java.lang.Exception: fail!
  at .failingFn(<console>:8)
  ...
```

We can prove that `y` is not referentially transparent. Recall that any RT expression may be substituted with the value it refers to, and this substitution should preserve program meaning. If we substitute `throw new Exception("fail!")` for `y` in `x + y`, it produces a different result, because the exception will now be raised inside a `try` block that will catch the exception and return 43:

```
def failingFn2(i: Int): Int = {
  try {
    val x = 42 + 5
    x + ((throw new Exception("fail!")): Int)   ◄
  }
  catch { case e: Exception => 43 }
}
```

> **A thrown Exception can be given any type; here we're annotating it with the type Int.**

We can demonstrate this in the REPL:

```
scala> failingFn2(12)
res1: Int = 43
```

Another way of understanding RT is that the meaning of RT expressions *does not depend on context* and may be reasoned about locally, whereas the meaning of non-RT expressions is *context-dependent* and requires more global reasoning. For instance, the meaning of the RT expression 42 + 5 doesn't depend on the larger expression it's embedded in—it's always and forever equal to 47. But the meaning of the expression `throw new Exception("fail")` is very context-dependent—as we just demonstrated, it takes on different meanings depending on which `try` block (if any) it's nested within.

There are two main problems with exceptions:

- As we just discussed, *exceptions break RT and introduce context dependence*, moving us away from the simple reasoning of the substitution model and making it possible to write confusing exception-based code. This is the source of the folklore advice that exceptions should be used only for error handling, not for control flow.

- *Exceptions are not type-safe.* The type of failingFn, Int => Int tells us nothing about the fact that exceptions may occur, and the compiler will certainly not force callers of failingFn to make a decision about how to handle those exceptions. If we forget to check for an exception in failingFn, this won't be detected until runtime.

Checked exceptions

Java's checked exceptions at least force a decision about whether to handle or reraise an error, but they result in significant boilerplate for callers. More importantly, *they don't work for higher-order functions*, which can't possibly be aware of the specific exceptions that could be raised by their arguments. For example, consider the map function we defined for List:

```
def map[A,B](l: List[A])(f: A => B): List[B]
```

This function is clearly useful, highly generic, and at odds with the use of checked exceptions—we can't have a version of map for every single checked exception that could possibly be thrown by f. Even if we wanted to do this, how would map even know what exceptions were possible? This is why generic code, even in Java, so often resorts to using RuntimeException or some common checked Exception type.

We'd like an alternative to exceptions without these drawbacks, but we don't want to lose out on the primary benefit of exceptions: they allow us to *consolidate and centralize error-handling logic*, rather than being forced to distribute this logic throughout our codebase. The technique we use is based on an old idea: instead of throwing an exception, we return a value indicating that an exceptional condition has occurred. This idea might be familiar to anyone who has used return codes in C to handle exceptions. But instead of using error codes, we introduce a new generic type for these "possibly defined values" and use higher-order functions to encapsulate common patterns of handling and propagating errors. Unlike C-style error codes, the error-handling strategy we use is *completely type-safe*, and we get full assistance from the type-checker in forcing us to deal with errors, with a minimum of syntactic noise. We'll see how all of this works shortly.

4.2   *Possible alternatives to exceptions*

Let's now consider a realistic situation where we might use an exception and look at different approaches we could use instead. Here's an implementation of a function that computes the mean of a list, which is undefined if the list is empty:

Seq is the common interface of various linear sequence-like collections. Check the API docs (http://mng.bz/f4k9) for more information.

sum is defined as a method on Seq only if the elements of the sequence are numeric. The standard library accomplishes this trick with implicits, which we won't go into here.

```
def mean(xs: Seq[Double]): Double =
  if (xs.isEmpty)
    throw new ArithmeticException("mean of empty list!")
  else xs.sum / xs.length
```

The mean function is an example of what's called a *partial function*: it's not defined for some inputs. A function is typically partial because it makes some assumptions about its inputs that aren't implied by the input types.[1] You may be used to throwing exceptions in this case, but we have a few other options. Let's look at these for our mean example.

The first possibility is to return some sort of bogus value of type Double. We could simply return xs.sum / xs.length in all cases, and have it result in 0.0/0.0 when the input is empty, which is Double.NaN; or we could return some other sentinel value. In other situations, we might return null instead of a value of the needed type. This general class of approaches is how error handling is often done in languages without exceptions, and we reject this solution for a few reasons:

- It allows errors to silently propagate—the caller can forget to check this condition and won't be alerted by the compiler, which might result in subsequent code not working properly. Often the error won't be detected until much later in the code.

- Besides being error-prone, it results in a fair amount of boilerplate code at call sites, with explicit if statements to check whether the caller has received a "real" result. This boilerplate is magnified if you happen to be calling several functions, each of which uses error codes that must be checked and aggregated in some way.

- It's not applicable to polymorphic code. For some output types, we might not even *have* a sentinel value of that type even if we wanted to! Consider a function like max, which finds the maximum value in a sequence according to a custom comparison function: def max[A](xs: Seq[A])(greater: (A,A) => Boolean): A. If the input is empty, we can't invent a value of type A. Nor can null be used here, since null is only valid for non-primitive types, and A may in fact be a primitive like Double or Int.

- It demands a special policy or calling convention of callers—proper use of the mean function would require that callers do something other than call mean and make use of the result. Giving functions special policies like this makes it difficult to pass them to higher-order functions, which must treat all arguments uniformly.

The second possibility is to force the caller to supply an argument that tells us what to do in case we don't know how to handle the input:

```
def mean_1(xs: IndexedSeq[Double], onEmpty: Double): Double =
  if (xs.isEmpty) onEmpty
  else xs.sum / xs.length
```

This makes mean into a total function, but it has drawbacks—it requires that *immediate* callers have direct knowledge of how to handle the undefined case and limits them to

---

[1] A function may also be partial if it doesn't terminate for some inputs. We won't discuss this form of partiality here, since it's not a recoverable error so there's no question of how best to handle it. See the chapter notes for more about partiality.

returning a `Double`. What if `mean` is called as part of a larger computation and we'd like to abort that computation if `mean` is undefined? Or perhaps we'd like to take some completely different branch in the larger computation in this case? Simply passing an `onEmpty` parameter doesn't give us this freedom.

We need a way to defer the decision of how to handle undefined cases so that they can be dealt with at the most appropriate level.

4.3   *The Option data type*

The solution is to represent explicitly in the return type that a function may not always have an answer. We can think of this as deferring to the caller for the error-handling strategy. We introduce a new type, `Option`. As we mentioned earlier, this type also exists in the Scala standard library, but we're re-creating it here for pedagogical purposes:

```scala
sealed trait Option[+A]
case class Some[+A](get: A) extends Option[A]
case object None extends Option[Nothing]
```

`Option` has two cases: it can be defined, in which case it will be a `Some`, or it can be undefined, in which case it will be `None`.

We can use `Option` for our definition of `mean` like so:

```scala
def mean(xs: Seq[Double]): Option[Double] =
  if (xs.isEmpty) None
  else Some(xs.sum / xs.length)
```

The return type now reflects the possibility that the result may not always be defined. We still always return a result of the declared type (now `Option[Double]`) from our function, so `mean` is now a *total function*. It takes each value of the input type to exactly one value of the output type.

Responding to invalid inputs

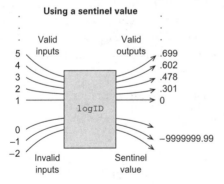

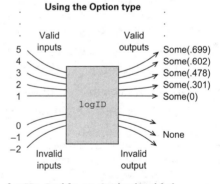

Mapping all invalid inputs to a special value of the same type as the valid outputs. Ambiguous, and compiler can't check that caller handles it correctly.

Every valid output is wrapped in Some. Invalid inputs are mapped to None. The compiler forces the caller to deal explicitly with the possibility of failure.

4.3.1 Usage patterns for Option

Partial functions abound in programming, and Option (and the Either data type that we'll discuss shortly) is typically how this partiality is dealt with in FP. You'll see Option used throughout the Scala standard library, for instance:

- Map lookup for a given key (http://mng.bz/ha64) returns Option.
- headOption and lastOption defined for lists and other iterables (http://mng.bz/Pz86) return an Option containing the first or last elements of a sequence if it's nonempty.

These aren't the only examples—we'll see Option come up in many different situations. What makes Option convenient is that we can factor out common patterns of error handling via higher-order functions, freeing us from writing the usual boilerplate that comes with exception-handling code. In this section, we'll cover some of the basic functions for working with Option. Our goal is not for you to attain fluency with all these functions, but just to get you familiar enough that you can revisit this chapter and make progress on your own when you have to write some functional code to deal with errors.

BASIC FUNCTIONS ON OPTION

Option can be thought of like a List that can contain at most one element, and many of the List functions we saw earlier have analogous functions on Option. Let's look at some of these functions.

We'll do something slightly different than in chapter 3 where we put all our List functions in the List companion object. Here we'll place our functions, when possible, inside the body of the Option trait, so they can be called with the syntax obj.fn(arg1) or obj fn arg1 instead of fn(obj, arg1). This is a stylistic choice with no real significance, and we'll use both styles throughout this book.[2]

This choice raises one additional complication with regard to variance that we'll discuss in a moment. Let's take a look.

Listing 4.2 The Option data type

Don't evaluate ob unless needed.

Apply f if the Option is not None.

```
trait Option[+A] {
  def map[B](f: A => B): Option[B]
  def flatMap[B](f: A => Option[B]): Option[B]
  def getOrElse[B >: A](default: => B): B
  def orElse[B >: A](ob: => Option[B]): Option[B]
  def filter(f: A => Boolean): Option[A]
}
```

Apply f, which may fail, to the Option if not None.

The B >: A says that the B type parameter must be a supertype of A.

Convert Some to None if the value doesn't satisfy f.

---

[2] In general, we'll use this object-oriented style of syntax where possible for functions that have a single, clear operand (like List.map), and the standalone function style otherwise.

There is some new syntax here. The `default: => B` type annotation in `getOrElse` (and the similar annotation in `orElse`) indicates that the argument is of type `B`, but won't be evaluated until it's needed by the function. Don't worry about this for now—we'll talk much more about this concept of *non-strictness* in the next chapter. Also, the `B >: A` type parameter on the `getOrElse` and `orElse` functions indicates that `B` must be equal to or a *supertype* of `A`. It's needed to convince Scala that it's still safe to declare `Option[+A]` as covariant in `A`. See the chapter notes for more detail—it's unfortunately somewhat complicated, but a necessary complication in Scala. Fortunately, fully understanding subtyping and variance isn't essential for our purposes here.

■ **EXERCISE 4.1**

Implement all of the preceding functions on `Option`. As you implement each function, try to think about what it means and in what situations you'd use it. We'll explore when to use each of these functions next. Here are a few hints for solving this exercise:

- It's fine to use pattern matching, though you should be able to implement all the functions besides `map` and `getOrElse` without resorting to pattern matching.
- For `map` and `flatMap`, the type signature should be enough to determine the implementation.
- `getOrElse` returns the result inside the `Some` case of the `Option`, or if the `Option` is `None`, returns the given default value.
- `orElse` returns the first `Option` if it's defined; otherwise, it returns the second `Option`.

USAGE SCENARIOS FOR THE BASIC OPTION FUNCTIONS

Although we can explicitly pattern match on an `Option`, we'll almost always use the above higher-order functions. Here, we'll try to give some guidance for when to use each one. Fluency with these functions will come with practice, but the objective here is to get some basic familiarity. Next time you try writing some functional code that uses `Option`, see if you can recognize the patterns these functions encapsulate before you resort to pattern matching.

Let's start with `map`. The `map` function can be used to transform the result inside an `Option`, if it exists. We can think of it as proceeding with a computation on the assumption that an error hasn't occurred; it's also a way of deferring the error handling to later code:

```scala
case class Employee(name: String, department: String)

def lookupByName(name: String): Option[Employee] = ...

val joeDepartment: Option[String] =
  lookupByName("Joe").map(_.department)
```

Here, `lookupByName("Joe")` returns an `Option[Employee]`, which we transform using `map` to pull out the `Option[String]` representing the department. Note that we don't need to explicitly check the result of `lookupByName("Joe")`; we simply continue the computation as if no error occurred, inside the argument to `map`. If `employeesBy-Name.get("Joe")` returns `None`, this will abort the rest of the computation and `map` will not call the `_.department` function at all.

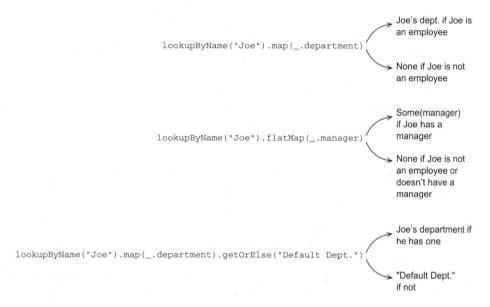

`flatMap` is similar, except that the function we provide to transform the result can itself fail.

■ **EXERCISE 4.2**

Implement the `variance` function in terms of `flatMap`. If the mean of a sequence is `m`, the variance is the mean of `math.pow(x - m, 2)` for each element `x` in the sequence. See the definition of variance on Wikipedia (http://mng.bz/0Qsr).

```
def variance(xs: Seq[Double]): Option[Double]
```

As the implementation of `variance` demonstrates, with `flatMap` we can construct a computation with multiple stages, any of which may fail, and the computation will abort as soon as the first failure is encountered, since `None.flatMap(f)` will immediately return `None`, without running `f`.

We can use `filter` to convert successes into failures if the successful values don't match the given predicate. A common pattern is to transform an `Option` via calls to `map`, `flatMap`, and/or `filter`, and then use `getOrElse` to do error handling at the end:

```
val dept: String =
  lookupByName("Joe").
  map(_.dept).
  filter(_ != "Accounting").
  getOrElse("Default Dept")
```

`getOrElse` is used here to convert from an `Option[String]` to a `String`, by providing a default department in case the key `"Joe"` didn't exist in the `Map` or if Joe's department was `"Accounting"`.

`orElse` is similar to `getOrElse`, except that we return another `Option` if the first is undefined. This is often useful when we need to chain together possibly failing computations, trying the second if the first hasn't succeeded.

A common idiom is to do `o.getOrElse(throw new Exception("FAIL"))` to convert the `None` case of an `Option` back to an exception. The general rule of thumb is that we use exceptions only if no reasonable program would ever catch the exception; if for some callers the exception might be a recoverable error, we use `Option` (or `Either`, discussed later) to give them flexibility.

As you can see, returning errors as ordinary values can be convenient and the use of higher-order functions lets us achieve the same sort of consolidation of error-handling logic we would get from using exceptions. Note that we don't have to check for `None` at each stage of the computation—we can apply several transformations and then check for and handle `None` when we're ready. But we also get additional safety, since `Option[A]` is a different type than `A`, and the compiler won't let us forget to explicitly defer or handle the possibility of `None`.

4.3.2 *Option composition, lifting, and wrapping exception-oriented APIs*

It may be easy to jump to the conclusion that once we start using `Option`, it infects our entire code base. One can imagine how any callers of methods that take or return `Option` will have to be modified to handle either `Some` or `None`. But this doesn't happen, and the reason is that we can *lift* ordinary functions to become functions that operate on `Option`.

For example, the `map` function lets us operate on values of type `Option[A]` using a function of type `A => B`, returning `Option[B]`. Another way of looking at this is that `map` turns a function `f` of type `A => B` into a function of type `Option[A] => Option[B]`. Let's make this explicit:

```
def lift[A,B](f: A => B): Option[A] => Option[B] = _ map f
```

This tells us that any function that we already have lying around can be transformed (via `lift`) to operate *within the context of* a single `Option` value. Let's look at an example:

```
val absO: Option[Double] => Option[Double] = lift(math.abs)
```

The `math` object contains various standalone mathematical functions including `abs`, `sqrt`, `exp`, and so on. We didn't need to rewrite the `math.abs` function to work with optional values; we just lifted it into the `Option` context after the fact. We can do this for *any* function. Let's look at another example. Suppose we're implementing the logic for a car insurance company's website, which contains a page where users can submit a form to request an instant online quote. We'd like to parse the information from this form and ultimately call our rate function:

```
/**
 * Top secret formula for computing an annual car
 * insurance premium from two key factors.
 */
def insuranceRateQuote(age: Int, numberOfSpeedingTickets: Int): Double
```

We want to be able to call this function, but if the user is submitting their age and number of speeding tickets in a web form, these fields will arrive as simple strings that we have to (try to) parse into integers. This parsing may fail; given a string, s, we can attempt to parse it into an `Int` using `s.toInt`, which throws a `NumberFormat-Exception` if the string isn't a valid integer:

```
scala> "112".toInt
res0: Int = 112

scala> "hello".toInt
java.lang.NumberFormatException: For input string: "hello"
  at java.lang.NumberFormatException.forInputString(...)
  ...
```

Lifting functions

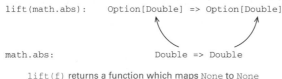

`lift(f)` returns a function which maps `None` to `None`
and applies `f` to the contents of `Some`. `f` need
not be aware of the `Option` type at all.

Let's convert the exception-based API of `toInt` to `Option` and see if we can implement a function `parseInsuranceRateQuote`, which takes the age and number of speeding tickets as strings, and attempts calling the `insuranceRateQuote` function if parsing both values is successful.

Listing 4.3 Using `Option`

```
def parseInsuranceRateQuote(
    age: String,
    numberOfSpeedingTickets: String): Option[Double] = {
  val optAge: Option[Int] = Try(age.toInt)
  val optTickets: Option[Int] = Try(numberOfSpeedingTickets.toInt)
```

The `toInt` method is available on any `String`.

```
        insuranceRateQuote(optAge, optTickets)
      }
```

Doesn't type check!
See following discussion.

We accept the A argument non-strictly,
so we can catch any exceptions that
occur while evaluating a and convert
them to None.

```
def Try[A](a: => A): Option[A] =
  try Some(a)
  catch { case e: Exception => None }
```

The Try function is a general-purpose function we can use to convert from an exception-based API to an Option-oriented API. This uses a non-strict or lazy argument, as indicated by the => A as the type of a. We'll discuss laziness much more in the next chapter.

But there's a problem—after we parse optAge and optTickets into Option[Int], how do we call insuranceRateQuote, which currently takes two Int values? Do we have to rewrite insuranceRateQuote to take Option[Int] values instead? No, and changing insuranceRateQuote would be entangling concerns, forcing it to be aware that a prior computation may have failed, not to mention that we may not have the ability to modify insuranceRateQuote—perhaps it's defined in a separate module that we don't have access to. Instead, we'd like to lift insuranceRateQuote to operate in the context of two optional values. We could do this using explicit pattern matching in the body of parseInsuranceRateQuote, but that's going to be tedious.

EXERCISE 4.3

Write a generic function map2 that combines two Option values using a binary function. If either Option value is None, then the return value is too. Here is its signature:

```
def map2[A,B,C](a: Option[A], b: Option[B])(f: (A, B) => C): Option[C]
```

With map2, we can now implement parseInsuranceRateQuote:

Functions accepting a single argument may
be called with braces instead of parentheses;
this is equivalent to Try(age.toInt).

```
def parseInsuranceRateQuote(
    age: String,
    numberOfSpeedingTickets: String): Option[Double] = {
  val optAge: Option[Int] = Try { age.toInt }
  val optTickets: Option[Int] = Try { numberOfSpeedingTickets.toInt }
  map2(optAge, optTickes)(insuranceRateQuote)
}
```

The map2 function means that we never need to modify any existing functions of two arguments to make them "Option-aware." We can lift them to operate in the context of Option after the fact. Can you already see how you might define map3, map4, and map5? Let's look at a few other similar cases.

Write a function `sequence` that combines a list of `Option`s into one `Option` containing a list of all the `Some` values in the original list. If the original list contains `None` even once, the result of the function should be `None`; otherwise the result should be `Some` with a list of all the values. Here is its signature:[3]

```
def sequence[A](a: List[Option[A]]): Option[List[A]]
```

Sometimes we'll want to map over a list using a function that might fail, returning `None` if applying it to any element of the list returns `None`. For example, what if we have a whole list of `String` values that we wish to parse to `Option[Int]`? In that case, we can simply sequence the results of the map:

```
def parseInts(a: List[String]): Option[List[Int]] =
  sequence(a map (i => Try(i.toInt)))
```

Unfortunately, this is inefficient, since it traverses the list twice, first to convert each `String` to an `Option[Int]`, and a second pass to combine these `Option[Int]` values into an `Option[List[Int]]`. Wanting to sequence the results of a map this way is a common enough occurrence to warrant a new generic function, `traverse`, with the following signature:

```
def traverse[A, B](a: List[A])(f: A => Option[B]): Option[List[B]]
```

Implement this function. It's straightforward to do using `map` and `sequence`, but try for a more efficient implementation that only looks at the list once. In fact, implement `sequence` in terms of `traverse`.

> ### For-comprehensions
> Since lifting functions is so common in Scala, Scala provides a syntactic construct called the *for-comprehension* that it expands automatically to a series of `flatMap` and `map` calls. Let's look at how `map2` could be implemented with for-comprehensions.

---

[3] This is a clear instance where it's not appropriate to define the function in the OO style. This shouldn't be a method on `List` (which shouldn't need to know anything about `Option`), and it can't be a method on `Option`, so it goes in the `Option` companion object.

(continued)
Here's our original version:

```scala
def map2[A,B,C](a: Option[A], b: Option[B])(f: (A, B) => C):
Option[C] =
  a flatMap (aa =>
  b map (bb =>
  f(aa, bb)))
```

And here's the *exact same code* written as a for-comprehension:

```scala
def map2[A,B,C](a: Option[A], b: Option[B])(f: (A, B) => C):
Option[C] =
  for {
    aa <- a
    bb <- b
  } yield f(aa, bb)
```

A for-comprehension consists of a sequence of bindings, like aa <- a, followed by a yield after the closing brace, where the yield may make use of any of the values on the left side of any previous <- binding. The compiler desugars the bindings to flatMap calls, with the final binding and yield being converted to a call to map.

You should feel free to use for-comprehensions in place of explicit calls to flatMap and map.

Between map, lift, sequence, traverse, map2, map3, and so on, you should *never* have to modify any existing functions to work with optional values.

4.4   *The Either data type*

The big idea in this chapter is that we can represent failures and exceptions with ordinary values, and write functions that abstract out common patterns of error handling and recovery. Option isn't the only data type we could use for this purpose, and although it gets used frequently, it's rather simplistic. One thing you may have noticed with Option is that it doesn't tell us anything about what went wrong in the case of an exceptional condition. All it can do is give us None, indicating that there's no value to be had. But sometimes we want to know more. For example, we might want a String that gives more information, or if an exception was raised, we might want to know what that error actually was.

We can craft a data type that encodes whatever information we want about failures. Sometimes just knowing whether a failure occurred is sufficient, in which case we can use Option; other times we want more information. In this section, we'll walk through a simple extension to Option, the Either data type, which lets us track a *reason* for the failure. Let's look at its definition:

```scala
sealed trait Either[+E, +A]
case class Left[+E](value: E) extends Either[E, Nothing]
case class Right[+A](value: A) extends Either[Nothing, A]
```

`Either` has only two cases, just like `Option`. The essential difference is that both cases carry a value. The `Either` data type represents, in a very general way, values that can be one of two things. We can say that it's a *disjoint union* of two types. When we use it to indicate success or failure, by convention the `Right` constructor is reserved for the success case (a pun on "right," meaning correct), and `Left` is used for failure. We've given the left type parameter the suggestive name E (for *error*).[4]

Option and Either in the standard library

As we mentioned earlier in this chapter, both `Option` and `Either` exist in the Scala standard library (`Option` API is at http://mng.bz/fiJ5; `Either` API is at http://mng.bz/106L), and most of the functions we've defined here in this chapter exist for the standard library versions.

You're encouraged to read through the API for `Option` and `Either` to understand the differences. There are a few missing functions, though, notably `sequence`, `traverse`, and `map2`. And `Either` doesn't define a right-biased `flatMap` directly like we do here. The standard library `Either` is slightly (but only slightly) more complicated. Read the API for details.

Let's look at the `mean` example again, this time returning a `String` in case of failure:

```
def mean(xs: IndexedSeq[Double]): Either[String, Double] =
  if (xs.isEmpty)
    Left("mean of empty list!")
  else
    Right(xs.sum / xs.length)
```

Sometimes we might want to include more information about the error, for example a stack trace showing the location of the error in the source code. In such cases we can simply return the exception in the `Left` side of an `Either`:

```
def safeDiv(x: Int, y: Int): Either[Exception, Int] =
  try Right(x / y)
  catch { case e: Exception => Left(e) }
```

As we did with `Option`, we can write a function, `Try`, which factors out this common pattern of converting thrown exceptions to values:

```
def Try[A](a: => A): Either[Exception, A] =
  try Right(a)
  catch { case e: Exception => Left(e) }
```

---

[4] `Either` is also often used more generally to encode one of two possibilities in cases where it isn't worth defining a fresh data type. We'll see some examples of this throughout the book.

EXERCISE 4.6

Implement versions of map, flatMap, orElse, and map2 on Either that operate on the Right value.

> When mapping over the right side, we must promote the left type parameter to some supertype, to satisfy the +E variance annotation.

Similarly for orElse.

```scala
trait Either[+E, +A] {
  def map[B](f: A => B): Either[E, B]
  def flatMap[EE >: E, B](f: A => Either[EE, B]): Either[EE, B]
  def orElse[EE >: E,B >: A](b: => Either[EE, B]): Either[EE, B]
  def map2[EE >: E, B, C](b: Either[EE, B])(f: (A, B) => C):
    Either[EE, C]
}
```

Note that with these definitions, Either can now be used in for-comprehensions. For instance:

```scala
def parseInsuranceRateQuote(
    age: String,
    numberOfSpeedingTickets: String): Either[Exception,Double] =
  for {
    a <- Try { age.toInt }
    tickets <- Try { numberOfSpeedingTickes.toInt }
  } yield insuranceRateQuote(a, tickets)
```

Now we get information about the actual exception that occurred, rather than just getting back None in the event of a failure.

EXERCISE 4.7

Implement sequence and traverse for Either. These should return the first error that's encountered, if there is one.

```scala
def sequence[E, A](es: List[Either[E, A]]): Either[E, List[A]]

def traverse[E, A, B](as: List[A])(
                      f: A => Either[E, B]): Either[E, List[B]]
```

As a final example, here's an application of map2, where the function mkPerson validates both the given name and the given age before constructing a valid Person.

Listing 4.4   Using `Either` to validate data

```scala
case class Person(name: Name, age: Age)
sealed class Name(val value: String)
sealed class Age(val value: Int)
```

```
def mkName(name: String): Either[String, Name] =
  if (name == "" || name == null) Left("Name is empty.")
  else Right(new Name(name))

def mkAge(age: Int): Either[String, Age] =
  if (age < 0) Left("Age is out of range.")
  else Right(new Age(age))

def mkPerson(name: String, age: Int): Either[String, Person] =
  mkName(name).map2(mkAge(age))(Person(_, _))
```

EXERCISE 4.8

In this implementation, map2 is only able to report one error, even if both the name and the age are invalid. What would you need to change in order to report *both* errors? Would you change map2 or the signature of mkPerson? Or could you create a new data type that captures this requirement better than Either does, with some additional structure? How would orElse, traverse, and sequence behave differently for that data type?

4.5 Summary

In this chapter, we noted some of the problems with using exceptions and introduced the basic principles of purely functional error handling. Although we focused on the algebraic data types Option and Either, the bigger idea is that we can represent exceptions as ordinary values and use higher-order functions to encapsulate common patterns of handling and propagating errors. This general idea, of representing effects as values, is something we'll see again and again throughout this book in various guises.

We don't expect you to be fluent with all the higher-order functions we wrote in this chapter, but you should now have enough familiarity to get started writing your own functional code complete with error handling. With these new tools in hand, exceptions should be reserved only for truly unrecoverable conditions.

Lastly, in this chapter we touched briefly on the notion of a *non-strict* function (recall the functions orElse, getOrElse, and Try). In the next chapter, we'll look more closely at why non-strictness is important and how it can buy us greater modularity and efficiency in our functional programs.

Strictness and laziness

In chapter 3 we talked about purely functional data structures, using singly linked lists as an example. We covered a number of bulk operations on lists—map, filter, foldLeft, foldRight, zipWith, and so on. We noted that each of these operations makes its own pass over the input and constructs a fresh list for the output.

Imagine if you had a deck of cards and you were asked to remove the odd-numbered cards and then flip over all the queens. Ideally, you'd make a single pass through the deck, looking for queens and odd-numbered cards at the same time. This is more efficient than removing the odd cards and then looking for queens in the remainder. And yet the latter is what Scala is doing in the following code:[1]

```scala
scala> List(1,2,3,4).map(_ + 10).filter(_ % 2 == 0).map(_ * 3)
List(36,42)
```

In this expression, map(_ + 10) will produce an intermediate list that then gets passed to filter(_ % 2 == 0), which in turn constructs a list that gets passed to map(_ * 3), which then produces the final list. In other words, each transformation will produce a temporary list that only ever gets used as input to the next transformation and is then immediately discarded.

Think about how this program will be evaluated. If we manually produce a trace of its evaluation, the steps would look something like this.

> **Listing 5.1   Program trace for List**

```scala
List(1,2,3,4).map(_ + 10).filter(_ % 2 == 0).map(_ * 3)

List(11,12,13,14).filter(_ % 2 == 0).map(_ * 3)
```

---

[1] We're now using the Scala standard library's List type here, where map and filter are methods on List rather than standalone functions like the ones we wrote in chapter 3.

```
List(12,14).map(_ * 3)
List(36,42)
```

Here we're showing the result of each substitution performed to evaluate our expression. For example, to go from the first line to the second, we've replaced `List(1,2,3,4).map(_ + 10)` with `List(11,12,13,14)`, based on the definition of map.[2] This view makes it clear how the calls to map and filter each perform their own traversal of the input and allocate lists for the output. Wouldn't it be nice if we could somehow fuse sequences of transformations like this into a single pass and avoid creating temporary data structures? We could rewrite the code into a while loop by hand, but ideally we'd like to have this done automatically while retaining the same high-level compositional style. We want to compose our programs using higher-order functions like map and filter instead of writing monolithic loops.

It turns out that we can accomplish this kind of automatic loop fusion through the use of *non-strictness* (or, less formally, *laziness*). In this chapter, we'll explain what exactly this means, and we'll work through the implementation of a lazy list type that fuses sequences of transformations. Although building a "better" list is the motivation for this chapter, we'll see that non-strictness is a fundamental technique for improving on the efficiency and modularity of functional programs in general.

5.1 Strict and non-strict functions

Before we get to our example of lazy lists, we need to cover some basics. What are strictness and non-strictness, and how are these concepts expressed in Scala?

Non-strictness is a property of a function. To say a function is non-strict just means that the function may choose *not* to evaluate one or more of its arguments. In contrast, a *strict* function always evaluates its arguments. Strict functions are the norm in most programming languages, and indeed most languages only support functions that expect their arguments fully evaluated. Unless we tell it otherwise, any function definition in Scala will be strict (and all the functions we've defined so far have been strict). As an example, consider the following function:

```
def square(x: Double): Double = x * x
```

When you invoke `square(41.0 + 1.0)`, the function square will receive the evaluated value of `42.0` because it's strict. If you invoke `square(sys.error("failure"))`, you'll get an exception before square has a chance to do anything, since the `sys.error ("failure")` expression will be evaluated before entering the body of square.

Although we haven't yet learned the syntax for indicating non-strictness in Scala, you're almost certainly familiar with the concept. For example, the short-circuiting Boolean functions `&&` and `||`, found in many programming languages including Scala, are non-strict. You may be used to thinking of `&&` and `||` as built-in syntax, part of the

---

[2] With program traces like these, it's often more illustrative to not fully trace the evaluation of every subexpression. In this case, we've omitted the full expansion of `List(1,2,3,4).map(_ + 10)`. We could "enter" the definition of map and trace its execution, but we chose to omit this level of detail here.

language, but you can also think of them as functions that may choose not to evaluate their arguments. The function `&&` takes two `Boolean` arguments, but only evaluates the second argument if the first is `true`:

```
scala> false && { println("!!"); true } // does not print anything
res0: Boolean = false
```

And `||` only evaluates its second argument if the first is `false`:

```
scala> true || { println("!!"); false } // doesn't print anything either
res1: Boolean = true
```

Another example of non-strictness is the `if` control construct in Scala:

```
val result = if (input.isEmpty) sys.error("empty input") else input
```

Even though `if` is a built-in language construct in Scala, it can be thought of as a function accepting three parameters: a condition of type `Boolean`, an expression of some type `A` to return in the case that the condition is `true`, and another expression of the same type `A` to return if the condition is `false`. This `if` function would be non-strict, since it won't evaluate all of its arguments. To be more precise, we'd say that the `if` function is strict in its condition parameter, since it'll always evaluate the condition to determine which branch to take, and non-strict in the two branches for the `true` and `false` cases, since it'll only evaluate one or the other based on the condition.

In Scala, we can write non-strict functions by accepting some of our arguments unevaluated. We'll show how this is done explicitly just to illustrate what's happening, and then show some nicer syntax for it that's built into Scala. Here's a non-strict `if` function:

```
def if2[A](cond: Boolean, onTrue: () => A, onFalse: () => A): A =
  if (cond) onTrue() else onFalse()

if2(a < 22,
  () => println("a"),          ⟵—————  The function literal syntax for
  () => println("b")                    creating a () => A
)
```

The arguments we'd like to pass unevaluated have a `()` `=>` immediately before their type. A value of type `()` `=> A` is a function that accepts zero arguments and returns an `A`.[3] In general, the unevaluated form of an expression is called a *thunk*, and we can *force* the thunk to evaluate the expression and get a result. We do so by invoking the function, passing an empty argument list, as in `onTrue()` or `onFalse()`. Likewise, callers of `if2` have to explicitly create thunks, and the syntax follows the same conventions as the function literal syntax we've already seen.

Overall, this syntax makes it very clear what's happening—we're passing a function of no arguments in place of each non-strict parameter, and then explicitly calling this function to obtain a result in the body. But this is such a common case that Scala provides some nicer syntax:

---

[3] In fact, the type `()` `=> A` is a syntactic alias for the type `Function0[A]`.

```
def if2[A](cond: Boolean, onTrue: => A, onFalse: => A): A =
  if (cond) onTrue else onFalse
```

The arguments we'd like to pass unevaluated have an arrow => immediately before their type. In the body of the function, we don't need to do anything special to evaluate an argument annotated with =>. We just reference the identifier as usual. Nor do we have to do anything special to call this function. We just use the normal function call syntax, and Scala takes care of wrapping the expression in a thunk for us:

```
scala> if2(false, sys.error("fail"), 3)
res2: Int = 3
```

With either syntax, an argument that's passed unevaluated to a function will be evaluated once for each place it's referenced in the body of the function. That is, Scala won't (by default) cache the result of evaluating an argument:

```
scala> def maybeTwice(b: Boolean, i: => Int) = if (b) i+i else 0
maybeTwice: (b: Boolean, i: => Int)Int

scala> val x = maybeTwice(true, { println("hi"); 1+41 })
hi
hi
x: Int = 84
```

Here, i is referenced twice in the body of maybeTwice, and we've made it particularly obvious that it's evaluated each time by passing the block {println("hi"); 1+41}, which prints hi as a side effect before returning a result of 42. The expression 1+41 will be computed twice as well. We can cache the value explicitly if we wish to only evaluate the result once, by using the lazy keyword:

```
scala> def maybeTwice2(b: Boolean, i: => Int) = {
     |    lazy val j = i
     |    if (b) j+j else 0
     | }
maybeTwice: (b: Boolean, i: => Int)Int

scala> val x = maybeTwice2(true, { println("hi"); 1+41 })
hi
x: Int = 84
```

Adding the lazy keyword to a val declaration will cause Scala to delay evaluation of the right-hand side of that lazy val declaration until it's first referenced. It will also cache the result so that subsequent references to it don't trigger repeated evaluation.

Formal definition of strictness
If the evaluation of an expression runs forever or throws an error instead of returning a definite value, we say that the expression doesn't *terminate*, or that it evaluates to *bottom*. A function f is *strict* if the expression f(x) evaluates to bottom for all x that evaluate to bottom.

As a final bit of terminology, we say that a non-strict function in Scala takes its arguments *by name* rather than *by value*.

5.2 An extended example: lazy lists

Let's now return to the problem posed at the beginning of this chapter. We'll explore how laziness can be used to improve the efficiency and modularity of functional programs using *lazy lists*, or *streams*, as an example. We'll see how chains of transformations on streams are fused into a single pass through the use of laziness. Here's a simple `Stream` definition. There are a few new things here we'll discuss next.

Listing 5.2 Simple definition for `Stream`

A nonempty stream consists of a head and a tail, which are both non-strict. Due to technical limitations, these are thunks that must be explicitly forced, rather than by-name parameters.

A smart constructor for creating a nonempty stream.

```scala
sealed trait Stream[+A]
case object Empty extends Stream[Nothing]
case class Cons[+A](h: () => A, t: () => Stream[A]) extends Stream[A]

object Stream {
  def cons[A](hd: => A, tl: => Stream[A]): Stream[A] = {
    lazy val head = hd
    lazy val tail = tl
    Cons(() => head, () => tail)
  }
  def empty[A]: Stream[A] = Empty

  def apply[A](as: A*): Stream[A] =
    if (as.isEmpty) empty else cons(as.head, apply(as.tail: _*))
}
```

We cache the head and tail as lazy values to avoid repeated evaluation.

A smart constructor for creating an empty stream of a particular type.

A convenient variable-argument method for constructing a `Stream` from multiple elements.

This type looks identical to our `List` type, except that the `Cons` data constructor takes *explicit* thunks (`() => A` and `() => Stream[A]`) instead of regular strict values. If we wish to examine or traverse the `Stream`, we need to force these thunks as we did earlier in our definition of `if2`. For instance, here's a function to optionally extract the head of a `Stream`:

```scala
def headOption: Option[A] = this match {
  case Empty => None
  case Cons(h, t) => Some(h())
}
```

Explicit forcing of the h thunk using `h()`

Note that we have to force h explicitly via `h()`, but other than that, the code works the same way as it would for `List`. But this ability of `Stream` to evaluate only the portion actually demanded (we don't evaluate the tail of the `Cons`) is useful, as we'll see.

5.2.1 *Memoizing streams and avoiding recomputation*

We typically want to cache the values of a `Cons` node, once they are forced. If we use the `Cons` data constructor directly, for instance, this code will actually compute `expensive(x)` twice:

```
val x = Cons(() => expensive(x), tl)
val h1 = x.headOption
val h2 = x.headOption
```

We typically avoid this problem by defining *smart* constructors, which is what we call a function for constructing a data type that ensures some additional invariant or provides a slightly different signature than the "real" constructors used for pattern matching. By convention, smart constructors typically lowercase the first letter of the corresponding data constructor. Here, our `cons` smart constructor takes care of memoizing the by-name arguments for the head and tail of the `Cons`. This is a common trick, and it ensures that our thunk will only do its work once, when forced for the first time. Subsequent forces will return the cached `lazy val`:

```
def cons[A](hd: => A, tl: => Stream[A]): Stream[A] = {
  lazy val head = hd
  lazy val tail = tl
  Cons(() => head, () => tail)
}
```

The `empty` smart constructor just returns `Empty`, but annotates `Empty` as a `Stream[A]`, which is better for type inference in some cases.[4] We can see how both smart constructors are used in the `Stream.apply` function:

```
def apply[A](as: A*): Stream[A] =
  if (as.isEmpty) empty
  else cons(as.head, apply(as.tail: _*))
```

Again, Scala takes care of wrapping the arguments to `cons` in thunks, so the `as.head` and `apply(as.tail: _*)` expressions won't be evaluated until we force the `Stream`.

5.2.2 *Helper functions for inspecting streams*

Before continuing, let's write a few helper functions to make inspecting streams easier.

■—(**EXERCISE 5.1**)——————————————————————

Write a function to convert a `Stream` to a `List`, which will force its evaluation and let you look at it in the REPL. You can convert to the regular `List` type in the standard library. You can place this and other functions that operate on a `Stream` inside the `Stream` trait.

```
def toList: List[A]
```

---

[4] Recall that Scala uses subtyping to represent data constructors, but we almost always want to infer `Stream` as the type, not `Cons` or `Empty`. Making smart constructors that return the base type is a common trick.

■   **EXERCISE 5.2**

Write the function `take(n)` for returning the first n elements of a `Stream`, and `drop(n)` for skipping the first n elements of a `Stream`.

■   **EXERCISE 5.3**

Write the function `takeWhile` for returning all starting elements of a `Stream` that match the given predicate.

```
def takeWhile(p: A => Boolean): Stream[A]
```

You can use `take` and `toList` together to inspect streams in the REPL. For example, try printing `Stream(1,2,3).take(2).toList`.

5.3 *Separating program description from evaluation*

A major theme in functional programming is *separation of concerns*. We want to separate the description of computations from actually running them. We've already touched on this theme in previous chapters in different ways. For example, first-class functions capture some computation in their bodies but only execute it once they receive their arguments. And we used `Option` to capture the fact that an error occurred, where the decision of what to do about it became a separate concern. With `Stream`, we're able to build up a computation that produces a sequence of elements without running the steps of that computation until we actually need those elements.

More generally speaking, laziness lets us separate the description of an expression from the evaluation of that expression. This gives us a powerful ability—we may choose to describe a "larger" expression than we need, and then evaluate only a portion of it. As an example, let's look at the function `exists` that checks whether an element matching a `Boolean` function exists in this `Stream`:

```
def exists(p: A => Boolean): Boolean = this match {
  case Cons(h, t) => p(h()) || t().exists(p)
  case _ => false
}
```

Note that `||` is non-strict in its second argument. If `p(h())` returns `true`, then `exists` terminates the traversal early and returns `true` as well. Remember also that the tail of the stream is a `lazy val`. So not only does the traversal terminate early, the tail of the stream is never evaluated at all! So whatever code would have generated the tail is never actually executed.

The `exists` function here is implemented using explicit recursion. But remember that with `List` in chapter 3, we could implement a general recursion in the form of `foldRight`. We can do the same thing for `Stream`, but lazily:

If f doesn't evaluate its second argument, the recursion never occurs.

```
def foldRight[B](z: => B)(f: (A, => B) => B): B =
  this match {
    case Cons(h,t) => f(h(), t().foldRight(z)(f))
    case _ => z
  }
```

The arrow => in front of the argument type B means that the function f takes its second argument by name and may choose not to evaluate it.

This looks very similar to the `foldRight` we wrote for `List`, but note how our combining function f is non-strict in its second parameter. If f chooses not to evaluate its second parameter, this terminates the traversal early. We can see this by using `foldRight` to implement `exists`:[5]

```
def exists(p: A => Boolean): Boolean =
  foldRight(false)((a, b) => p(a) || b)
```

Here b is the unevaluated recursive step that folds the tail of the stream. If p(a) returns true, b will never be evaluated and the computation terminates early.

Since `foldRight` can terminate the traversal early, we can reuse it to implement `exists`. We can't do that with a strict version of `foldRight`. We'd have to write a specialized recursive `exists` function to handle early termination. Laziness makes our code more reusable.

■ EXERCISE 5.4 ───

Implement `forAll`, which checks that all elements in the `Stream` match a given predicate. Your implementation should terminate the traversal as soon as it encounters a nonmatching value.

```
def forAll(p: A => Boolean): Boolean
```

■ EXERCISE 5.5 ───

Use `foldRight` to implement `takeWhile`.

■ EXERCISE 5.6 ───

Hard: Implement `headOption` using `foldRight`.

───────────────────────────────

[5] This definition of `exists`, though illustrative, isn't stack-safe if the stream is large and all elements test `false`.

◼ ── **EXERCISE 5.7** ───

Implement `map`, `filter`, `append`, and `flatMap` using `foldRight`. The `append` method should be non-strict in its argument.

───

Note that these implementations are *incremental*—they don't fully generate their answers. It's not until some other computation looks at the elements of the resulting `Stream` that the computation to generate that `Stream` actually takes place—and then it will do just enough work to generate the requested elements. Because of this incremental nature, we can call these functions one after another without fully instantiating the intermediate results.

Let's look at a simplified program trace for (a fragment of) the motivating example we started this chapter with, `Stream(1,2,3,4).map(_ + 10).filter(_ % 2 == 0)`. We'll convert this expression to a `List` to force evaluation. Take a minute to work through this trace to understand what's happening. It's a bit more challenging than the trace we looked at earlier in this chapter. Remember, a trace like this is just the same expression over and over again, evaluated by one more step each time.

Listing 5.3 Program trace for `Stream`

Apply map to the first element.

```
Stream(1,2,3,4).map(_ + 10).filter(_ % 2 == 0).toList
```

Apply **filter to the first element.**

```
cons(11, Stream(2,3,4).map(_ + 10)).filter(_ % 2 == 0).toList
```

Apply map to the second element.

```
Stream(2,3,4).map(_ + 10).filter(_ % 2 == 0).toList
```

```
cons(12, Stream(3,4).map(_ + 10)).filter(_ % 2 == 0).toList
```

Apply **filter to the second element.** **Produce the first element of the result.**

```
12 :: Stream(3,4).map(_ + 10).filter(_ % 2 == 0).toList
```

```
12 :: cons(13, Stream(4).map(_ + 10)).filter(_ % 2 == 0).toList
```

Apply **filter to the fourth element and produce the final element of the result.**

```
12 :: Stream(4).map(_ + 10).filter(_ % 2 == 0).toList
```

```
12 :: cons(14, Stream().map(_ + 10)).filter(_ % 2 == 0).toList
```

```
12 :: 14 :: Stream().map(_ + 10).filter(_ % 2 == 0).toList
```

```
12 :: 14 :: List()
```

map and filter have no more work to do, and the empty stream becomes the empty list.

The thing to notice in this trace is how the `filter` and `map` transformations are interleaved—the computation alternates between generating a single element of the output of map, and testing with `filter` to see if that element is divisible by 2 (adding it to the output list if it is). Note that we don't fully instantiate the intermediate stream that results from the map. It's exactly as if we had interleaved the logic using a special-purpose loop. For this reason, people sometimes describe streams as "first-class loops" whose logic can be combined using higher-order functions like map and filter.

Since intermediate streams aren't instantiated, it's easy to reuse existing combinators in novel ways without having to worry that we're doing more processing of the stream than necessary. For example, we can reuse filter to define find, a method to return just the first element that matches if it exists. Even though filter transforms the whole stream, that transformation is done lazily, so find terminates as soon as a match is found:

```
def find(p: A => Boolean): Option[A] =
  filter(p).headOption
```

The incremental nature of stream transformations also has important consequences for memory usage. Because intermediate streams aren't generated, a transformation of the stream requires only enough working memory to store and transform the current element. For instance, in the transformation Stream(1,2,3,4).map(_ + 10).filter (_ % 2 == 0), the garbage collector can reclaim the space allocated for the values 11 and 13 emitted by map as soon as filter determines they aren't needed. Of course, this is a simple example; in other situations we might be dealing with larger numbers of elements, and the stream elements themselves could be large objects that retain significant amounts of memory. Being able to reclaim this memory as quickly as possible can cut down on the amount of memory required by your program as a whole.

We'll have a lot more to say about defining memory-efficient streaming calculations, in particular calculations that require I/O, in part 4 of this book.

5.4 *Infinite streams and corecursion*

Because they're incremental, the functions we've written also work for *infinite streams*. Here's an example of an infinite Stream of 1s:

```
val ones: Stream[Int] = Stream.cons(1, ones)
```

Although ones is infinite, the functions we've written so far only inspect the portion of the stream needed to generate the demanded output. For example:

```
scala> ones.take(5).toList
res0: List[Int] = List(1, 1, 1, 1, 1)

scala> ones.exists(_ % 2 != 0)
res1: Boolean = true
```

Try playing with a few other examples:

- ones.map(_ + 1).exists(_ % 2 == 0)
- ones.takeWhile(_ == 1)
- ones.forAll(_ != 1)

In each case, we get back a result immediately. Be careful though, since it's easy to write expressions that never terminate or aren't stack-safe. For example, `ones.forAll(_ == 1)` will forever need to inspect more of the series since it'll never encounter an element that allows it to terminate with a definite answer (this will manifest as a stack overflow rather than an infinite loop).[6]

An infinite stream

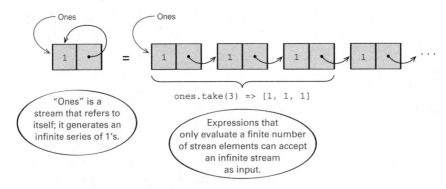

Many functions can be evaluated using finite resources even if their inputs generate infinite sequences.

Let's see what other functions we can discover for generating streams.

EXERCISE 5.8

Generalize `ones` slightly to the function `constant`, which returns an infinite `Stream` of a given value.

```
def constant[A](a: A): Stream[A]
```

EXERCISE 5.9

Write a function that generates an infinite stream of integers, starting from n, then n + 1, n + 2, and so on.[7]

```
def from(n: Int): Stream[Int]
```

---

[6] It's possible to define a stack-safe version of `forAll` using an ordinary recursive loop.

[7] In Scala, the `Int` type is a 32-bit signed integer, so this stream will switch from positive to negative values at some point, and will repeat itself after about four billion elements.

EXERCISE 5.10 ───

Write a function `fibs` that generates the infinite stream of Fibonacci numbers: 0, 1, 1, 2, 3, 5, 8, and so on.

EXERCISE 5.11 ───

Write a more general stream-building function called `unfold`. It takes an initial state, and a function for producing both the next state and the next value in the generated stream.

```
def unfold[A, S](z: S)(f: S => Option[(A, S)]): Stream[A]
```

`Option` is used to indicate when the `Stream` should be terminated, if at all. The function `unfold` is a very general `Stream`-building function.

The `unfold` function is an example of what's sometimes called a *corecursive* function. Whereas a recursive function consumes data, a corecursive function *produces* data. And whereas recursive functions terminate by recursing on smaller inputs, corecursive functions need not terminate so long as they remain *productive*, which just means that we can always evaluate more of the result in a finite amount of time. The `unfold` function is productive as long as f terminates, since we just need to run the function f one more time to generate the next element of the `Stream`. Corecursion is also sometimes called *guarded recursion*, and productivity is also sometimes called *cotermination*. These terms aren't that important to our discussion, but you'll hear them used sometimes in the context of functional programming. If you're curious to learn where they come from and understand some of the deeper connections, follow the references in the chapter notes.

EXERCISE 5.12 ───

Write `fibs`, `from`, `constant`, and `ones` in terms of `unfold`.[8]

───────────────────────────────

[8] Using `unfold` to define `constant` and `ones` means that we don't get sharing as in the recursive definition `val ones: Stream[Int] = cons(1, ones)`. The recursive definition consumes constant memory even if we keep a reference to it around while traversing it, while the `unfold`-based implementation does not. Preserving sharing isn't something we usually rely on when programming with streams, since it's extremely delicate and not tracked by the types. For instance, sharing is destroyed when calling even `xs.map(x => x)`.

■ **EXERCISE 5.13**

Use `unfold` to implement `map`, `take`, `takeWhile`, `zipWith` (as in chapter 3), and `zipAll`. The `zipAll` function should continue the traversal as long as either stream has more elements—it uses `Option` to indicate whether each stream has been exhausted.

```
def zipAll[B](s2: Stream[B]): Stream[(Option[A],Option[B])]
```

Now that we have some practice writing stream functions, let's return to the exercise we covered at the end of chapter 3—a function, `hasSubsequence`, to check whether a list contains a given subsequence. With strict lists and list-processing functions, we were forced to write a rather tricky monolithic loop to implement this function without doing extra work. Using lazy lists, can you see how you could implement `hasSubsequence` by combining some other functions we've already written?[9] Try to think about it on your own before continuing.

■ **EXERCISE 5.14**

Hard: Implement `startsWith` using functions you've written. It should check if one `Stream` is a prefix of another. For instance, `Stream(1,2,3) startsWith Stream(1,2)` would be `true`.

```
def startsWith[A](s: Stream[A]): Boolean
```

■ **EXERCISE 5.15**

Implement `tails` using `unfold`. For a given `Stream`, `tails` returns the `Stream` of suffixes of the input sequence, starting with the original `Stream`. For example, given `Stream(1,2,3)`, it would return `Stream(Stream(1,2,3), Stream(2,3), Stream(3), Stream())`.

```
def tails: Stream[Stream[A]]
```

We can now implement `hasSubsequence` using functions we've written:

```
def hasSubsequence[A](s: Stream[A]): Boolean =
  tails exists (_ startsWith s)
```

---

[9] This small example, of assembling hasSubsequence from simpler functions using laziness, is from Cale Gibbard. See this post: http://lambda-the-ultimate.org/node/1277#comment-14313.

This implementation performs the same number of steps as a more monolithic implementation using nested loops with logic for breaking out of each loop early. By using laziness, we can compose this function from simpler components and still retain the efficiency of the more specialized (and verbose) implementation.

EXERCISE 5.16

Hard: Generalize `tails` to the function `scanRight`, which is like a `foldRight` that returns a stream of the intermediate results. For example:

```scala
scala> Stream(1,2,3).scanRight(0)(_ + _).toList
res0: List[Int] = List(6,5,3,0)
```

This example should be equivalent to the expression `List(1+2+3+0, 2+3+0, 3+0, 0)`. Your function should reuse intermediate results so that traversing a `Stream` with n elements always takes time linear in n. Can it be implemented using `unfold`? How, or why not? Could it be implemented using another function we've written?

5.5 *Summary*

In this chapter, we introduced non-strictness as a fundamental technique for implementing efficient and modular functional programs. Non-strictness can be thought of as a technique for recovering some efficiency when writing functional code, but it's also a much bigger idea—non-strictness can improve modularity by separating the description of an expression from the how-and-when of its evaluation. Keeping these concerns separate lets us reuse a description in multiple contexts, evaluating different portions of our expression to obtain different results. We weren't able to do that when description and evaluation were intertwined as they are in strict code. We saw a number of examples of this principle in action over the course of the chapter, and we'll see many more in the remainder of the book.

We'll switch gears in the next chapter and talk about purely functional approaches to *state*. This is the last building block needed before we begin exploring the process of functional design.

Purely functional state

In this chapter, we'll see how to write purely functional programs that manipulate state, using the simple domain of *random number generation* as the example. Although by itself it's not the most compelling use case for the techniques in this chapter, the simplicity of random number generation makes it a good first example. We'll see more compelling use cases in parts 3 and 4 of the book, especially part 4, where we'll say a lot more about dealing with state and effects. The goal here is to give you the basic pattern for how to make *any* stateful API purely functional. As you start writing your own functional APIs, you'll likely run into many of the same questions that we'll explore here.

6.1 Generating random numbers using side effects

If you need to generate random[1] numbers in Scala, there's a class in the standard library, scala.util.Random,[2] with a pretty typical imperative API that relies on side effects. Here's an example of its use.

> **Listing 6.1 Using scala.util.Random to generate random numbers**

```
scala> val rng = new scala.util.Random

scala> rng.nextDouble
res1: Double = 0.9867076608154569

scala> rng.nextDouble
res2: Double = 0.8455696498024141

scala> rng.nextInt
```

Creates a new random number generator seeded with the current system time

---

[1] Actually, pseudo-random, but we'll ignore this distinction.
[2] Scala API link: http://mng.bz/3DP7.

```
res3: Int = -623297295

scala> rng.nextInt(10)          Gets a random integer
 res4: Int = 4                  between 0 and 9
```

Even if we didn't know anything about what happens inside `scala.util.Random`, we can assume that the object `rng` has some internal state that gets updated after each invocation, since we'd otherwise get the same value each time we called `nextInt` or `nextDouble`. Because the state updates are performed as a side effect, these methods aren't referentially transparent. And as we know, this implies that they aren't as testable, composable, modular, and easily parallelized as they could be.

Let's just take testability as an example. If we want to write a method that makes use of randomness, we need tests to be reproducible. Let's say we had the following side-effecting method, intended to simulate the rolling of a single six-sided die, which *should* return a value between 1 and 6, inclusive:

```
def rollDie: Int = {
  val rng = new scala.util.Random      Returns a random
  rng.nextInt(6)                       number from 0 to 5
}
```

This method has an off-by-one error. Whereas it's supposed to return a value between 1 and 6, it actually returns a value from 0 to 5. But even though it doesn't work properly, five out of six times a test of this method will meet the specification! And if a test did fail, it would be ideal if we could reliably reproduce the failure.

Note that what's important here is not this specific example, but the general idea. In this case, the bug is obvious and easy to reproduce. But we can easily imagine a situation where the method is much more complicated and the bug far more subtle. The more complex the program and the subtler the bug, the more important it is to be able to reproduce bugs in a reliable way.

One suggestion might be to pass in the random number generator. That way, when we want to reproduce a failed test, we can pass the same generator that caused the test to fail:

```
def rollDie(rng: scala.util.Random): Int = rng.nextInt(6)
```

But there's a problem with this solution. The "same" generator has to be both created with the same seed, and also be in the same state, which means that its methods have been called a certain number of times since it was created. That will be really difficult to guarantee, because every time we call `nextInt`, for example, the previous state of the random number generator is destroyed. Do we now need a separate mechanism to keep track of how many times we've called the methods on `Random`?

No! The answer to all of this, of course, is that we should eschew side effects on principle!

6.2   *Purely functional random number generation*

The key to recovering referential transparency is to make the state updates *explicit*. Don't update the state as a side effect, but simply return the new state along with the value that we're generating. Here's one possible interface to a random number generator:

```
trait RNG {
  def nextInt: (Int, RNG)
}
```

This method should generate a random Int. We'll later define other functions in terms of nextInt. Rather than returning only the generated random number (as is done in scala.util.Random) and updating some internal state by *mutating* it in place, we return the random number and the new state, leaving the old state unmodified.[3] In effect, we separate the concern of *computing* what the next state is from the concern of *communicating* the new state to the rest of the program. No global mutable memory is being used—we simply return the next state back to the caller. This leaves the caller of nextInt in complete control of what to do with the new state. Note that we're still *encapsulating* the state, in the sense that users of this API don't know anything about the implementation of the random number generator itself.

A functional RNG

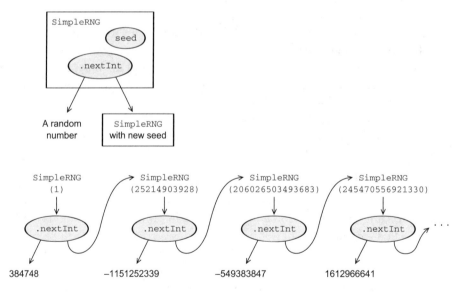

Each call to SimpleRNG.nextInt returns the next random number in the sequence and the SimpleRNG object needed to continue the sequence.

---

[3]   Recall that (A, B) is the type of two-element tuples, and given p: (A, B), you can use p._1 to extract the A and p._2 to extract the B.

But we do need to have an implementation, so let's pick a simple one. The following is a simple random number generator that uses the same algorithm as `scala.util.Random`, which happens to be what's called a *linear congruential generator* (http://mng.bz/r046). The details of this implementation aren't really important, but notice that `nextInt` returns both the generated value and a new RNG to use for generating the next value.

Listing 6.2 A purely functional random number generator

The next state, which is an RNG instance created from the new seed.

& is bitwise **AND**. We use the current seed to generate a new seed.

```
case class SimpleRNG(seed: Long) extends RNG {
  def nextInt: (Int, RNG) = {
    val newSeed = (seed * 0x5DEECE66DL + 0xBL) & 0xFFFFFFFFFFFFL
    val nextRNG = SimpleRNG(newSeed)
    val n = (newSeed >>> 16).toInt
    (n, nextRNG)
  }
}
```

>>> is right binary shift with zero fill. The value n is the new pseudo-random integer.

The return value is a tuple containing both a pseudo-random integer and the next RNG state.

Here's an example of using this API from the interpreter:

```
scala> val rng = SimpleRNG(42)
rng: SimpleRNG = SimpleRNG(42)
```

Let's choose an arbitrary seed value, 42.

```
scala> val (n1, rng2) = rng.nextInt
n1: Int = 16159453
rng2: RNG = SimpleRNG(1059025964525)
```

Syntax for declaring two values by deconstructing the pair returned by `rng.nextInt`.

```
scala> val (n2, rng3) = rng2.nextInt
n2: Int = -1281479697
rng3: RNG = SimpleRNG(197491923327988)
```

We can run this sequence of statements as many times as we want and we'll always get the same values. When we call `rng.nextInt`, it will always return `16159453` and a new RNG, whose `nextInt` will always return `-1281479697`. In other words, this API is pure.

6.3 *Making stateful APIs pure*

This problem of making seemingly stateful APIs pure and its solution (having the API *compute* the next state rather than actually mutate anything) aren't unique to random number generation. It comes up frequently, and we can always deal with it in this same way.[4]

---

[4] An efficiency loss comes with computing next states using pure functions, because it means we can't actually mutate the data in place. (Here, it's not really a problem since the state is just a single `Long` that must be copied.) This loss of efficiency can be mitigated by using efficient purely functional data structures. It's also possible in some cases to mutate the data in place without breaking referential transparency, which we'll talk about in part 4.

For instance, suppose you have a class like this:

```
class Foo {
  private var s: FooState = ...
  def bar: Bar
  def baz: Int
}
```

Suppose `bar` and `baz` each mutate `s` in some way. We can mechanically translate this to the purely functional API by making explicit the transition from one state to the next:

```
trait Foo {
  def bar: (Bar, Foo)
  def baz: (Int, Foo)
}
```

Whenever we use this pattern, we make the caller responsible for passing the computed next state through the rest of the program. For the pure `RNG` interface just shown, if we reuse a previous `RNG`, it will always generate the same value it generated before. For instance:

```
def randomPair(rng: RNG): (Int,Int) = {
  val (i1,_) = rng.nextInt
  val (i2,_) = rng.nextInt
  (i1,i2)
}
```

Here `i1` and `i2` will be the same! If we want to generate two distinct numbers, we need to use the `RNG` returned by the first call to `nextInt` to generate the second `Int`:

```
def randomPair(rng: RNG): ((Int,Int), RNG) = {
  val (i1,rng2) = rng.nextInt         ← Note use of rng2 here.
  val (i2,rng3) = rng2.nextInt
  ((i1,i2), rng3)          ← We return the final state after generating the two
}                            random numbers. This lets the caller generate
                             more random values using the new state.
```

You can see the general pattern, and perhaps you can also see how it might get tedious to use this API directly. Let's write a few functions to generate random values and see if we notice any repetition that we can factor out.

EXERCISE 6.1

Write a function that uses `RNG.nextInt` to generate a random integer between 0 and `Int.maxValue` (inclusive). Make sure to handle the corner case when `nextInt` returns `Int.MinValue`, which doesn't have a non-negative counterpart.

```
def nonNegativeInt(rng: RNG): (Int, RNG)
```

Dealing with awkwardness in functional programming

As you write more functional programs, you'll sometimes encounter situations like this where the functional way of expressing a program feels awkward or tedious. Does this imply that purity is the equivalent of trying to write an entire novel without using the letter *E*? Of course not. Awkwardness like this is almost always a sign of some missing abstraction waiting to be discovered.

When you encounter these situations, we encourage you to plow ahead and look for common patterns that you can factor out. Most likely, this is a problem that others have encountered, and you may even rediscover the "standard" solution yourself. Even if you get stuck, struggling to puzzle out a clean solution yourself will help you to better understand what solutions others have discovered to deal with similar problems.

With practice, experience, and more familiarity with the idioms contained in this book, expressing a program functionally will become effortless and natural. Of course, good design is still hard, but programming using pure functions greatly simplifies the design space.

EXERCISE 6.2

Write a function to generate a Double between 0 and 1, not including 1. Note: You can use Int.MaxValue to obtain the maximum positive integer value, and you can use x.toDouble to convert an x: Int to a Double.

```
def double(rng: RNG): (Double, RNG)
```

EXERCISE 6.3

Write functions to generate an (Int, Double) pair, a (Double, Int) pair, and a (Double, Double, Double) 3-tuple. You should be able to reuse the functions you've already written.

```
def intDouble(rng: RNG): ((Int,Double), RNG)
def doubleInt(rng: RNG): ((Double,Int), RNG)
def double3(rng: RNG): ((Double,Double,Double), RNG)
```

EXERCISE 6.4

Write a function to generate a list of random integers.

```
def ints(count: Int)(rng: RNG): (List[Int], RNG)
```

6.4   *A better API for state actions*

Looking back at our implementations, we'll notice a common pattern: each of our functions has a type of the form `RNG => (A, RNG)` for some type `A`. Functions of this type are called *state actions* or *state transitions* because they transform `RNG` states from one to the next. These state actions can be combined using *combinators*, which are higher-order functions that we'll define in this section. Since it's pretty tedious and repetitive to pass the state along ourselves, we want our combinators to pass the state from one action to the next automatically.

To make the type of actions convenient to talk about, and to simplify our thinking about them, let's make a type alias for the `RNG` state action data type:

```
type Rand[+A] = RNG => (A, RNG)
```

We can think of a value of type `Rand[A]` as "a randomly generated `A`," although that's not really precise. It's really a state action—a *program* that depends on some `RNG`, uses it to generate an `A`, and also transitions the `RNG` to a new state that can be used by another action later.

We can now turn methods such as `RNG`'s `nextInt` into values of this new type:

```
val int: Rand[Int] = _.nextInt
```

We want to write combinators that let us combine `Rand` actions while avoiding explicitly passing along the `RNG` state. We'll end up with a kind of domain-specific language that does all of the passing for us. For example, a simple `RNG` state transition is the `unit` action, which passes the `RNG` state through without using it, always returning a constant value rather than a random value:

```
def unit[A](a: A): Rand[A] =
  rng => (a, rng)
```

There's also `map` for transforming the output of a state action without modifying the state itself. Remember, `Rand[A]` is just a type alias for a function type `RNG => (A, RNG)`, so this is just a kind of function composition:

```
def map[A,B](s: Rand[A])(f: A => B): Rand[B] =
  rng => {
    val (a, rng2) = s(rng)
    (f(a), rng2)
  }
```

As an example of how `map` is used, here's `nonNegativeEven`, which reuses `nonNegative-Int` to generate an `Int` that's greater than or equal to zero and divisible by two:

```
def nonNegativeEven: Rand[Int] =
  map(nonNegativeInt)(i => i - i % 2)
```

■ **EXERCISE 6.5**

Use map to reimplement double in a more elegant way. See exercise 6.2.

6.4.1 Combining state actions

Unfortunately, map isn't powerful enough to implement intDouble and doubleInt from exercise 6.3. What we need is a new combinator map2 that can combine two RNG actions into one using a binary rather than unary function.

■ **EXERCISE 6.6**

Write the implementation of map2 based on the following signature. This function takes two actions, ra and rb, and a function f for combining their results, and returns a new action that combines them:

```
def map2[A,B,C](ra: Rand[A], rb: Rand[B])(f: (A, B) => C): Rand[C]
```

We only have to write the map2 combinator once, and then we can use it to combine arbitrary RNG state actions. For example, if we have an action that generates values of type A and an action to generate values of type B, then we can combine them into one action that generates pairs of both A and B:

```
def both[A,B](ra: Rand[A], rb: Rand[B]): Rand[(A,B)] =
  map2(ra, rb)((_, _))
```

We can use this to reimplement intDouble and doubleInt from exercise 6.3 more succinctly:

```
val randIntDouble: Rand[(Int, Double)] =
  both(int, double)

val randDoubleInt: Rand[(Double, Int)] =
  both(double, int)
```

■ **EXERCISE 6.7**

Hard: If you can combine two RNG transitions, you should be able to combine a whole list of them. Implement sequence for combining a List of transitions into a single transition. Use it to reimplement the ints function you wrote before. For the latter, you can use the standard library function `List.fill(n)(x)` to make a list with `x` repeated `n` times.

```
def sequence[A](fs: List[Rand[A]]): Rand[List[A]]
```

6.4.2 *Nesting state actions*

A pattern is beginning to emerge: we're progressing toward implementations that don't explicitly mention or pass along the RNG value. The `map` and `map2` combinators allowed us to implement, in a rather succinct and elegant way, functions that were otherwise tedious and error-prone to write. But there are some functions that we can't very well write in terms of `map` and `map2`.

One such function is `nonNegativeLessThan`, which generates an integer between 0 (inclusive) and n (exclusive):

```
def nonNegativeLessThan(n: Int): Rand[Int]
```

A first stab at an implementation might be to generate a non-negative integer modulo n:

```
def nonNegativeLessThan(n: Int): Rand[Int] =
  map(nonNegativeInt) { _ % n }
```

This will certainly generate a number in the range, but it'll be skewed because `Int.MaxValue` may not be exactly divisible by n. So numbers that are less than the remainder of that division will come up more frequently. When `nonNegativeInt` generates numbers higher than the largest multiple of n that fits in a 32-bit integer, we should *retry* the generator and hope to get a smaller number. We might attempt this:

```
def nonNegativeLessThan(n: Int): Rand[Int] =
  map(nonNegativeInt) { i =>
    val mod = i % n
    if (i + (n-1) - mod >= 0) mod else nonNegativeLessThan(n)(???)
  }
```

Retry recursively if the `Int` we got is higher than the largest multiple of n that fits in a 32-bit `Int`.

This is moving in the right direction, but `nonNegativeLessThan(n)` has the wrong type to be used right there. Remember, it should return a `Rand[Int]` which *is a function* that expects an RNG! But we don't have one right there. What we would like is to chain things together so that the RNG that's returned by `nonNegativeInt` is passed along to the recursive call to `nonNegativeLessThan`. We could pass it along explicitly instead of using `map`, like this:

```
def nonNegativeLessThan(n: Int): Rand[Int] = { rng =>
  val (i, rng2) = nonNegativeInt(rng)
  val mod = i % n
  if (i + (n-1) - mod >= 0)
    (mod, rng2)
  else nonNegativeLessThan(n)(rng)
}
```

But it would be better to have a combinator that does this passing along for us. Neither map nor map2 will cut it. We need a more powerful combinator, flatMap.

■ **EXERCISE 6.8** ──

Implement flatMap, and then use it to implement nonNegativeLessThan.

```
def flatMap[A,B](f: Rand[A])(g: A => Rand[B]): Rand[B]
```

---

flatMap allows us to generate a random A with Rand[A], and then take that A and choose a Rand[B] based on its value. In nonNegativeLessThan, we use it to choose whether to retry or not, based on the value generated by nonNegativeInt.

■ **EXERCISE 6.9** ──

Reimplement map and map2 in terms of flatMap. The fact that this is possible is what we're referring to when we say that flatMap is *more powerful* than map and map2.

We can now revisit our example from the beginning of this chapter. Can we make a more testable die roll using our purely functional API?

Here's an implementation of rollDie using nonNegativeLessThan, including the off-by-one error we had before:

```
def rollDie: Rand[Int] = nonNegativeLessThan(6)
```

If we test this function with various RNG states, we'll pretty soon find an RNG that causes this function to return 0:

```
scala> val zero = rollDie(SimpleRNG(5))._1
zero: Int = 0
```

And we can re-create this reliably by using the same SimpleRNG(5) random generator, without having to worry that its state is destroyed after it's been used.

Fixing the bug is trivial:

```
def rollDie: Rand[Int] = map(nonNegativeLessThan(6))(_ + 1)
```

6.5 *A general state action data type*

The functions we've just written—unit, map, map2, flatMap, and sequence—aren't really specific to random number generation at all. They're general-purpose functions for working with state actions, and don't care about the type of the state. Note that, for instance, map doesn't care that it's dealing with RNG state actions, and we can give it a more general signature:

```
def map[S,A,B](a: S => (A,S))(f: A => B): S => (B,S)
```

Changing this signature doesn't require modifying the implementation of `map`! The more general signature was there all along; we just didn't see it.

We should then come up with a more general type than `Rand`, for handling any type of state:

```
type State[S,+A] = S => (A,S)
```

Here `State` is short for *computation that carries some state along*, or *state action, state transition*, or even *statement* (see the next section). We might want to write it as its own class, wrapping the underlying function like this:

```
case class State[S,+A](run: S => (A,S))
```

The representation doesn't matter too much. What's important is that we have a single, general-purpose type, and using this type we can write general-purpose functions for capturing common patterns of stateful programs.

We can now just make `Rand` a type alias for `State`:

```
type Rand[A] = State[RNG, A]
```

■ **EXERCISE 6.10**

Generalize the functions `unit`, `map`, `map2`, `flatMap`, and `sequence`. Add them as methods on the `State` case class where possible. Otherwise you should put them in a `State` companion object.

The functions we've written here capture only a few of the most common patterns. As you write more functional code, you'll likely encounter other patterns and discover other functions to capture them.

6.6   *Purely functional imperative programming*

In the preceding sections, we were writing functions that followed a definite pattern. We'd run a state action, assign its result to a `val`, then run another state action that used that `val`, assign its result to another `val`, and so on. It looks a lot like *imperative* programming.

In the imperative programming paradigm, a program is a sequence of statements where each statement may modify the program state. That's exactly what we've been doing, except that our "statements" are really `State` actions, which are really functions. As functions, they read the current program state simply by receiving it in their argument, and they write to the program state simply by returning a value.

> ### Aren't imperative and functional programming opposites?
>
> Absolutely not. Remember, functional programming is simply programming without side effects. Imperative programming is about programming with statements that modify some program state, and as we've seen, it's entirely reasonable to maintain state without side effects.
>
> Functional programming has excellent support for writing imperative programs, with the added benefit that such programs can be reasoned about equationally because they're referentially transparent. We'll have much more to say about equational reasoning about programs in part 2, and imperative programs in particular in parts 3 and 4.

We implemented some combinators like map, map2, and ultimately flatMap to handle the propagation of the state from one statement to the next. But in doing so, we seem to have lost a bit of the imperative mood.

Consider as an example the following (which assumes that we've made Rand[A] a type alias for State[RNG, A]):

```
val ns: Rand[List[Int]] =
  int.flatMap(x =>
    int.flatMap(y =>
      ints(x).map(xs =>
        xs.map(_ % y))))
```

int is a value of type Rand[Int] that generates a single random integer.

ints(x) generates a list of length x.

Replaces every element in the list with its remainder when divided by y.

It's not clear what's going on here. But since we have map and flatMap defined, we can use a for-comprehension to recover the imperative style:

```
val ns: Rand[List[Int]] = for {
  x <- int
  y <- int
  xs <- ints(x)
} yield xs.map(_ % y)
```

Generates an integer x.

Generates another integer y.

Generates a list xs of length x.

Returns the list xs with each element replaced with its remainder when divided by y.

This code is much easier to read (and write), and it looks like what it is—an imperative program that maintains some state. But it's *the same code*. We get the next Int and assign it to x, get the next Int after that and assign it to y, then generate a list of length x, and finally return the list with all of its elements modulo y.

To facilitate this kind of imperative programming with for-comprehensions (or flatMaps), we really only need two primitive State combinators—one for reading the state and one for writing the state. If we imagine that we have a combinator get for getting the current state, and a combinator `set` for setting a new state, we could implement a combinator that can modify the state in arbitrary ways:

```
def modify[S](f: S => S): State[S, Unit] = for {
  s <- get
  _ <- set(f(s))
} yield ()
```

Gets the current state and assigns it to s (annotation pointing to `s <- get`)

Sets the new state to f applied to s (annotation pointing to `_ <- set(f(s))`)

This method returns a `State` action that modifies the incoming state by the function `f`. It yields `Unit` to indicate that it doesn't have a return value other than the state.

What would the `get` and `set` actions look like? They're exceedingly simple. The `get` action simply passes the incoming state along and returns it as the value:

```
def get[S]: State[S, S] = State(s => (s, s))
```

The `set` action is constructed with a new state `s`. The resulting action ignores the incoming state, replaces it with the new state, and returns `()` instead of a meaningful value:

```
def set[S](s: S): State[S, Unit] = State(_ => ((), s))
```

These two simple actions, together with the `State` combinators that we wrote—unit, map, map2, and flatMap—are all the tools we need to implement any kind of state machine or stateful program in a purely functional way.

EXERCISE 6.11

Hard: To gain experience with the use of `State`, implement a finite state automaton that models a simple candy dispenser. The machine has two types of input: you can insert a coin, or you can turn the knob to dispense candy. It can be in one of two states: locked or unlocked. It also tracks how many candies are left and how many coins it contains.

```
sealed trait Input
case object Coin extends Input
case object Turn extends Input

case class Machine(locked: Boolean, candies: Int, coins: Int)
```

The rules of the machine are as follows:

- Inserting a coin into a locked machine will cause it to unlock if there's any candy left.
- Turning the knob on an unlocked machine will cause it to dispense candy and become locked.
- Turning the knob on a locked machine or inserting a coin into an unlocked machine does nothing.
- A machine that's out of candy ignores all inputs.

The method `simulateMachine` should operate the machine based on the list of inputs and return the number of coins and candies left in the machine at the end. For example, if the input `Machine` has 10 coins and 5 candies, and a total of 4 candies are successfully bought, the output should be `(14, 1)`.

```
def simulateMachine(inputs: List[Input]): State[Machine, (Int, Int)]
```

6.7   *Summary*

In this chapter, we touched on the subject of how to write purely functional programs that have state. We used random number generation as the motivating example, but the overall pattern comes up in many different domains. The idea is simple: use a pure function that accepts a state as its argument, and it returns the new state alongside its result. Next time you encounter an imperative API that relies on side effects, see if you can provide a purely functional version of it, and use some of the functions we wrote here to make working with it more convenient.

Part 2

Functional design and combinator libraries

We said in chapter 1 that functional programming is a radical premise that affects how we write and organize programs at every level. In part 1, we covered the fundamentals of FP and saw how the commitment to using only pure functions affects the basic building blocks of programs: loops, data structures, exceptions, and so on. In part 2, we'll see how the assumptions of functional programming affect *library design*.

We'll create three useful libraries in part 2—one for parallel and asynchronous computation, another for testing programs, and a third for parsing text. There won't be much in the way of new syntax or language features, but we'll make heavy use of the material already covered. Our primary goal isn't to teach you about parallelism, testing, and parsing. The primary goal is *to help you develop skill in designing functional libraries*, even for domains that look nothing like the ones here.

This part of the book will be a somewhat meandering journey. Functional design can be a messy, iterative process. We hope to show at least a stylized view of how functional design proceeds in the real world. Don't worry if you don't follow every bit of discussion. These chapters should be like peering over the shoulder of someone as they think through possible designs. And because no two people approach this process the same way, the particular path we walk in each case might not strike you as the most natural one—perhaps it considers issues in what seems like an odd order, skips too fast, or goes too slow. Keep in mind that when you design your own functional libraries, you get to do it at your own pace, take whatever path you want, and, whenever questions come up about design choices, you get to think through the consequences in whatever way makes sense for you, which could include running little experiments, creating prototypes, and so on.

There are no right answers in functional library design. Instead, we have a collection of *design choices*, each with different trade-offs. Our goal is that you start to understand these trade-offs and what different choices mean. Sometimes, when designing a library, we'll come to a fork in the road. In this text we may, for pedagogical purposes, deliberately make a choice with undesirable consequences that we'll uncover later. We want you to see this process first-hand, because it's part of what actually occurs when designing functional programs. We're less interested in the particular libraries covered here in part 2, and more interested in giving you insight into how functional design proceeds and how to navigate situations that you will likely encounter. Library design is not something that only a select few people get to do; it's part of the day-to-day work of ordinary functional programming. In these chapters and beyond, you should absolutely feel free to experiment, play with different design choices, and develop your own aesthetic.

One final note: as you work through part 2, you may notice repeated patterns of similar-looking code. Keep this in the back of your mind. When we get to part 3, we'll discuss how to remove this duplication, and we'll discover an entire world of fundamental abstractions that are common to *all libraries*.

Purely functional parallelism

7

Because modern computers have multiple cores per CPU, and often multiple CPUs, it's more important than ever to design programs in such a way that they can take advantage of this parallel processing power. But the interaction of programs that run with parallelism is complex, and the traditional mechanism for communication among execution threads—shared mutable memory—is notoriously difficult to reason about. This can all too easily result in programs that have race conditions and deadlocks, aren't readily testable, and don't scale well.

In this chapter, we'll build a purely functional library for creating parallel and asynchronous computations. We'll rein in the complexity inherent in parallel programs by describing them using only pure functions. This will let us use the substitution model to simplify our reasoning and hopefully make working with concurrent computations both easy and enjoyable.

What you should take away from this chapter is not only how to write a library for purely functional parallelism, but *how to approach the problem of designing a purely functional library*. Our main concern will be to make our library highly composable and modular. To this end, we'll keep with our theme of separating the concern of *describing* a computation from actually *running* it. We want to allow users of our library to write programs at a very high level, insulating them from the nitty-gritty of how their programs will be executed. For example, towards the end of the chapter we'll develop a combinator, parMap, that will let us easily apply a function f to every element in a collection simultaneously:

```
val outputList = parMap(inputList)(f)
```

95

To get there, we'll work iteratively. We'll begin with a simple use case that we'd like our library to handle, and then develop an interface that facilitates this use case. Only then will we consider what our implementation of this interface should be. As we keep refining our design, we'll oscillate between the interface and implementation as we gain a better understanding of the domain and the design space through progressively more complex use cases. We'll emphasize *algebraic reasoning* and introduce the idea that an API can be described by *an algebra* that obeys specific *laws*.

Why design our own library? Why not just use the concurrency primitives that come with Scala's standard library in the scala.concurrent package? This is partially for pedagogical purposes—we want to show you how easy it is to design your own practical libraries. But there's another reason: we want to encourage the view that no existing library is authoritative or beyond reexamination, even if designed by experts and labeled "standard." There's a certain safety in doing what everybody else does, but what's conventional isn't necessarily the most practical. Most libraries contain a lot of arbitrary design choices, many made unintentionally. When you start from scratch, you get to revisit all the fundamental assumptions that went into designing the library, take a different path, and discover things about the problem space that others may not have even considered. As a result, you might arrive at your own design that suits your purposes better. In this particular case, our fundamental assumption will be that our library admits *absolutely no side effects*.

We'll write a lot of code in this chapter, largely posed as exercises for you, the reader. As always, you can find the answers in the downloadable content that goes along with the book.

7.1 *Choosing data types and functions*

When you begin designing a functional library, you usually have some general ideas about what you want to be able to do, and the difficulty in the design process is in refining these ideas and finding a data type that enables the functionality you want. In our case, we'd like to be able to "create parallel computations," but what does that mean exactly? Let's try to refine this into something we can implement by examining a simple, parallelizable computation—summing a list of integers. The usual left fold for this would be as follows:

```scala
def sum(ints: Seq[Int]): Int =
  ints.foldLeft(0)((a,b) => a + b)
```

Here Seq is a superclass of lists and other sequences in the standard library. Importantly, it has a foldLeft method.

Instead of folding sequentially, we could use a divide-and-conquer algorithm; see the following listing.

IndexedSeq is a superclass of random-access sequences like Vector in the standard library. Unlike lists, these sequences provide an efficient splitAt method for dividing them into two parts at a particular index.

Divides the sequence in half using the splitAt function.

```
def sum(ints: IndexedSeq[Int]): Int =
  if (ints.size <= 1)
    ints.headOption getOrElse 0
  else {
    val (l,r) = ints.splitAt(ints.length/2)
    sum(l) + sum(r)
  }
```

headOption is a method defined on all collections in Scala. We saw this function in chapter 4.

Recursively sums both halves and adds the results together.

We divide the sequence in half using the splitAt function, recursively sum both halves, and then combine their results. And unlike the foldLeft-based implementation, this implementation can be parallelized—the two halves can be summed in parallel.

The importance of simple examples

Summing integers is in practice probably so fast that parallelization imposes more overhead than it saves. But simple examples like this are exactly the kind that are most helpful to consider when designing a functional library. Complicated examples include all sorts of incidental structure and extraneous detail that can confuse the initial design process. We're trying to explain the essence of the problem domain, and a good way to do this is to start with trivial examples, factor out common concerns across these examples, and gradually add complexity. In functional design, our goal is to achieve expressiveness not with mountains of special cases, but by building a simple and composable set of core data types and functions.

As we think about what sort of data types and functions could enable parallelizing this computation, we can shift our perspective. Rather than focusing on how this parallelism will ultimately be implemented and forcing ourselves to work with the implementation APIs directly (likely related to java.lang.Thread and the java.util.concurrent library), we'll instead design our own ideal API as illuminated by our examples and work backward from there to an implementation.

7.1.1   A data type for parallel computations

Look at the line sum(l) + sum(r), which invokes sum on the two halves recursively. Just from looking at this single line, we can see that any data type we might choose to represent our parallel computations needs to be able to *contain a result*. That result will have some meaningful type (in this case Int), and we require some way of extracting this result. Let's apply this newfound knowledge to our design. For now, we can just *invent* a container type for our result, `Par[A]` (for *parallel*), and legislate the existence of the functions we need:

- `def unit[A](a: => A): Par[A]`, for taking an unevaluated `A` and returning a computation that might evaluate it in a separate thread. We call it *unit* because in a sense it creates a unit of parallelism that just wraps a single value.
- `def get[A](a: Par[A]): A`, for extracting the resulting value from a parallel computation.

Can we really do this? Yes, of course! For now, we don't need to worry about what other functions we require, what the internal representation of `Par` might be, or how these functions are implemented. We're simply reading off the needed data types and functions by inspecting our simple example. Let's update this example now.

> **Listing 7.2   Updating sum with our custom data type**

```scala
def sum(ints: IndexedSeq[Int]): Int =
  if (ints.size <= 1)
    ints headOption getOrElse 0
  else {
    val (l,r) = ints.splitAt(ints.length/2)
    val sumL: Par[Int] = Par.unit(sum(l))      Computes the left
    val sumR: Par[Int] = Par.unit(sum(r))      half in parallel.
    Par.get(sumL) + Par.get(sumR)              Computes the right half in parallel.
  }
```

Extracts both results
and sums them.

We've wrapped the two recursive calls to `sum` in calls to `unit`, and we're calling `get` to extract the two results from the two subcomputations.

The problem with using concurrency primitives directly

What of `java.lang.Thread` and `Runnable`? Let's take a look at these classes. Here's a partial excerpt of their API, transcribed into Scala:

```scala
trait Runnable { def run: Unit }

class Thread(r: Runnable) {           Begins running r in
  def start: Unit                     a separate thread.
  def join: Unit                      Blocks the calling thread
}                                      until r finishes running.
```

Already, we can see a problem with both of these types—none of the methods return a meaningful value. Therefore, if we want to get any information out of a `Runnable`, it has to have some side effect, like mutating some state that we can inspect. This is bad for compositionality—we can't manipulate `Runnable` objects generically since we always need to know something about their internal behavior. `Thread` also has the disadvantage that it maps directly onto operating system threads, which are a scarce resource. It would be preferable to create as many "logical threads" as is natural for our problem, and later deal with mapping these onto actual OS threads.

This kind of thing can be handled by something like `java.util.concurrent` `.Future`, `ExecutorService`, and friends. Why don't we use them directly? Here's a portion of their API:

```
class ExecutorService {
  def submit[A](a: Callable[A]): Future[A]
}
trait Future[A] {
  def get: A
}
```

Though these are a tremendous help in abstracting over physical threads, these primitives are still at a much lower level of abstraction than the library we want to create in this chapter. A call to `Future.get`, for example, blocks the calling thread until the `ExecutorService` has finished executing it, and its API provides no means of *composing* futures. Of course, we can build the *implementation* of our library on top of these tools (and this is in fact what we end up doing later in the chapter), but they don't present a modular and compositional API that we'd want to use directly from functional programs.

We now have a choice about the meaning of `unit` and `get`—`unit` could begin evaluating its argument immediately in a separate (logical) thread,[1] or it could simply hold onto its argument until `get` is called and begin evaluation then. But note that in this example, if we want to obtain any degree of parallelism, we require that `unit` begin evaluating its argument concurrently and return immediately. Can you see why?[2]

But if `unit` begins evaluating its argument concurrently, then calling `get` arguably breaks referential transparency. We can see this by replacing `sumL` and `sumR` with their definitions—if we do so, we still get the same result, but our program is no longer parallel:

```
Par.get(Par.unit(sum(l))) + Par.get(Par.unit(sum(r)))
```

If `unit` starts evaluating its argument right away, the next thing to happen is that `get` will wait for that evaluation to complete. So the two sides of the + sign won't run in parallel if we simply inline the `sumL` and `sumR` variables. We can see that `unit` has a definite side effect, but only *with regard to* `get`. That is, `unit` simply returns a `Par[Int]` in this case, representing an asynchronous computation. But as soon as we pass that `Par` to `get`, we explicitly wait for it, exposing the side effect. So it seems that we want to avoid calling `get`, or at least delay calling it until the very end. We want to be able to combine asynchronous computations without waiting for them to finish.

---

[1] We'll use the term *logical thread* somewhat informally throughout this chapter to mean a computation that runs concurrently with the main execution thread of our program. There need not be a one-to-one correspondence between logical threads and OS threads. We may have a large number of logical threads mapped onto a smaller number of OS threads via thread pooling, for instance.

[2] Function arguments in Scala are strictly evaluated from left to right, so if `unit` delays execution until `get` is called, we will both spawn the parallel computation and wait for it to finish before spawning the second parallel computation. This means the computation is effectively sequential!

Before we continue, note what we've done. First, we conjured up a simple, almost trivial example. We next explored this example a bit to uncover a design choice. Then, via some experimentation, we discovered an interesting consequence of one option and in the process learned something fundamental about the nature of our problem domain! The overall design process is a series of these little adventures. You don't need any special license to do this sort of exploration, and you don't need to be an expert in functional programming either. Just dive in and see what you find.

7.1.2   *Combining parallel computations*

Let's see if we can avoid the aforementioned pitfall of combining unit and get. If we don't call get, that implies that our sum function must return a Par[Int]. What consequences does this change reveal? Again, let's just invent functions with the required signatures:

```
def sum(ints: IndexedSeq[Int]): Par[Int] =
  if (ints.size <= 1)
    Par.unit(ints.headOption getOrElse 0)
  else {
    val (l,r) = ints.splitAt(ints.length/2)
    Par.map2(sum(l), sum(r))(_ + _)
  }
```

EXERCISE 7.1

Par.map2 is a new higher-order function for combining the result of two parallel computations. What is its signature? Give the most general signature possible (don't assume it works only for Int).

Observe that we're no longer calling unit in the recursive case, and it isn't clear whether unit should accept its argument lazily anymore. In this example, accepting the argument lazily doesn't seem to provide any benefit, but perhaps this isn't always the case. Let's come back to this question later.

What about map2—should it take its arguments lazily? It would make sense for map2 to run both sides of the computation in parallel, giving each side equal opportunity to run (it would seem arbitrary for the order of the map2 arguments to matter—we simply want map2 to indicate that the two computations being combined are independent, and can be run in parallel). What choice lets us implement this meaning? As a simple test case, consider what happens if map2 is strict in both arguments, and we're evaluating sum(IndexedSeq(1,2,3,4)). Take a minute to work through and understand the following (somewhat stylized) program trace.

Listing 7.3 Program trace for sum

```
sum(IndexedSeq(1,2,3,4))
map2(
  sum(IndexedSeq(1,2)),
  sum(IndexedSeq(3,4)))(_ + _)
map2(
  map2(
    sum(IndexedSeq(1)),
    sum(IndexedSeq(2)))(_ + _),
  sum(IndexedSeq(3,4)))(_ + _)
map2(
  map2(
    unit(1),
    unit(2))(_ + _),
  sum(IndexedSeq(3,4)))(_ + _)
map2(
  map2(
    unit(1),
    unit(2))(_ + _),
  map2(
    sum(IndexedSeq(3)),
    sum(IndexedSeq(4)))(_ + _))(_ + _)
...
```

In this trace, to evaluate sum(x), we substitute x into the definition of sum, as we've done in previous chapters. Because map2 is strict, and Scala evaluates arguments left to right, whenever we encounter map2(sum(x),sum(y))(_ + _), we have to then evaluate sum(x) and so on recursively. This has the rather unfortunate consequence that we'll strictly construct the entire left half of the tree of summations first before moving on to (strictly) constructing the right half. Here sum(IndexedSeq(1,2)) gets fully expanded before we consider sum(IndexedSeq(3,4)). And if map2 evaluates its arguments in parallel (using whatever resource is being used to implement the parallelism, like a thread pool), that implies the left half of our computation will start executing before we even begin constructing the right half of our computation.

What if we keep map2 strict, but *don't* have it begin execution immediately? Does this help? If map2 doesn't begin evaluation immediately, this implies a Par value is merely constructing a *description* of what needs to be computed in parallel. Nothing actually occurs until we *evaluate* this description, perhaps using a get-like function. The problem is that if we construct our descriptions strictly, they'll be rather heavyweight objects. Looking back at our trace, our description will have to contain the full tree of operations to be performed:

```
map2(
  map2(
    unit(1),
    unit(2))(_ + _),
  map2(
    unit(3),
    unit(4))(_ + _))(_ + _)
```

Whatever data structure we use to store this description, it'll likely occupy more space than the original list itself! It would be nice if our descriptions were more lightweight.

It seems we should make `map2` lazy and have it begin immediate execution of both sides in parallel. This also addresses the problem of giving neither side priority over the other.

7.1.3   *Explicit forking*

Something still doesn't feel right about our latest choice. Is it *always* the case that we want to evaluate the two arguments to `map2` in parallel? Probably not. Consider this simple hypothetical example:

```
Par.map2(Par.unit(1), Par.unit(1))(_ + _)
```

In this case, we happen to know that the two computations we're combining will execute so quickly that there isn't much point in spawning off a separate logical thread to evaluate them. But our API doesn't give us any way of providing this sort of information. That is, our current API is very *inexplicit* about when computations get forked off the main thread—the programmer doesn't get to specify where this forking should occur. What if we make the forking more explicit? We can do that by inventing another function, `def fork[A](a: => Par[A]): Par[A]`, which we can take to mean that the given `Par` should be run in a separate logical thread:

```
def sum(ints: IndexedSeq[Int]): Par[Int] =
  if (ints.length <= 1)
    Par.unit(ints.headOption getOrElse 0)
  else {
    val (l,r) = ints.splitAt(ints.length/2)
    Par.map2(Par.fork(sum(l)), Par.fork(sum(r)))(_ + _)
  }
```

With `fork`, we can now make `map2` strict, leaving it up to the programmer to wrap arguments if they wish. A function like `fork` solves the problem of instantiating our parallel computations too strictly, but more fundamentally it puts the parallelism explicitly under programmer control. We're addressing two concerns here. The first is that we need some way to indicate that the results of the two parallel tasks should be combined. Separate from this, we have the choice of whether a particular task should be performed asynchronously. By keeping these concerns separate, we avoid having any sort of global policy for parallelism attached to `map2` and other combinators we write, which would mean making tough (and ultimately arbitrary) choices about what global policy is best.

Let's now return to the question of whether `unit` should be strict or lazy. With `fork`, we can now make `unit` strict without any loss of expressiveness. A non-strict version of it, let's call it `lazyUnit`, can be implemented using `unit` and `fork`:

```
def unit[A](a: A): Par[A]
def lazyUnit[A](a: => A): Par[A] = fork(unit(a))
```

The function lazyUnit is a simple example of a *derived* combinator, as opposed to a *primitive* combinator like unit. We were able to define lazyUnit just in terms of other operations. Later, when we pick a representation for Par, lazyUnit won't need to know anything about this representation—its only knowledge of Par is through the operations fork and unit that are defined on Par.[3]

We know we want fork to signal that its argument gets evaluated in a separate logical thread. But we still have the question of whether it should begin doing so *immediately* upon being called, or hold on to its argument, to be evaluated in a logical thread later, when the computation is *forced* using something like get. In other words, should evaluation be the responsibility of fork or of get? Should evaluation be eager or lazy? When you're unsure about a meaning to assign to some function in your API, you can always continue with the design process—at some point later the trade-offs of different choices of meaning may become clear. Here we make use of a helpful trick—we'll think about what *sort of information* is required to implement fork and get with various meanings.

If fork begins evaluating its argument immediately in parallel, the implementation must clearly know something, either directly or indirectly, about how to create threads or submit tasks to some sort of thread pool. Moreover, this implies that the thread pool (or whatever resource we use to implement the parallelism) must be (globally) accessible and properly initialized wherever we want to call fork.[4] This means we lose the ability to control the parallelism strategy used for different parts of our program. And though there's nothing inherently wrong with having a global resource for executing parallel tasks, we can imagine how it would be useful to have more fine-grained control over what implementations are used where (we might like for each subsystem of a large application to get its own thread pool with different parameters, for example). It seems much more appropriate to give get the responsibility of creating threads and submitting execution tasks.

Note that coming to these conclusions didn't require knowing exactly how fork and get will be implemented, or even what the representation of Par will be. We just reasoned informally about the sort of information required to actually spawn a parallel task, and examined the consequences of having Par values know about this information.

In contrast, if fork simply holds on to its unevaluated argument until later, it requires no access to the mechanism for implementing parallelism. It just takes an unevaluated Par and "marks" it for concurrent evaluation. Let's now assume this meaning for fork. With this model, Par itself doesn't need to know how to actually *implement* the parallelism. It's more a *description* of a parallel computation that gets *interpreted* at a later time by something like the get function. This is a shift from before, where we were considering Par to be a *container* of a value that we could simply

---

[3] This sort of indifference to representation is a hint that the operations are actually more general, and can be abstracted to work for types other than just Par. We'll explore this topic in detail in part 3.

[4] Much like the credit card processing system was accessible to the buyCoffee method in our Cafe example in chapter 1.

get when it becomes available. Now it's more of a first-class *program* that we can *run*. So let's rename our get function to run, and dictate that this is where the parallelism actually gets implemented:

```
def run[A](a: Par[A]): A
```

Because Par is now just a pure data structure, run has to have some means of implementing the parallelism, whether it spawns new threads, delegates tasks to a thread pool, or uses some other mechanism.

7.2   *Picking a representation*

Just by exploring this simple example and thinking through the consequences of different choices, we've sketched out the following API.

> **Listing 7.4   Basic sketch for an API for Par**

Marks a computation for concurrent evaluation by run.

Creates a computation that immediately results in the value a.

Combines the results of two parallel computations with a binary function.

```
def unit[A](a: A): Par[A]
def map2[A,B,C](a: Par[A], b: Par[B])(f: (A,B) => C): Par[C]
def fork[A](a: => Par[A]): Par[A]
def lazyUnit[A](a: => A): Par[A] = fork(unit(a))
def run[A](a: Par[A]): A
```

Wraps the expression a for concurrent evaluation by run.

Fully evaluates a given Par, spawning parallel computations as requested by fork and extracting the resulting value.

We've also loosely assigned meaning to these various functions:

- unit promotes a constant value to a parallel computation.
- map2 combines the results of two parallel computations with a binary function.
- fork marks a computation for concurrent evaluation. The evaluation won't actually occur until forced by run.
- lazyUnit wraps its unevaluated argument in a Par and marks it for concurrent evaluation.
- run extracts a value from a Par by actually performing the computation.

At any point while sketching out an API, you can start thinking about possible *representations* for the abstract types that appear.

 EXERCISE 7.2

Before continuing, try to come up with representations for Par that make it possible to implement the functions of our API.

Let's see if we can come up with a representation. We know `run` needs to execute asynchronous tasks somehow. We could write our own low-level API, but there's already a class that we can use in the Java Standard Library, `java.util.concurrent.ExecutorService`. Here is its API, excerpted and transcribed to Scala:

```scala
class ExecutorService {
  def submit[A](a: Callable[A]): Future[A]
}
trait Callable[A] { def call: A }          ⟵          Essentially just a lazy A
trait Future[A] {
  def get: A
  def get(timeout: Long, unit: TimeUnit): A
  def cancel(evenIfRunning: Boolean): Boolean
  def isDone: Boolean
  def isCancelled: Boolean
}
```

So `ExecutorService` lets us submit a `Callable` value (in Scala we'd probably just use a lazy argument to `submit`) and get back a corresponding `Future` that's a handle to a computation that's potentially running in a separate thread. We can obtain a value from a `Future` with its `get` method (which blocks the current thread until the value is available), and it has some extra features for cancellation (throwing an exception after blocking for a certain amount of time, and so on).

Let's try assuming that our `run` function has access to an `ExecutorService` and see if that suggests anything about the representation for `Par`:

```scala
def run[A](s: ExecutorService)(a: Par[A]): A
```

The simplest possible model for `Par[A]` might be `ExecutorService => A`. This would obviously make `run` trivial to implement. But it might be nice to defer the decision of how long to wait for a computation, or whether to cancel it, to the caller of `run`. So `Par[A]` becomes `ExecutorService => Future[A]`, and `run` simply returns the `Future`:

```scala
type Par[A] = ExecutorService => Future[A]

def run[A](s: ExecutorService)(a: Par[A]): Future[A] = a(s)
```

Note that since `Par` is represented by *a function* that needs an `ExecutorService`, the creation of the `Future` doesn't actually happen until this `ExectorService` is provided.

Is it really that simple? Let's assume it is for now, and revise our model if we find it doesn't allow some functionality we'd like.

7.3 *Refining the API*

The way we've worked so far is a bit artificial. In practice, there aren't such clear boundaries between designing the API and choosing a representation, and one doesn't necessarily precede the other. Ideas for a representation can inform the API, the API can inform the choice of representation, and it's natural to shift fluidly between these two perspectives, run experiments as questions arise, build prototypes, and so on.

We'll devote this section to exploring our API. Though we got a lot of mileage out of considering a simple example, before we add any new primitive operations, let's try to learn more about what's expressible using those we already have. With our primitives and choices of meaning for them, we've carved out a little universe for ourselves. We now get to discover what ideas are expressible in this universe. This can and should be a fluid process—we can change the rules of our universe at any time, make a fundamental change to our representation or introduce a new primitive, and explore how our creation then behaves.

Let's begin by implementing the functions of the API that we've developed so far. Now that we have a representation for `Par`, a first crack at it should be straightforward. What follows is a simplistic implementation using the representation of `Par` that we've chosen.

Listing 7.5   Basic implementation for `Par`

unit is represented as a function that returns a `UnitFuture`, which is a simple implementation of `Future` that just wraps a constant value. It doesn't use the `ExecutorService` at all. It's always done and can't be cancelled. Its `get` method simply returns the value that we gave it.

```scala
object Par {
  def unit[A](a: A): Par[A] = (es: ExecutorService) => UnitFuture(a)

  private case class UnitFuture[A](get: A) extends Future[A] {
    def isDone = true
    def get(timeout: Long, units: TimeUnit) = get
    def isCancelled = false
    def cancel(evenIfRunning: Boolean): Boolean = false
  }
```

map2 doesn't evaluate the call to `f` in a separate logical thread, in accord with our design choice of having `fork` be the sole function in the API for controlling parallelism. We can always do `fork(map2(a,b)(f))` if we want the evaluation of `f` to occur in a separate thread.

```scala
  def map2[A,B,C](a: Par[A], b: Par[B])(f: (A,B) => C): Par[C] =
    (es: ExecutorService) => {
      val af = a(es)
      val bf = b(es)
      UnitFuture(f(af.get, bf.get))
    }
```

This implementation of `map2` does *not* respect timeouts. It simply passes the `ExecutorService` on to both `Par` values, waits for the results of the Futures `af` and `bf`, applies `f` to them, and wraps them in a `UnitFuture`. In order to respect timeouts, we'd need a new `Future` implementation that records the amount of time spent evaluating `af`, and then subtracts that time from the available time allocated for evaluating `bf`.

```
def fork[A](a: => Par[A]): Par[A] =
  es => es.submit(new Callable[A] {
    def call = a(es).get
  })
}
```

This is the simplest and most natural implementation of `fork`, but there are some problems with it—for one, the outer `Callable` will block waiting for the "inner" task to complete. Since this blocking occupies a thread in our thread pool, or whatever resource backs the `ExecutorService`, this implies that we're losing out on some potential parallelism. Essentially, we're using two threads when one should suffice. This is a symptom of a more serious problem with the implementation that we'll discuss later in the chapter.

We should note that `Future` doesn't have a purely functional interface. This is part of the reason why we don't want users of our library to deal with `Future` directly. But importantly, even though methods on `Future` rely on side effects, our entire Par API remains pure. It's only after the user calls `run` and the implementation receives an `ExecutorService` that we expose the `Future` machinery. Our users therefore program to a pure interface whose implementation nevertheless relies on effects at the end of the day. But since our API remains pure, these effects aren't *side* effects. In part 4 we'll discuss this distinction in detail.

EXERCISE 7.3

Hard: Fix the implementation of map2 so that it respects the contract of timeouts on `Future`.

EXERCISE 7.4

This API already enables a rich set of operations. Here's a simple example: using `lazyUnit`, write a function to convert any function A => B to one that evaluates its result asynchronously.

```
def asyncF[A,B](f: A => B): A => Par[B]
```

Adding infix syntax using implicit conversions

If `Par` were an actual data type, functions like `map2` could be placed in the class body and then called with infix syntax like `x.map2(y)(f)` (much like we did for `Stream` and `Option`). But since `Par` is just a type alias, we can't do this directly. There's a trick to add infix syntax to *any* type using *implicit conversions*. We won't discuss that here since it isn't that relevant to what we're trying to cover, but if you're interested, check out the answer code associated with this chapter.

What else can we express with our existing combinators? Let's look at a more concrete example.

Suppose we have a `Par[List[Int]]` representing a parallel computation that produces a `List[Int]`, and we'd like to convert this to a `Par[List[Int]]` whose result is sorted:

```
def sortPar(parList: Par[List[Int]]): Par[List[Int]]
```

We could of course run the `Par`, sort the resulting list, and repackage it in a `Par` with `unit`. But we want to avoid calling `run`. The only other combinator we have that allows us to manipulate the value of a `Par` in any way is `map2`. So if we passed `parList` to one side of `map2`, we'd be able to gain access to the `List` inside and sort it. And we can pass whatever we want to the other side of `map2`, so let's just pass a no-op:

```
def sortPar(parList: Par[List[Int]]): Par[List[Int]] =
  map2(parList, unit(()))((a, _) => a.sorted)
```

That was easy. We can now tell a `Par[List[Int]]` that we'd like that list sorted. But we might as well generalize this further. We can "lift" any function of type `A => B` to become a function that takes `Par[A]` and returns `Par[B]`; we can `map` any function over a `Par`:

```
def map[A,B](pa: Par[A])(f: A => B): Par[B] =
  map2(pa, unit(()))((a,_) => f(a))
```

For instance, `sortPar` is now simply this:

```
def sortPar(parList: Par[List[Int]]) = map(parList)(_.sorted)
```

That's terse and clear. We just combined the operations to make the types line up. And yet, if you look at the implementations of `map2` and `unit`, it should be clear this implementation of `map` *means* something sensible.

Was it cheating to pass a bogus value, `unit(())`, as an argument to `map2`, only to ignore its value? Not at all! The fact that we can implement `map` in terms of `map2`, but not the other way around, just shows that `map2` is strictly more powerful than `map`. This sort of thing happens a lot when we're designing libraries—often, a function that seems to be primitive will turn out to be expressible using some more powerful primitive.

What else can we implement using our API? Could we `map` over a list in parallel? Unlike `map2`, which combines two parallel computations, `parMap` (let's call it) needs to combine *N* parallel computations. It seems like this should somehow be expressible:

```
def parMap[A,B](ps: List[A])(f: A => B): Par[List[B]]
```

We could always just write `parMap` as a new primitive. Remember that `Par[A]` is simply an alias for `ExecutorService => Future[A]`.

There's nothing wrong with implementing operations as new primitives. In some cases, we can even implement the operations more efficiently by assuming something about the underlying representation of the data types we're working with. But right now we're interested in exploring what operations are expressible using our existing

API, and grasping the relationships between the various operations we've defined. Understanding what combinators are truly primitive will become more important in part 3, when we show how to abstract over common patterns across libraries.[5]

Let's see how far we can get implementing parMap in terms of existing combinators:

```
def parMap[A,B](ps: List[A])(f: A => B): Par[List[B]] = {
  val fbs: List[Par[B]] = ps.map(asyncF(f))
  ...
}
```

Remember, asyncF converts an A => B to an A => Par[B] by forking a parallel computation to produce the result. So we can fork off our *N* parallel computations pretty easily, but we need some way of collecting their results. Are we stuck? Well, just from inspecting the types, we can see that we need some way of converting our List[Par[B]] to the Par[List[B]] required by the return type of parMap.

EXERCISE 7.5

Hard: Write this function, called sequence. No additional primitives are required. Do not call run.

```
def sequence[A](ps: List[Par[A]]): Par[List[A]]
```

Once we have sequence, we can complete our implementation of parMap:

```
def parMap[A,B](ps: List[A])(f: A => B): Par[List[B]] = fork {
  val fbs: List[Par[B]] = ps.map(asyncF(f))
  sequence(fbs)
}
```

Note that we've wrapped our implementation in a call to fork. With this implementation, parMap will return immediately, even for a huge input list. When we later call run, it will fork a single asynchronous computation which itself spawns *N* parallel computations, and then waits for these computations to finish, collecting their results into a list.

EXERCISE 7.6

Implement parFilter, which filters elements of a list in parallel.

```
def parFilter[A](as: List[A])(f: A => Boolean): Par[List[A]]
```

---

[5] In this case, there's another good reason not to implement parMap as a new primitive—it's challenging to do correctly, particularly if we want to properly respect timeouts. It's frequently the case that primitive combinators encapsulate some rather tricky logic, and reusing them means we don't have to duplicate this logic.

Can you think of any other useful functions to write? Experiment with writing a few parallel computations of your own to see which ones can be expressed without additional primitives. Here are some ideas to try:

- Is there a more general version of the parallel summation function we wrote at the beginning of this chapter? Try using it to find the maximum value of an `IndexedSeq` in parallel.
- Write a function that takes a list of paragraphs (a `List[String]`) and returns the total number of words across all paragraphs, in parallel. Generalize this function as much as possible.
- Implement `map3`, `map4`, and `map5`, in terms of `map2`.

7.4 The algebra of an API

As the previous section demonstrates, we often get far just by writing down the type signature for an operation we want, and then "following the types" to an implementation. When working this way, we can almost forget the concrete domain (for instance, when we implemented `map` in terms of `map2` and `unit`) and just focus on lining up types. This isn't cheating; it's a natural style of reasoning, analogous to the reasoning one does when simplifying an algebraic equation. We're treating the API as an *algebra*,[6] or an abstract set of operations along with a set of *laws* or properties we assume to be true, and simply doing formal symbol manipulation following the rules of the game specified by this algebra.

Up until now, we've been reasoning somewhat informally about our API. There's nothing wrong with this, but it can be helpful to take a step back and formalize what laws you expect to hold (or would like to hold) for your API.[7] Without realizing it, you've probably mentally built up a model of what properties or laws you expect. Actually writing these down and making them precise can highlight design choices that wouldn't be otherwise apparent when reasoning informally.

7.4.1 The law of mapping

Like any design choice, choosing laws has *consequences*—it places constraints on what the operations can mean, determines what implementation choices are possible, and affects what other properties can be true. Let's look at an example. We'll just make up a possible law that seems reasonable. This might be used as a test case if we were writing tests for our library:

```
map(unit(1))(_ + 1) == unit(2)
```

---

[6] We do mean algebra in the mathematical sense of one or more sets, together with a collection of functions operating on objects of these sets, and a set of *axioms*. Axioms are statements assumed true from which we can derive other *theorems* that must also be true. In our case, the sets are particular types like `Par[A]` and `List[Par[A]]`, and the functions are operations like `map2`, `unit`, and `sequence`.

[7] We'll have much more to say about this throughout the rest of this book. In the next chapter, we'll design a declarative testing library that lets us define properties we expect functions to satisfy, and automatically generates test cases to check these properties. And in part 3 we'll introduce abstract interfaces specified *only* by sets of laws.

We're saying that mapping over unit(1) with the _ + 1 function is in some sense equivalent to unit(2). (Laws often start out this way, as concrete examples of *identities*[8] we expect to hold.) In what sense are they equivalent? This is an interesting question. For now, let's say two Par objects are equivalent if *for any valid* ExecutorService argument, their Future results have the same value.

We can check that this holds for a particular ExecutorService with a function like this:

```
def equal[A](e: ExecutorService)(p: Par[A], p2: Par[A]): Boolean =
  p(e).get == p2(e).get
```

Laws and functions share much in common. Just as we can generalize functions, we can generalize laws. For instance, the preceding could be generalized this way:

```
map(unit(x))(f) == unit(f(x))
```

Here we're saying this should hold for *any* choice of x and f, not just 1 and the _ + 1 function. This places some constraints on our implementation. Our implementation of unit can't, say, inspect the value it receives and decide to return a parallel computation with a result of 42 when the input is 1—it can only pass along whatever it receives. Similarly for our ExecutorService—when we submit Callable objects to it for execution, it can't make any assumptions or change behavior based on the values it receives. More concretely, this law disallows downcasting or isInstanceOf checks (often grouped under the term *typecasing*) in the implementations of map and unit.

Much like we strive to define functions in terms of simpler functions, each of which *do* just one thing, we can define laws in terms of simpler laws that each *say* just one thing. Let's see if we can simplify this law further. We said we wanted this law to hold for *any* choice of x and f. Something interesting happens if we substitute the identity function for f.[9] We can simplify both sides of the equation and get a new law that's considerably simpler:[10]

```
map(unit(x))(f) == unit(f(x))       ←——————  Initial law.
map(unit(x))(id) == unit(id(x))     ←——————  Substitute identity function for f.
map(unit(x))(id) == unit(x)         ←——————  Simplify.
map(y)(id) == y                     ←——
                                     Substitute y for unit(x) on both sides.
```

Fascinating! Our new, simpler law talks only about map—apparently the mention of unit was an extraneous detail. To get some insight into what this new law is saying, let's think about what map *can't* do. It can't, say, throw an exception and crash the computation before applying the function to the result (can you see why this violates the law?). All it can do is apply the function f to the result of y, which of course leaves y

---

[8] Here we mean *identity* in the mathematical sense of a statement that two expressions are identical or equivalent.

[9] The identity function is defined as def id[A](a: A): A = a.

[10] This is the same sort of substitution and simplification one might do when solving an algebraic equation.

unaffected when that function is `id`.[11] Even more interestingly, given `map(y)(id) == y`, we can perform the substitutions in the other direction to get back our original, more complex law. (Try it!) Logically, we have the freedom to do so because `map` can't possibly behave differently for different function types it receives. Thus, given `map(y)(id) == y`, it must be true that `map(unit(x))(f) == unit(f(x))`. Since we get this second law or theorem for free, simply because of the parametricity of `map`, it's sometimes called a *free theorem*.[12]

EXERCISE 7.7

Hard: Given `map(y)(id) == y`, it's a free theorem that `map(map(y)(g))(f) == map(y)(f compose g)`. (This is sometimes called *map fusion*, and it can be used as an optimization—rather than spawning a separate parallel computation to compute the second mapping, we can fold it into the first mapping.)[13] Can you prove it? You may want to read the paper "Theorems for Free!" (http://mng.bz/Z9f1) to better understand the "trick" of free theorems.

7.4.2   *The law of forking*

As interesting as all this is, this particular law doesn't do much to constrain our implementation. You've probably been assuming these properties without even realizing it (it would be strange to have any special cases in the implementations of `map`, `unit`, or `ExecutorService.submit`, or have `map` randomly throwing exceptions). Let's consider a stronger property—that `fork` should not affect the result of a parallel computation:

```
fork(x) == x
```

This seems like it should be obviously true of our implementation, and it is clearly a desirable property, consistent with our expectation of how `fork` should work. `fork(x)` should do the same thing as `x`, but asynchronously, in a logical thread separate from the main thread. If this law didn't always hold, we'd have to somehow know when it was safe to call without changing meaning, without any help from the type system.

Surprisingly, this simple property places strong constraints on our implementation of `fork`. After you've written down a law like this, take off your implementer hat, put on your debugger hat, and try to break your law. Think through any possible corner cases, try to come up with counterexamples, and even construct an informal proof that the law holds—at least enough to convince a skeptical fellow programmer.

---

[11] We say that `map` is required to be *structure-preserving* in that it doesn't alter the structure of the parallel computation, only the value "inside" the computation.

[12] The idea of free theorems was introduced by Philip Wadler in the classic paper "Theorems for Free!" (http://mng.bz/Z9f1).

[13] Our representation of `Par` doesn't give us the ability to implement this optimization, since it's an opaque function. If it were reified as a data type, we could pattern match and discover opportunities to apply this rule. You may want to try experimenting with this idea on your own.

7.4.3   *Breaking the law: a subtle bug*

Let's try this mode of thinking. We're expecting that fork(x) == x for *all* choices of x, and any choice of ExecutorService. We have a good sense of what x could be—it's some expression making use of fork, unit, and map2 (and other combinators derived from these). What about ExecutorService? What are some possible implementations of it? There's a good listing of different implementations in the class java.util .concurrent.Executors (API link: http://mng.bz/urQd).

> **EXERCISE 7.8**
>
> *Hard:* Take a look through the various static methods in Executors to get a feel for the different implementations of ExecutorService that exist. Then, before continuing, go back and revisit your implementation of fork and try to find a counterexample or convince yourself that the law holds for your implementation.

> **Why laws about code and proofs are important**
>
> It may seem unusual to state and prove properties about an API. This certainly isn't something typically done in ordinary programming. Why is it important in FP?
>
> In functional programming it's easy, and expected, to factor out common functionality into generic, reusable components that can be *composed*. Side effects hurt compositionality, but more generally, any hidden or out-of-band assumption or behavior that prevents us from treating our components (be they functions or anything else) as *black boxes* makes composition difficult or impossible.
>
> In our example of the law for fork, we can see that if the law we posited didn't hold, many of our general-purpose combinators, like parMap, would no longer be sound (and their usage might be dangerous, since they could, depending on the broader parallel computation they were used in, result in deadlocks).
>
> Giving our APIs an algebra, with laws that are meaningful and aid reasoning, makes the APIs more usable for clients, but also means we can treat the objects of our APIs as black boxes. As we'll see in part 3, this is crucial for our ability to factor out common patterns across the different libraries we've written.

There's actually a rather subtle problem that will occur in most implementations of fork. When using an ExecutorService backed by a thread pool of bounded size (see Executors.newFixedThreadPool), it's very easy to run into a deadlock.[14] Suppose we have an ExecutorService backed by a thread pool where the maximum number of threads is 1. Try running the following example using our current implementation:

---

[14] In the next chapter, we'll write a combinator library for testing that can help discover problems like these automatically.

```
val a = lazyUnit(42 + 1)
val S = Executors.newFixedThreadPool(1)
println(Par.equal(S)(a, fork(a)))
```

Most implementations of `fork` will result in this code deadlocking. Can you see why? Let's look again at our implementation of `fork`:

```
def fork[A](a: => Par[A]): Par[A] =                    Waits for the result of
  es => es.submit(new Callable[A] {                    one Callable inside
    def call = a(es).get          ←                    another Callable.
  })
```

Note that we're submitting the `Callable` first, and *within that* `Callable`, we're submitting another `Callable` to the `ExecutorService` and blocking on its result (recall that `a(es)` will submit a `Callable` to the `ExecutorService` and get back a `Future`). This is a problem if our thread pool has size 1. The outer `Callable` gets submitted and picked up by the sole thread. Within that thread, before it will complete, we submit and block waiting for the result of another `Callable`. But there are no threads available to run this `Callable`. They're waiting on each other and therefore our code deadlocks.

EXERCISE 7.9

Hard: Show that any fixed-size thread pool can be made to deadlock given this implementation of `fork`.

When you find counterexamples like this, you have two choices—you can try to fix your implementation such that the law holds, or you can refine your law a bit, to state more explicitly the conditions under which it holds (you could simply stipulate that you require thread pools that can grow unbounded). Even this is a good exercise—it forces you to document invariants or assumptions that were previously implicit.

Can we fix `fork` to work on fixed-size thread pools? Let's look at a different implementation:

```
def fork[A](fa: => Par[A]): Par[A] =
  es => fa(es)
```

This certainly avoids deadlock. The only problem is that we aren't actually forking a separate logical thread to evaluate `fa`. So `fork(hugeComputation)(es)` for some `ExecutorService` es, would run `hugeComputation` in the main thread, which is exactly what we wanted to avoid by calling `fork`. This is still a useful combinator, though, since it lets us delay instantiation of a computation until it's actually needed. Let's give it a name, `delay`:

```
def delay[A](fa: => Par[A]): Par[A] =
  es => fa(es)
```

But we'd really like to be able to run arbitrary computations over fixed-size thread pools. In order to do that, we'll need to pick a different representation of `Par`.

7.4.4 A fully non-blocking Par implementation using actors

In this section, we'll develop a fully non-blocking implementation of `Par` that works for fixed-size thread pools. Since this isn't essential to our overall goals of discussing various aspects of functional design, you may skip to the next section if you prefer. Otherwise, read on.

The essential problem with the current representation is that we can't get a value *out* of a `Future` without the current thread blocking on its `get` method. A representation of `Par` that doesn't leak resources this way has to be *non-blocking* in the sense that the implementations of `fork` and `map2` must never call a method that blocks the current thread like `Future.get`. Writing such an implementation correctly can be challenging. Fortunately we have our laws with which to test our implementation, and we only have to get it right *once*. After that, the users of our library can enjoy a composable and abstract API that does the right thing every time.

In the code that follows, you don't need to understand exactly what's going on with every part of it. We just want to show you, using real code, what a correct representation of `Par` that respects the laws might look like.

THE BASIC IDEA

How can we implement a non-blocking representation of `Par`? The idea is simple. Instead of turning a `Par` into a `java.util.concurrent.Future` that we can get a value *out* of (which requires blocking), we'll introduce our own version of `Future` with which we can *register a callback that will be invoked when the result is ready*. This is a slight shift in perspective:

The `apply` method is declared `private` to the `fpinscala.parallelism` package, which means that it can only be accessed by code within that package.

```
sealed trait Future[A] {
  private[parallelism] def apply(k: A => Unit): Unit
}
type Par[+A] = ExecutorService => Future[A]
```

`Par` looks the same, but we're using our new non-blocking `Future` instead of the one in `java.util.concurrent`.

Our `Par` type looks identical, except we're now using our new version of `Future`, which has a different API than the one in `java.util.concurrent`. Rather than calling `get` to obtain the result from our `Future`, our `Future` instead has an `apply` method that receives a function `k` that expects the result of type `A` and uses it to perform some effect. This kind of function is sometimes called a *continuation* or a *callback*.

The `apply` method is marked `private[parallelism]` so that we don't expose it to users of our library. Marking it `private[parallelism]` ensures that it can only be accessed from code within the `fpinscala.parallelism` package. This is so that our API remains pure and we can guarantee that our laws hold.

> ### Using local side effects for a pure API
>
> The `Future` type we defined here is rather imperative. An `A => Unit`? Such a function can only be useful for executing some side effect using the given `A`, as we certainly aren't using the returned result. Are we still doing functional programming in using a type like `Future`? Yes, but we're making use of a common technique of using side effects as an implementation detail for a purely functional API. We can get away with this because the side effects we use are *not observable* to code that uses `Par`. Note that `Future.apply` is protected and can't even be called by outside code.
>
> As we go through the rest of our implementation of the non-blocking `Par`, you may want to convince yourself that the side effects employed can't be observed by outside code. The notion of local effects, observability, and subtleties of our definitions of purity and referential transparency are discussed in much more detail in chapter 14, but for now an informal understanding is fine.

With this representation of `Par`, let's look at how we might implement the run function first, which we'll change to just return an `A`. Since it goes from `Par[A]` to `A`, it will have to construct a continuation and pass it to the `Future` value's `apply` method.

Listing 7.6   Implementing `run` for `Par`

A mutable, thread-safe reference to use for storing the result. See the `java.util.concurrent.atomic` package for more information about these classes.

When we receive the value, sets the result and releases the latch.

```
def run[A](es: ExecutorService)(p: Par[A]): A = {

  val ref = new AtomicReference[A]

  val latch = new CountDownLatch(1)

  p(es) { a => ref.set(a); latch.countDown }

  latch.await

  ref.get

}
```

A `java.util.concurrent.CountDownLatch` allows threads to wait until its `countDown` method is called a certain number of times. Here the `countDown` method will be called once when we've received the value of type `A` from `p`, and we want the `run` implementation to block until that happens.

Waits until the result becomes available and the latch is released.

Once we've passed the latch, we know `ref` has been set, and we return its value.

It should be noted that `run` blocks the calling thread while waiting for the `latch`. It's not possible to write an implementation of `run` that doesn't block. Since it needs to return a value of type `A`, it has to wait for that value to become available before it can return. For this reason, we want users of our API to avoid calling `run` until they definitely want to wait for a result. We could even go so far as to remove `run` from our API altogether and expose the `apply` method on `Par` instead so that users can register asynchronous callbacks. That would certainly be a valid design choice, but we'll leave our API as it is for now.

Let's look at an example of actually creating a `Par`. The simplest one is `unit`:

```
def unit[A](a: A): Par[A] =
  es => new Future[A] {
    def apply(cb: A => Unit): Unit =
      cb(a)
  }
```

Simply passes the value to the continuation. Note that the `ExecutorService` isn't needed.

Since `unit` already has a value of type `A` available, all it needs to do is call the continuation `cb`, passing it this value. If that continuation is the one from our `run` implementation, for example, this will release the latch and make the result available immediately.

What about `fork`? This is where we introduce the actual parallelism:

```
def fork[A](a: => Par[A]): Par[A] =
  es => new Future[A] {
    def apply(cb: A => Unit): Unit =
      eval(es)(a(es)(cb))
  }

def eval(es: ExecutorService)(r: => Unit): Unit =
  es.submit(new Callable[Unit] { def call = r })
```

`eval` forks off evaluation of `a` and returns immediately. The callback will be invoked asynchronously on another thread.

A helper function to evaluate an action asynchronously using some `ExecutorService`.

When the `Future` returned by `fork` receives its continuation `cb`, it will fork off a task to evaluate the by-name argument `a`. Once the argument has been evaluated and called to produce a `Future[A]`, we register `cb` to be invoked when that `Future` has its resulting `A`.

What about `map2`? Recall the signature:

```
def map2[A,B,C](a: Par[A], b: Par[B])(f: (A,B) => C): Par[C]
```

Here, a non-blocking implementation is considerably trickier. Conceptually, we'd like `map2` to run both `Par` arguments in parallel. When both results have arrived, we want to invoke `f` and then pass the resulting `C` to the continuation. But there are several race conditions to worry about here, and a correct non-blocking implementation is difficult using only the low-level primitives of `java.util.concurrent`.

A BRIEF INTRODUCTION TO ACTORS

To implement `map2`, we'll use a non-blocking concurrency primitive called *actors*. An `Actor` is essentially a concurrent process that doesn't constantly occupy a thread. Instead, it only occupies a thread when it receives a *message*. Importantly, although multiple threads may be concurrently sending messages to an actor, the actor processes only one message at a time, queueing other messages for subsequent processing. This makes them useful as a concurrency primitive when writing tricky code that must be accessed by multiple threads, and which would otherwise be prone to race conditions or deadlocks.

It's best to illustrate this with an example. Many implementations of actors would suit our purposes just fine, including one in the Scala standard library (see scala.actors.Actor), but in the interest of simplicity we'll use our own minimal actor implementation included with the chapter code in the file Actor.scala:

```
scala> import fpinscala.parallelism._

scala> val S = Executors.newFixedThreadPool(4)
S: java.util.concurrent.ExecutorService = ...

scala> val echoer = Actor[String](S) {
   |    msg => println (s"Got message: '$msg'")
   | }
echoer: fpinscala.parallelism.Actor[String] = ...
```

An actor uses an ExecutorService to process messages when they arrive, so we create one here.

This is a very simple actor that just echoes the String messages it receives. Note we supply S, an ExecutorService to use for processing messages.

Let's try out this Actor:

```
scala> echoer ! "hello"
Got message: 'hello'
```
Sends the "hello" message to the actor.

```
scala>
```
Note that echoer doesn't occupy a thread at this point, since it has no further messages to process.

```
scala> echoer ! "goodbye"
Got message: 'goodbye'
```
Sends the "goodbye" message to the actor. The actor reacts by submitting a task to its ExecutorService to process that message.

```
scala> echoer ! "You're just repeating everything I say, aren't you?"
Got message: 'You're just repeating everything I say, aren't you?'
```

It's not at all essential to understand the Actor *implementation*. A correct, efficient implementation is rather subtle, but if you're curious, see the Actor.scala file in the chapter code. The implementation is just under 100 lines of ordinary Scala code.[15]

IMPLEMENTING MAP2 VIA ACTORS

We can now implement map2 using an Actor to collect the result from both arguments. The code is straightforward, and there are no race conditions to worry about, since we know that the Actor will only process one message at a time.

Listing 7.7 Implementing map2 with Actor

```
def map2[A,B,C](p: Par[A], p2: Par[B])(f: (A,B) => C): Par[C] =
  es => new Future[C] {
    def apply(cb: C => Unit): Unit = {
      var ar: Option[A] = None
      var br: Option[B] = None
```
Two mutable vars are used to store the two results.

---

[15] The main trickiness in an actor implementation has to do with the fact that multiple threads may be messaging the actor simultaneously. The implementation needs to ensure that messages are processed only one at a time, and also that all messages sent to the actor will be processed eventually rather than queued indefinitely. Even so, the code ends up being short.

An actor that awaits both results, combines them with f, and passes the result to cb.

```scala
val combiner = Actor[Either[A,B]](es) {
  case Left(a) => br match {
    case None => ar = Some(a)
    case Some(b) => eval(es)(cb(f(a, b)))
  }

  case Right(b) => ar match {
    case None => br = Some(b)
    case Some(a) => eval(es)(cb(f(a, b)))
  }
}

p(es)(a => combiner ! Left(a))
p2(es)(b => combiner ! Right(b))
}
}
```

If the A result came in first, stores it in `ar` and waits for the B. If the A result came last and we already have our B, calls f with both results and passes the resulting C to the callback, `cb`.

Analogously, if the B result came in first, stores it in `br` and waits for the A. If the B result came last and we already have our A, calls f with both results and passes the resulting C to the callback, `cb`.

Passes the actor as a continuation to both sides. On the A side, we wrap the result in `Left`, and on the B side, we wrap it in `Right`. These are the constructors of the `Either` data type, and they serve to indicate to the actor where the result came from.

Given these implementations, we should now be able to run `Par` values of arbitrary complexity without having to worry about running out of threads, even if the actors only have access to a single JVM thread.

Let's try this out in the REPL:

```scala
scala> import java.util.concurrent.Executors

scala> val p = parMap(List.range(1, 100000))(math.sqrt(_))
p: ExecutorService => Future[List[Double]] = < function >

scala> val x = run(Executors.newFixedThreadPool(2))(p)
x: List[Double] = List(1.0, 1.4142135623730951, 1.7320508075688772,
2.0, 2.23606797749979, 2.449489742783178, 2.6457513110645907, 2.828
4271247461903, 3.0, 3.1622776601683795, 3.3166247903554, 3.46410...
```

That will call `fork` about 100,000 times, starting that many actors to combine these values two at a time. Thanks to our non-blocking `Actor` implementation, we don't need 100,000 JVM threads to do that in.

Fantastic. Our law of forking now holds for fixed-size thread pools.

EXERCISE 7.10

Hard: Our non-blocking representation doesn't currently handle errors at all. If at any point our computation throws an exception, the `run` implementation's `latch` never counts down and the exception is simply swallowed. Can you fix that?

Taking a step back, the purpose of this section hasn't necessarily been to figure out the best non-blocking implementation of `fork`, but more to show that laws are important. They give us another angle to consider when thinking about the design of a library. If we hadn't tried writing out some of the laws of our API, we may not have discovered the thread resource leak in our first implementation until much later.

In general, there are multiple approaches you can consider when choosing laws for your API. You can think about your conceptual model, and reason from there to postulate laws that should hold. You can also just *invent* laws you think might be useful or instructive (like we did with our `fork` law), and see if it's possible and sensible to ensure that they hold for your model. And lastly, you can look at your *implementation* and come up with laws you expect to hold based on that.[16]

7.5   *Refining combinators to their most general form*

Functional design is an iterative process. After you write down your API and have at least a prototype implementation, try using it for progressively more complex or realistic scenarios. Sometimes you'll find that these scenarios require new combinators. But before jumping right to implementation, it's a good idea to see if you can refine the combinator you need to *its most general form*. It may be that what you need is just a specific case of some more general combinator.

About the exercises in this section

The exercises and answers in this section use our original simpler (blocking) representation of `Par[A]`. If you'd like to work through the exercises and answers using the non-blocking implementation we developed in the previous section instead, see the file `Nonblocking.scala` in both the `exercises` and `answers` projects.

Let's look at an example of this. Suppose we want a function to choose between two forking computations based on the result of an initial computation:

```
def choice[A](cond: Par[Boolean])(t: Par[A], f: Par[A]): Par[A]
```

This constructs a computation that proceeds with t if cond results in `true`, or f if cond results in `false`. We can certainly implement this by blocking on the result of the cond, and then using this result to determine whether to run t or f. Here's a simple blocking implementation:[17]

```
def choice[A](cond: Par[Boolean])(t: Par[A], f: Par[A]): Par[A] =
  es =>
    if (run(es)(cond).get) t(es)      ⟵ Notice we are blocking
    else f(es)                           on the result of cond.
```

But before we call ourselves good and move on, let's think about this combinator a bit. What is it doing? It's running cond and then, when the result is available, it runs either t or f. This seems reasonable, but let's see if we can think of some variations to get at

---

[16] This last way of generating laws is probably the weakest, since it can be too easy to just have the laws reflect the implementation, even if the implementation is buggy or requires all sorts of unusual side conditions that make composition difficult.

[17] See `Nonblocking.scala` in the chapter code for the non-blocking implementation.

the essence of this combinator. There's something rather arbitrary about the use of `Boolean` here, and the fact that we're only selecting among *two* possible parallel computations, t and f. Why just two? If it's useful to be able to choose between two parallel computations based on the results of a first, it should be certainly be useful to choose between *N* computations:

```
def choiceN[A](n: Par[Int])(choices: List[Par[A]]): Par[A]
```

Let's say that choiceN runs n, and then uses that to select a parallel computation from choices. This is a bit more general than choice.

EXERCISE 7.11

Implement choiceN and then choice in terms of choiceN.

Note what we've done so far. We've refined our original combinator, choice, to choiceN, which turns out to be more general, capable of expressing choice as well as other use cases not supported by choice. But let's keep going to see if we can refine choice to an even more general combinator.

EXERCISE 7.12

There's still something rather arbitrary about choiceN. The choice of List seems overly specific. Why does it matter what sort of container we have? For instance, what if, instead of a list of computations, we have a Map of them:[18]

```
def choiceMap[K,V](key: Par[K])(choices: Map[K,Par[V]]): Par[V]
```

If you want, stop reading here and see if you can come up with a new and more general combinator in terms of which you can implement choice, choiceN, and choiceMap.

The Map encoding of the set of possible choices feels overly specific, just like List. If we look at our implementation of choiceMap, we can see we aren't really using much of the API of Map. Really, the Map[A,Par[B]] is used to provide a function, A => Par[B]. And now that we've spotted that, looking back at choice and choiceN, we can see that for choice, the pair of arguments was just being used as a function of type Boolean => Par[A] (where the Boolean selects one of the two Par[A] arguments), and for choiceN the list was just being used as a function of type Int => Par[A]!

---

[18] Map[K,V] (API link: http://mng.bz/eZ4l) is a purely functional data structure in the Scala standard library. It associates keys of type K with values of type V in a one-to-one relationship, and allows us to look up the value by the associated key.

Let's make a more general signature that unifies them all:

```
def chooser[A,B](pa: Par[A])(choices: A => Par[B]): Par[B]
```

■ EXERCISE 7.13

Implement this new primitive `chooser`, and then use it to implement `choice` and `choiceN`.

Whenever you generalize functions like this, take a critical look at your generalized function when you're finished. Although the function may have been motivated by some specific use case, the signature and implementation may have a more general meaning. In this case, `chooser` is perhaps no longer the most appropriate name for this operation, which is actually quite general—it's a parallel computation that, when run, will run an initial computation whose result is used to determine a second computation. Nothing says that this second computation needs to even exist before the first computation's result is available. It doesn't need to be stored in a container like `List` or `Map`. Perhaps it's being *generated* from whole cloth using the result of the first computation. This function, which comes up often in functional libraries, is usually called `bind` or `flatMap`:

```
def flatMap[A,B](a: Par[A])(f: A => Par[B]): Par[B]
```

Is `flatMap` really the most primitive possible function, or can we generalize further? Let's play around with it a bit more. The name `flatMap` is suggestive of the fact that this operation could be decomposed into two steps: *mapping* f: A => Par[B] over our Par[A], which generates a Par[Par[B]], and then *flattening* this nested Par[Par[B]] to a Par[B]. But this is interesting—it suggests that all we needed to do was add an *even simpler* combinator, let's call it `join`, for converting a Par[Par[X]] to Par[X] for *any* choice of X:

```
def join[A](a: Par[Par[A]]): Par[A]
```

Again we're just following the types. We have an example that demands a function with the given signature, and so we just bring it into existence. Now that it exists, we can think about what the signature means. We call it `join` since conceptually it's a parallel computation that, when run, will execute the inner computation, wait for it to finish (much like `Thread.join`), and then return its result.

■ EXERCISE 7.14

Implement `join`. Can you see how to implement `flatMap` using `join`? And can you implement `join` using `flatMap`?

We'll stop here, but you're encouraged to explore this algebra further. Try more complicated examples, discover new combinators, and see what you find! Here are some questions to consider:

- Can you implement a function with the same signature as `map2`, but using `flatMap` and `unit`? How is its meaning different than that of `map2`?
- Can you think of laws relating `join` to the other primitives of the algebra?
- Are there parallel computations that can't be expressed using this algebra? Can you think of any computations that can't even be expressed by adding new primitives to the algebra?

Recognizing the expressiveness and limitations of an algebra

As you practice more functional programming, one of the skills you'll develop is the ability to recognize *what functions are expressible from an algebra*, and what the limitations of that algebra are. For instance, in the preceding example, it may not have been obvious at first that a function like `choice` couldn't be expressed purely in terms of `map`, `map2`, and `unit`, and it may not have been obvious that `choice` was just a special case of `flatMap`. Over time, observations like this will come quickly, and you'll also get better at spotting how to modify your algebra to make some needed combinator expressible. These skills will be helpful for all of your API design work.

As a practical consideration, being able to reduce an API to a minimal set of primitive functions is extremely useful. As we noted earlier when we implemented `parMap` in terms of existing combinators, it's frequently the case that primitive combinators encapsulate some rather tricky logic, and reusing them means we don't have to duplicate this logic.

7.6 Summary

We've now completed the design of a library for defining parallel and asynchronous computations in a purely functional way. Although this domain is interesting, the primary goal of this chapter was to give you a window into the process of functional design, a sense of the sorts of issues you're likely to encounter, and ideas for how you can handle those issues.

Chapters 4 through 6 had a strong theme of *separation of concerns*: specifically, the idea of separating the description of a computation from the interpreter that then runs it. In this chapter, we saw that principle in action in the design of a library that describes parallel computations as values of a data type `Par`, with a separate interpreter `run` to actually spawn the threads to execute them.

In the next chapter, we'll look at a completely different domain, take another meandering journey toward an API for that domain, and draw further lessons about functional design.

Property-based testing

8

In chapter 7 we worked through the design of a functional library for expressing parallel computations. There we introduced the idea that an API should form an *algebra*—that is, a collection of data types, functions over these data types, and importantly, *laws* or *properties* that express relationships between these functions. We also hinted at the idea that it might be possible to somehow check these laws automatically.

This chapter will take us toward a simple but powerful library for *property-based testing*. The general idea of such a library is to decouple the specification of program behavior from the creation of test cases. The programmer focuses on specifying the behavior of programs and giving high-level constraints on the test cases; the framework then automatically generates test cases that satisfy these constraints, and runs tests to ensure that programs behave as specified.

Although a library for testing has a very different purpose than a library for parallel computations, we'll discover that these libraries have a lot of surprisingly similar combinators. This similarity is something we'll return to in part 3.

8.1 A brief tour of property-based testing

As an example, in ScalaCheck (http://mng.bz/n2j9), a property-based testing library for Scala, a property looks something like this.

Listing 8.1 ScalaCheck properties

A *generator* of lists of integers between 0 and 100.

A property that specifies the behavior of the `List.reverse` method.

```
val intList = Gen.listOf(Gen.choose(0,100))
val prop =
    forAll(intList)(ns => ns.reverse.reverse == ns) &&
```

Check that reversing a list twice gives back the original list.

124

A property which is obviously false.

```
forAll(intList)(ns => ns.headOption == ns.reverse.lastOption)
val failingProp = forAll(intList)(ns => ns.reverse == ns)
```

Check that the first element becomes the last element after reversal.

And we can check properties like so:

```
scala> prop.check
+ OK, passed 100 tests.

scala> failingProp.check
! Falsified after 6 passed tests.
> ARG_0: List(0, 1)
```

Here, `intList` is not a `List[Int]`, but a `Gen[List[Int]]`, which is something that knows how to generate test data of type `List[Int]`. We can *sample* from this generator, and it will produce lists of different lengths, filled with random numbers between 0 and 100. Generators in a property-based testing library have a rich API. We can combine and compose generators in different ways, reuse them, and so on.

The function `forAll` creates a *property* by combining a generator of type `Gen[A]` with some predicate of type `A => Boolean`. The property asserts that all values produced by the generator should satisfy the predicate. Like generators, properties can also have a rich API. In this simple example we've used `&&` to combine two properties. The resulting property will hold only if neither property can be *falsified* by any of the generated test cases. Together, the two properties form a partial specification of the correct behavior of the `reverse` method.[1]

Generators and properties

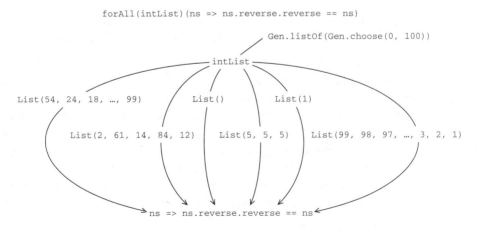

A `Gen` object generates a variety of different objects to pass to a Boolean expression, searching for one that will make it false.

---

[1] The goal of this sort of testing is not necessarily to fully specify program behavior, but to give greater confidence in the code. Like testing in general, we can always make our properties more *complete*, but we should do the usual cost-benefit analysis to determine if the additional work is worth doing.

When we invoke `prop.check`, ScalaCheck will randomly generate `List[Int]` values to try to find a case that falsifies the predicates that we've supplied. The output indicates that ScalaCheck has generated 100 test cases (of type `List[Int]`) and that they all satisfied the predicates. Properties can of course fail—the output of `failingProp.check` indicates that the predicate tested false for some input, which is helpfully printed out to facilitate further testing or debugging.

EXERCISE 8.1

To get used to thinking about testing in this way, come up with properties that specify the implementation of a `sum: List[Int] => Int` function. You don't have to write your properties down as executable ScalaCheck code—an informal description is fine. Here are some ideas to get you started:

- Reversing a list and summing it should give the same result as summing the original, nonreversed list.
- What should the sum be if all elements of the list are the same value?
- Can you think of other properties?

EXERCISE 8.2

What properties specify a function that finds the maximum of a `List[Int]`?

Property-based testing libraries often come equipped with other useful features. We'll talk more about some of these features later, but just to give an idea of what's possible:

- *Test case minimization*—In the event of a failing test, the framework tries smaller sizes until it finds the *smallest* test case that also fails, which is more illuminating for debugging purposes. For instance, if a property fails for a list of size 10, the framework tries smaller lists and reports the smallest list that fails the test.
- *Exhaustive test case generation*—We call the set of values that could be produced by some `Gen[A]` the *domain*.[2] When the domain is small enough (for instance, if it's all even integers less than 100), we may exhaustively test all its values, rather than generate sample values. If the property holds for all values in a domain, we have an actual *proof*, rather than just the absence of evidence to the contrary.

---

[2] This is the same usage of "domain" as the domain of a function (http://mng.bz/ZP8q)—generators describe possible inputs to functions we'd like to test. Note that we'll also still sometimes use "domain" in the more colloquial sense, to refer to a subject or area of interest, for example, "the domain of functional parallelism" or "the error-handling domain."

ScalaCheck is just one property-based testing library. And while there's nothing wrong with it, we'll derive our own library in this chapter, starting from scratch. Like in chapter 7, this is mostly for pedagogical purposes, but also partly because we should consider no library to be the final word on any subject. There's certainly nothing wrong with using an existing library like ScalaCheck, and existing libraries can be a good source of ideas. But even if you decide you like the existing library's solution, spending an hour or two playing with designs and writing down some type signatures is a great way to learn more about the domain and understand the design trade-offs.

8.2 Choosing data types and functions

This section will be another messy and iterative process of discovering data types and functions for our library. This time around, we're designing a library for property-based testing. As before, this is a chance to peer over the shoulder of someone working through possible designs. The particular path we take and the library we arrive at isn't necessarily the same as what you would come up with on your own. If property-based testing is unfamiliar to you, even better; this is a chance to explore a new domain and its design space, and make your own discoveries about it. If at any point you're feeling inspired or have ideas of your own about how to design a library like this, don't wait for an exercise to prompt you—*put the book down* and go off to play with your ideas. You can always come back to the chapter if you run out of ideas or get stuck.

8.2.1 Initial snippets of an API

With that said, let's get started. What data types should we use for our testing library? What primitives should we define, and what might they mean? What laws should our functions satisfy? As before, we can look at a simple example and "read off" the needed data types and functions, and see what we find. For inspiration, let's look at the ScalaCheck example we showed earlier:

```
val intList = Gen.listOf(Gen.choose(0,100))
val prop =
  forAll(intList)(ns => ns.reverse.reverse == ns) &&
  forAll(intList)(ns => ns.headOption == ns.reverse.lastOption)
```

Without knowing anything about the implementation of `Gen.choose` or `Gen.listOf`, we can guess that whatever data type they return (let's call it Gen, short for *generator*) must be parametric in some type. That is, `Gen.choose(0,100)` probably returns a `Gen[Int]`, and `Gen.listOf` is then a function with the signature `Gen[Int] => Gen[List[Int]]`. But since it doesn't seem like `Gen.listOf` should care about the type of the `Gen` it receives as input (it would be odd to require separate combinators for creating lists of `Int`, `Double`, `String`, and so on), let's go ahead and make it polymorphic:

```
def listOf[A](a: Gen[A]): Gen[List[A]]
```

We can learn many things by looking at this signature. Notice what we're *not* specifying—the size of the list to generate. For this to be implementable, our generator must therefore either assume or be told the size. Assuming a size seems a bit inflexible—any assumption is unlikely to be appropriate in all contexts. So it seems that generators must be told the size of test cases to generate. We can imagine an API where this is made explicit:

```
def listOfN[A](n: Int, a: Gen[A]): Gen[List[A]]
```

This would certainly be a useful combinator, but *not* having to explicitly specify sizes is powerful as well. It means that whatever function runs the tests has the freedom to choose test case sizes, which opens up the possibility of doing the test case minimization we mentioned earlier. If the sizes are always fixed and specified by the programmer, the test runner won't have this flexibility. Keep this concern in mind as we get further along in our design.

What about the rest of this example? The `forAll` function looks interesting. We can see that it accepts a `Gen[List[Int]]` and what looks to be a corresponding predicate, `List[Int] => Boolean`. But again, it doesn't seem like `forAll` should care about the types of the generator and the predicate, as long as they match up. We can express this with the type:

```
def forAll[A](a: Gen[A])(f: A => Boolean): Prop
```

Here, we've simply invented a new type, `Prop` (short for *property*, following the ScalaCheck naming), for the result of binding a `Gen` to a predicate. We might not know the internal representation of `Prop` or what other functions it supports, but based on this example we can see that it has an `&&` operator, so let's introduce that:

```
trait Prop { def &&(p: Prop): Prop }
```

8.2.2 The meaning and API of properties

Now that we have a few fragments of an API, let's discuss what we want our types and functions to *mean*. First, consider `Prop`. We know there exist functions `forAll` (for creating a property), `&&` (for composing properties), and `check` (for running a property). In ScalaCheck, this `check` method has a side effect of printing to the console. It's fine to expose this as a convenience function, but it's not a basis for composition. For instance, we couldn't implement `&&` for `Prop` if its representation were just the `check` method:[3]

```
trait Prop {
  def check: Unit
  def &&(p: Prop): Prop = ???
}
```

Since `check` has a side effect, the only option for implementing `&&` in this case would be to run both `check` methods. So if `check` prints out a test report, then we would get two of them, and they would print failures and successes independently of each other.

---

[3] This might remind you of similar problems that we discussed in chapter 7, when we looked at using `Thread` and `Runnable` for parallelism.

That's likely not a correct implementation. The problem is not so much that check has a side effect, but more generally that it throws away information.

In order to combine Prop values using combinators like &&, we need check (or whatever function "runs" properties) to return some meaningful value. What type should that value have? Well, let's consider what sort of information we'd like to get out of checking our properties. At a minimum, we need to know whether the property succeeded or failed. This lets us implement &&.

■ EXERCISE 8.3

Assuming the following representation of Prop, implement && as a method of Prop.

```
trait Prop { def check: Boolean }
```

In this representation, Prop is nothing more than a non-strict Boolean, and any of the usual Boolean functions (AND, OR, NOT, XOR, and so on) can be defined for Prop. But a Boolean alone is probably insufficient. If a property fails, we might want to know how many tests succeeded first, and what arguments produced the failure. And if a property succeeds, it would be useful to know how many tests it ran. Let's try returning an Either to indicate success or failure:

```
object Prop {
  type SuccessCount = Int          ←——— Type aliases like this can help
  ...                                    the readability of an API.
}
trait Prop { def check: Either[???,SuccessCount] }
```

What type shall we return in the failure case? We don't know anything about the type of the test cases being generated. Should we add a type parameter to Prop and make it Prop[A]? Then check could return Either[A,Int]. Before going too far down this path, let's ask ourselves whether we really care about the *type* of the value that caused the property to fail. We don't really. We would only care about the type if we were going to do further computation with the failure. Most likely we're just going to end up printing it to the screen for inspection by the person running the tests. After all, the goal here is to find bugs, and to indicate to someone what test cases trigger those bugs so they can go and fix them. As a general rule, we shouldn't use String to represent data that we want to compute with. But for values that we're just going to show to human beings, a String is absolutely appropriate. This suggests that we can get away with the following representation for Prop:

```
object Prop {
  type FailedCase = String
  type SuccessCount = Int
}
```

```
trait Prop {
  def check: Either[(FailedCase, SuccessCount), SuccessCount]
}
```

In the case of failure, check returns a Left((s,n)), where s is some String that represents the value that caused the property to fail, and n is the number of cases that succeeded before the failure occurred.

That takes care of the return value of check, at least for now, but what about the arguments to check? Right now, the check method takes no arguments. Is this sufficient? We can think about what information Prop will have access to just by inspecting the way Prop values are created. In particular, let's look at forAll:

```
def forAll[A](a: Gen[A])(f: A => Boolean): Prop
```

Without knowing more about the representation of Gen, it's hard to say whether there's enough information here to be able to generate values of type A (which is what we need to implement check). So for now let's turn our attention to Gen, to get a better idea of what it means and what its dependencies might be.

8.2.3 *The meaning and API of generators*

We determined earlier that a Gen[A] was something that knows how to generate values of type A. What are some ways it could do that? Well, it could *randomly* generate these values. Look back at the example from chapter 6—there, we gave an interface for a purely functional random number generator RNG and showed how to make it convenient to combine computations that made use of it. We could just make Gen a type that wraps a State transition over a random number generator:[4]

```
case class Gen[A](sample: State[RNG,A])
```

EXERCISE 8.4

Implement Gen.choose using this representation of Gen. It should generate integers in the range start to stopExclusive. Feel free to use functions you've already written.

```
def choose(start: Int, stopExclusive: Int): Gen[Int]
```

EXERCISE 8.5

Let's see what else we can implement using this representation of Gen. Try implementing unit, boolean, and listOfN.

```
def unit[A](a: => A): Gen[A]        ←————  Always generates the value a
```

---

[4] Recall the definition: case class State[S,A](run: S => (A,S)).

```
def boolean: Gen[Boolean]
def listOfN[A](n: Int, g: Gen[A]): Gen[List[A]]
```
Generates lists of length n using the generator g

As we discussed in chapter 7, we're interested in understanding what operations are *primitive* and what operations are *derived*, and in finding a small yet expressive set of primitives. A good way to explore what is expressible with a given set of primitives is to pick some concrete examples you'd like to express, and see if you can assemble the functionality you want. As you do so, look for patterns, try factoring out these patterns into combinators, and refine your set of primitives. We encourage you to stop reading here and simply *play* with the primitives and combinators we've written so far. If you want some concrete examples to inspire you, here are some ideas:

- If we can generate a single Int in some range, do we need a new primitive to generate an (Int, Int) pair in some range?
- Can we produce a Gen[Option[A]] from a Gen[A]? What about a Gen[A] from a Gen[Option[A]]?
- Can we generate strings somehow using our existing primitives?

The importance of play

You don't have to wait around for a concrete example to force exploration of the design space. In fact, if you rely exclusively on concrete, obviously useful or important examples to design your API, you'll often miss out on aspects of the design space and generate APIs with ad hoc, overly specific features. We don't want to *overfit* our design to the particular examples we happen to think of right now. We want to reduce the problem to its *essence*, and sometimes the best way to do this is *play*. Don't try to solve important problems or produce useful functionality. Not right away. Just experiment with different representations, primitives, and operations, let questions naturally arise, and explore whatever piques your curiosity. ("These two functions seem similar. I wonder if there's some more general operation hiding inside," or "Would it make sense to make this data type polymorphic?" or "What would it mean to change this aspect of the representation from a single value to a List of values?") There's no right or wrong way to do this, but there are so many different design choices that it's impossible *not* to run headlong into fascinating questions to play with. It doesn't matter where you begin—if you keep playing, the domain will inexorably guide you to make all the design choices that are required.

8.2.4 *Generators that depend on generated values*

Suppose we'd like a Gen[(String, String)] that generates pairs where the second string contains only characters from the first. Or that we had a Gen[Int] that chooses an integer between 0 and 11, and we'd like to make a Gen[List[Double]] that then generates lists of whatever length is chosen. In both of these cases there's a dependency—we generate a value, and then use that value to determine what generator to use next. For this we need `flatMap`, which lets one generator depend on another.

■ **EXERCISE 8.6** ───

Implement `flatMap`, and then use it to implement this more dynamic version of `listOfN`. Put `flatMap` and `listOfN` in the `Gen` class.

```
def flatMap[B](f: A => Gen[B]): Gen[B]
def listOfN(size: Gen[Int]): Gen[List[A]]
```

■ **EXERCISE 8.7** ───

Implement `union`, for combining two generators of the same type into one, by pulling values from each generator with equal likelihood.

```
def union[A](g1: Gen[A], g2: Gen[A]): Gen[A]
```

□ **EXERCISE 8.8** ───

Implement `weighted`, a version of `union` that accepts a weight for each `Gen` and generates values from each `Gen` with probability proportional to its weight.

```
def weighted[A](g1: (Gen[A],Double), g2: (Gen[A],Double)): Gen[A]
```

8.2.5   *Refining the Prop data type*

Now that we know more about our representation of generators, let's return to our definition of `Prop`. Our `Gen` representation has revealed information about the requirements for `Prop`. Our current definition of `Prop` looks like this:

```
trait Prop {
  def check: Either[(FailedCase, SuccessCount), SuccessCount]
}
```

`Prop` is nothing more than a non-strict `Either`. But it's missing some information. We have the number of successful test cases in `SuccessCount`, but we haven't specified how many test cases to examine before we consider the property to have *passed* the test. We could certainly hardcode something, but it would be better to abstract over this dependency:

```
type TestCases = Int
type Result = Either[(FailedCase, SuccessCount), SuccessCount]
case class Prop(run: TestCases => Result)
```

Also, we're recording the number of successful tests on both sides of that `Either`. But when a property passes, it's implied that the number of passed tests will be equal to the argument to `run`. So the caller of `run` learns nothing new by being told the success count. Since we don't currently need any information in the `Right` case of that `Either`, we can turn it into an `Option`:

```
type Result = Option[(FailedCase, SuccessCount)]
case class Prop(run: TestCases => Result)
```

This seems a little weird, since `None` will mean that all tests succeeded and the property passed and `Some` will indicate a failure. Until now, we've only used the `None` case of `Option` to indicate failure. But in this case we're using it to represent the *absence* of a failure. That's a perfectly legitimate use for `Option`, but its intent isn't very clear. So let's make a new data type, equivalent to `Option[(FailedCase, SuccessCount)]`, that shows our intent very clearly.

Listing 8.2 Creating a `Result` data type

```
sealed trait Result {
  def isFalsified: Boolean
}
case object Passed extends Result {        ←  Indicates that all tests passed
  def isFalsified = false
}
case class Falsified(failure: FailedCase,  ←  Indicates that one of the test
                     successes: SuccessCount) extends Result {   cases falsified the property
  def isFalsified = true
}
```

Is this now a sufficient representation of `Prop`? Let's take another look at `forAll`. Can `forAll` be implemented? Why not?

```
def forAll[A](a: Gen[A])(f: A => Boolean): Prop
```

We can see that `forAll` doesn't have enough information to return a `Prop`. Besides the number of test cases to try, `Prop.run` must have all the information needed to generate test cases. If it needs to generate random test cases using our current representation of `Gen`, it's going to need an `RNG`. Let's go ahead and propagate that dependency to `Prop`:

```
case class Prop(run: (TestCases,RNG) => Result)
```

If we think of other dependencies that it might need, besides the number of test cases and the source of randomness, we can just add these as extra parameters to `Prop.run` later.

We now have enough information to actually implement `forAll`. Here's a simple implementation.

Listing 8.3   Implementing `forAll`

A stream of pairs `(a, i)` where `a` is a random value and `i` is its index in the stream.

```
def forAll[A](as: Gen[A])(f: A => Boolean): Prop = Prop {
  (n,rng) => randomStream(as)(rng).zip(Stream.from(0)).take(n).map {
    case (a, i) => try {
      if (f(a)) Passed else Falsified(a.toString, i)
    } catch { case e: Exception => Falsified(buildMsg(a, e), i) }
  }.find(_.isFalsified).getOrElse(Passed)
}

def randomStream[A](g: Gen[A])(rng: RNG): Stream[A] =
  Stream.unfold(rng)(rng => Some(g.sample.run(rng)))

def buildMsg[A](s: A, e: Exception): String =
  s"test case: $s\n" +
  s"generated an exception: ${e.getMessage}\n" +
  s"stack trace:\n ${e.getStackTrace.mkString("\n")}"
```

If a test case generates an exception, record it in the result.

Generates an infinite stream of `A` values by repeatedly sampling a generator.

When a test fails, record the failed case and its index so we know how many tests succeeded before it.

String interpolation syntax. A string starting with `s"` can refer to a Scala value `v` as `$v` or `${v}` in the string. The Scala compiler will expand this to `v.toString`.

Notice that we're catching exceptions and reporting them as test failures, rather than letting the `run` throw the error (which would lose information about what argument triggered the failure).

EXERCISE 8.9

Now that we have a representation of `Prop`, implement `&&` and `||` for composing `Prop` values. Notice that in the case of failure we don't know which property was responsible, the left or the right. Can you devise a way of handling this, perhaps by allowing `Prop` values to be assigned a tag or label which gets displayed in the event of a failure?

```
def &&(p: Prop): Prop
def ||(p: Prop): Prop
```

8.3 *Test case minimization*

Earlier, we mentioned the idea of test case minimization. That is, ideally we'd like our framework to find the smallest or simplest failing test case, to better illustrate the problem and facilitate debugging. Let's see if we can tweak our representations to support this outcome. There are two general approaches we could take:

- *Shrinking*—After we've found a failing test case, we can run a separate procedure to minimize the test case by successively decreasing its "size" until it no longer fails. This is called *shrinking*, and it usually requires us to write separate code for each data type to implement this minimization process.

- *Sized generation*—Rather than shrinking test cases after the fact, we simply generate our test cases in order of increasing size and complexity. So we start small and increase the size until we find a failure. This idea can be extended in various ways to allow the test runner to make larger jumps in the space of possible sizes while still making it possible to find the smallest failing test.

ScalaCheck, incidentally, takes the first approach: shrinking. There's nothing wrong with this approach (it's also used by the Haskell library QuickCheck that ScalaCheck is based on: http://mng.bz/E24n), but we'll see what we can do with sized generation. It's a bit simpler and in some ways more modular, because our generators only need to know how to generate a test case of a given size. They don't need to be aware of the "schedule" used to search the space of test cases, and the function that runs the tests therefore has the freedom to choose this schedule. We'll see how this plays out shortly.

Instead of modifying our Gen data type, for which we've already written a number of useful combinators, let's introduce sized generation as a separate layer in our library. A simple representation of a sized generator is just a function that takes a size and produces a generator:

```scala
case class SGen[+A](forSize: Int => Gen[A])
```

EXERCISE 8.10

Implement helper functions for converting Gen to SGen. You can add this as a method on Gen.

```scala
def unsized: SGen[A]
```

EXERCISE 8.11

Not surprisingly, SGen at a minimum supports many of the same operations as Gen, and the implementations are rather mechanical. Define some convenience functions on SGen that simply delegate to the corresponding functions on Gen.[5]

EXERCISE 8.12

Implement a listOf combinator that doesn't accept an explicit size. It should return an SGen instead of a Gen. The implementation should generate lists of the requested size.

```scala
def listOf[A](g: Gen[A]): SGen[List[A]]
```

---

[5] In part 3 we'll discuss ways of factoring out this sort of duplication.

Let's see how SGen affects the definition of Prop and Prop.forAll. The SGen version of forAll looks like this:

```
def forAll[A](g: SGen[A])(f: A => Boolean): Prop
```

Can you see why it's not possible to implement this function? SGen is expecting to be told a size, but Prop doesn't receive any size information. Much like we did with the source of randomness and number of test cases, we simply need to add this as a dependency to Prop. But since we want to put Prop in charge of invoking the underlying generators with various sizes, we'll have Prop accept a *maximum* size. Prop will then generate test cases up to and including the maximum specified size. This will also allow it to search for the smallest failing test case. Let's see how this works out.[6]

Listing 8.4   Generating test cases up to a given maximum size

```
type MaxSize = Int
case class Prop(run: (MaxSize,TestCases,RNG) => Result)

def forAll[A](g: SGen[A])(f: A => Boolean): Prop =
  forAll(g(_))(f)

def forAll[A](g: Int => Gen[A])(f: A => Boolean): Prop = Prop {
  (max,n,rng) =>
    val casesPerSize = (n + (max - 1)) / max
    val props: Stream[Prop] =
      Stream.from(0).take((n min max) + 1).map(i => forAll(g(i))(f))
    val prop: Prop =
      props.map(p => Prop { (max, _, rng) =>
        p.run(max, casesPerSize, rng)
      }).toList.reduce(_ && _)
    prop.run(max,n,rng)
}
```

> For each size, generate this many random cases.

> Make one property per size, but no more than n properties.

> Combine them all into one property.

8.4   *Using the library and improving its usability*

We've converged on what seems like a reasonable API. We could keep tinkering with it, but at this point let's try *using* the library to construct tests and see if we notice any deficiencies, either in what it can express or in its general usability. Usability is somewhat subjective, but we generally like to have convenient syntax and appropriate helper functions for common usage patterns. We aren't necessarily aiming to make the library more expressive, but we want to make it pleasant to use.

---

[6] This rather simplistic implementation gives an equal number of test cases to each size being generated, and increases the size by 1 starting from 0. We could imagine a more sophisticated implementation that does something more like a binary search for a failing test case size—starting with sizes 0,1,2,4,8,16..., and then narrowing the search space in the event of a failure.

8.4.1 *Some simple examples*

Let's revisit an example that we mentioned at the start of this chapter—specifying the behavior of the function max, available as a method on List (API docs link: http://mng.bz/Pz86). The maximum of a list should be greater than or equal to every other element in the list. Let's specify this:

```
val smallInt = Gen.choose(-10,10)
val maxProp = forAll(listOf(smallInt)) { ns =>
  val max = ns.max
  !ns.exists(_ > max)
}
```

No value greater than max should exist in ns.

At this point, calling run directly on a Prop is rather cumbersome. We can introduce a helper function for running our Prop values and printing their result to the console in a useful format. Let's make this a method on the Prop companion object.

Listing 8.5　A run helper function for Prop

```
def run(p: Prop,
        maxSize: Int = 100,
        testCases: Int = 100,
        rng: RNG = RNG.Simple(System.currentTimeMillis)): Unit =
  p.run(maxSize, testCases, rng) match {
    case Falsified(msg, n) =>
      println(s"! Falsified after $n passed tests:\n $msg")
    case Passed =>
      println(s"+ OK, passed $testCases tests.")
  }
```

A default argument of 100

We're taking advantage of default arguments here. This makes the method more convenient to call. We want the default number of tests to be enough to get good coverage, but not too many or they'll take too long to run.

If we try running run(maxProp), we notice that the property fails! Property-based testing has a way of revealing hidden assumptions that we have about our code, and forcing us to be more explicit about these assumptions. The standard library's implementation of max crashes when given the empty list. We need to fix our property to take this into account.

EXERCISE 8.13

Define listOf1 for generating nonempty lists, and then update your specification of max to use this generator.

Let's try a few more examples.

■   **EXERCISE 8.14**
───

Write a property to verify the behavior of `List.sorted` (API docs link: http://mng.bz/ Pz86), which you can use to sort (among other things) a `List[Int]`.[7] For instance, `List(2,1,3).sorted` is equal to `List(1,2,3)`.

8.4.2 *Writing a test suite for parallel computations*

Recall that in chapter 7 we discovered laws that should hold for our parallel computations. Can we express these laws with our library? The first "law" we looked at was actually a particular test case:

```
map(unit(1))(_ + 1) == unit(2)
```

We certainly can express this, but the result is somewhat ugly.[8]

```
val ES: ExecutorService = Executors.newCachedThreadPool
val p1 = Prop.forAll(Gen.unit(Par.unit(1)))(i =>
  Par.map(i)(_ + 1)(ES).get == Par.unit(2)(ES).get)
```

We've expressed the test, but it's verbose, cluttered, and the *idea* of the test is obscured by details that aren't really relevant here. Notice that this isn't a question of the API being expressive enough—yes, we can express what we want, but a combination of missing helper functions and poor syntax obscures the intent.

PROVING PROPERTIES

Let's improve on this. Our first observation is that `forAll` is a bit too general for this test case. We aren't varying the input to this test, we just have a hardcoded example. Hardcoded examples should be just as convenient to write as in a traditional unit testing library. Let's introduce a combinator for it (on the `Prop` companion object):

```
def check(p: => Boolean): Prop
```

How would we implement this? One possible way is to use `forAll`:

```
def check(p: => Boolean): Prop = {          ←──────  Note that we are non-strict here.
  lazy val result = p                ←──────
  forAll(unit(()))(_ => result)                 Result is memoized to
}                                               avoid recomputation.
```

But this doesn't seem quite right. We're providing a unit generator that only generates a single value, and then we're proceeding to ignore that value just to drive the evaluation of the given `Boolean`.

Even though we memoize the result so that it's not evaluated more than once, the test runner will still generate multiple test cases and test the `Boolean` multiple times.

───────────────────────────────

[7] `sorted` takes an *implicit* `Ordering` for the elements of the list, to control the sorting strategy.

[8] This is assuming our representation of `Par[A]` that's just an alias for the function type `ExecutorService => Future[A]`.

For example, if we say `run(check(true))`, this will test the property 100 times and print "OK, passed 100 tests." But checking a property that is always `true` 100 times is a terrible waste of effort. What we need is a new primitive.

Remember, the representation of `Prop` that we have so far is just a function of type `(MaxSize, TestCases, RNG) => Result`, where `Result` is either `Passed` or `Falsified`. A simple implementation of a `check` primitive is to construct a `Prop` that ignores the number of test cases:

```
def check(p: => Boolean): Prop = Prop { (_, _, _) =>
  if (p) Passed else Falsified("()", 0)
}
```

This is certainly better than using `forAll`, but `run(check(true))` will still *print* "passed 100 tests" even though it only tests the property once. It's not really true that such a property has "passed" in the sense that it remains unfalsified after a number of tests. It is *proved* after just one test. It seems that we want a new kind of `Result`:

```
case object Proved extends Result
```

Then we can just return `Proved` instead of `Passed` in a property created by `check`. We'll need to modify the test runner to take this case into account.

> **Listing 8.6 Using `run` to return a `Proved` object**

```
def run(p: Prop,
        maxSize: Int = 100,
        testCases: Int = 100,
        rng: RNG = RNG.Simple(System.currentTimeMillis)): Unit =
  p.run(maxSize, testCases, rng) match {
    case Falsified((msg, n)) =>
      println(s"! Falsified after $n passed tests:\n $msg")
    case Passed =>
      println(s"+ OK, passed $testCases tests.")
    case Proved =>
      println(s"+ OK, proved property.")
  }
```

We also have to modify our implementations of `Prop` combinators like `&&`. These changes are quite trivial, since such combinators don't need to distinguish between `Passed` and `Proved` results.

EXERCISE 8.15

Hard: A check property is easy to prove conclusively because the test just involves evaluating the `Boolean` argument. But some `forAll` properties can be proved as well. For instance, if the domain of the property is `Boolean`, then there are really only two cases to test. If a property `forAll(p)` passes for both `p(true)` and `p(false)`, then it is proved. Some domains (like `Boolean` and `Byte`) are so small that they can be exhaustively checked. And with sized generators, even infinite domains can be exhaustively checked up to the maximum size. Automated testing is very useful, but it's even better if we can *automatically prove our code correct*. Modify our library to incorporate this kind of exhaustive checking of finite domains and sized generators. This is less of an exercise and more of an extensive, open-ended design project.

TESTING PAR

Getting back to proving the property that `Par.map(Par.unit(1))(_ + 1)` is equal to `Par.unit(2)`, we can use our new `Prop.check` primitive to express this in a way that doesn't obscure the intent:

```
val p2 = Prop.check {
  val p = Par.map(Par.unit(1))(_ + 1)
  val p2 = Par.unit(2)
  p(ES).get == p2(ES).get
}
```

This is now pretty clear. But can we do something about the `p(ES).get` and `p2(ES).get` noise? There's something rather unsatisfying about it. For one, we're forcing this code to be aware of the internal implementation details of `Par` simply to compare two `Par` values for equality. One improvement is to *lift* the equality comparison into `Par` using `map2`, which means we only have to run a single `Par` at the end to get our result:

```
def equal[A](p: Par[A], p2: Par[A]): Par[Boolean] =
  Par.map2(p,p2)(_ == _)

val p3 = check {
  equal(
    Par.map(Par.unit(1))(_ + 1),
    Par.unit(2)
  )(ES).get
}
```

This is a bit nicer than having to run each side separately. But while we're at it, why don't we move the running of `Par` out into a separate function, `forAllPar`. This also gives us a good place to insert variation across different parallel strategies, without it cluttering up the property we're specifying:

```
val S = weighted(                                          ←
  choose(1,4).map(Executors.newFixedThreadPool) -> .75,
  unit(Executors.newCachedThreadPool) -> .25)

def forAllPar[A](g: Gen[A])(f: A => Par[Boolean]): Prop =
  forAll(S.map2(g)((_,_))) { case (s,a) => f(a)(s).get }
```

a -> b is syntactic sugar for (a,b).

This generator creates a fixed thread pool executor 75% of the time and an unbounded one 25% of the time.

S.map2(g)((_,_)) is a rather noisy way of combining two generators to produce a pair of their outputs. Let's quickly introduce a combinator to clean that up:[9]

```
def **[B](g: Gen[B]): Gen[(A,B)] =
  (this map2 g)((_,_))
```

Much nicer:

```
def forAllPar[A](g: Gen[A])(f: A => Par[Boolean]): Prop =
  forAll(S ** g) { case (s,a) => f(a)(s).get }
```

We can even introduce ** as a pattern using custom extractors (http://mng.bz/4pUc), which lets us write this:

```
def forAllPar[A](g: Gen[A])(f: A => Par[Boolean]): Prop =
  forAll(S ** g) { case s ** a => f(a)(s).get }
```

This syntax works nicely when tupling up multiple generators—when pattern matching, we don't have to nest parentheses like using the tuple pattern directly would require. To enable ** as a pattern, we define an object called ** with an unapply function:

```
object ** {
  def unapply[A,B](p: (A,B)) = Some(p)
}
```

See the custom extractors documentation for more details on this technique.

So S is a Gen[ExecutorService] that will vary over fixed-size thread pools from 1–4 threads, and also consider an unbounded thread pool. And now our property looks a lot cleaner:[10]

```
val p2 = checkPar {
  equal (
    Par.map(Par.unit(1))(_ + 1),
    Par.unit(2)
  )
}
```

These might seem like minor changes, but this sort of factoring and cleanup can greatly improve the usability of our library, and the helper functions we've written make the properties easier to read and more pleasant to write. You may want to add a forAllPar version for sized generators as well.

Let's look at some other properties from chapter 7. Recall that we generalized our test case:

```
map(unit(x))(f) == unit(f(x))
```

---

[9] Calling this ** is actually appropriate, since this function is taking the *product* of two generators, in the sense we discussed in chapter 3.

[10] We can't use the standard Java/Scala equals method, or the == method in Scala (which delegates to the equals method), since that method returns a Boolean directly, and we need to return a Par[Boolean]. Some infix syntax for equal might be nice. See the answer file for chapter 7 for an example of how to do this.

We then simplified it to the law that mapping the identity function over a computation should have no effect:

```
map(y)(x => x) == y
```

Can we express this? Not exactly. This property implicitly states that the equality holds *for all* choices of y, for all types. We're forced to pick particular values for y:

```
val pint = Gen.choose(0,10) map (Par.unit(_))
val p4 =
  forAllPar(pint)(n => equal(Par.map(n)(y => y), n))
```

We can certainly range over more choices of y, but what we have here is probably good enough. The implementation of `map` can't care about the values of our parallel computation, so there isn't much point in constructing the same test for `Double`, `String`, and so on. What *can* affect `map` is the *structure* of the parallel computation. If we wanted greater assurance that our property held, we could provide richer generators for the structure. Here, we're only supplying `Par` expressions with one level of nesting.

EXERCISE 8.16

Hard: Write a richer generator for `Par[Int]`, which builds more deeply nested parallel computations than the simple ones we gave previously.

EXERCISE 8.17

Express the property about `fork` from chapter 7, that `fork(x) == x`.

8.5   *Testing higher-order functions and future directions*

So far, our library seems quite expressive, but there's one area where it's lacking: we don't currently have a good way to test higher-order functions. While we have lots of ways of generating *data* using our generators, we don't really have a good way of generating *functions*.

For instance, let's consider the `takeWhile` function defined for `List` and `Stream`. Recall that this function returns the longest prefix of its input whose elements all satisfy a predicate. For instance, `List(1,2,3).takeWhile(_ < 3)` results in `List(1,2)`. A simple property we'd like to check is that for any list, `s: List[A]`, and any `f: A => Boolean`, the expression `s.takeWhile(f).forall(f)` evaluates to true. That is, every element in the returned list satisfies the predicate.[11]

---

[11] In the Scala standard library, `forall` is a method on `List` and `Stream` with the signature `def forall[A] (f: A => Boolean): Boolean`.

■ **EXERCISE 8.18**

Come up with some other properties that takeWhile should satisfy. Can you think of a good property expressing the relationship between takeWhile and dropWhile?

We could certainly take the approach of only examining *particular* arguments when testing higher-order functions. For instance, here's a more specific property for takeWhile:

```
val isEven = (i: Int) => i%2 == 0
val takeWhileProp =
  Prop.forAll(Gen.listOf(int))(ns => ns.takeWhile(isEven).forall(isEven))
```

This works, but is there a way we could let the testing framework handle generating functions to use with takeWhile?[12] Let's consider our options. To make this concrete, let's suppose we have a Gen[Int] and would like to produce a Gen[String => Int]. What are some ways we could do that? Well, we could produce String => Int functions that simply ignore their input string and delegate to the underlying Gen[Int]:

```
def genStringIntFn(g: Gen[Int]): Gen[String => Int] =
  g map (i => (s => i))
```

This approach isn't sufficient though. We're simply generating *constant* functions that ignore their input. In the case of takeWhile, where we need a function that returns a Boolean, this will be a function that always returns true or always returns false—clearly not very interesting for testing the behavior of our function.

☐ **EXERCISE 8.19**

Hard: We want to generate a function that *uses its argument* in some way to select which Int to return. Can you think of a good way of expressing this? This is a very open-ended and challenging design exercise. See what you can discover about this problem and if there's a nice general solution that you can incorporate into the library we've developed so far.

☐ **EXERCISE 8.20**

You're strongly encouraged to venture out and try using the library we've developed! See what else you can test with it, and see if you discover any new idioms for its use or

---

[12] Recall that in chapter 7 we introduced the idea of *free theorems* and discussed how parametricity frees us from having to inspect the behavior of a function for every type of argument. Still, there are many situations where being able to generate functions for testing is useful.

perhaps ways it could be extended further or made more convenient. Here are a few ideas to get you started:

- Write properties to specify the behavior of some of the other functions we wrote for `List` and `Stream`, for instance, `take`, `drop`, `filter`, and `unfold`.
- Write a sized generator for producing the `Tree` data type defined in chapter 3, and then use this to specify the behavior of the `fold` function we defined for `Tree`. Can you think of ways to improve the API to make this easier?
- Write properties to specify the behavior of the `sequence` function we defined for `Option` and `Either`.

8.6 *The laws of generators*

Isn't it interesting that many of the functions we've implemented for our `Gen` type look quite similar to other functions we defined on `Par`, `List`, `Stream`, and `Option`? As an example, for `Par` we defined this:

```
def map[A,B](a: Par[A])(f: A => B): Par[B]
```

And in this chapter we defined `map` for `Gen` (as a method on `Gen[A]`):

```
def map[B](f: A => B): Gen[B]
```

We've also defined similar-looking functions for `Option`, `List`, `Stream`, and `State`. We have to wonder, is it merely that our functions share similar-looking signatures, or do they satisfy the same *laws* as well? Let's look at a law we introduced for `Par` in chapter 7:

```
map(x)(id) == x
```

Does this law hold for our implementation of `Gen.map`? What about for `Stream`, `List`, `Option`, and `State`? Yes, it does! Try it and see. This indicates that not only do these functions share similar-looking signatures, they also in some sense have analogous meanings in their respective domains. It appears there are deeper forces at work! We're uncovering some fundamental patterns that cut across domains. In part 3, we'll learn the names for these patterns, discover the laws that govern them, and understand what it all means.

8.7 *Summary*

In this chapter, we worked through another extended exercise in functional library design, using the domain of property-based testing as inspiration.

We reiterate that our goal was not necessarily to learn about property-based testing as such, but to highlight particular aspects of functional design. First, we saw that oscillating between the abstract algebra and the concrete representation lets the two inform each other. This avoids overfitting the library to a particular representation, and also avoids ending up with a floating abstraction disconnected from the end goal.

Second, we noticed that this domain led us to discover many of the same combinators we've now seen a few times before: map, flatMap, and so on. Not only are the signatures of these functions analogous, the *laws* satisfied by the implementations are analogous too. There are a great many seemingly distinct *problems* being solved in the world of software, yet the space of functional *solutions* is much smaller. Many libraries are just simple combinations of certain fundamental structures that appear over and over again across a variety of different domains. This is an opportunity for code reuse that we'll exploit in part 3, when we learn both the names of some of these structures and how to spot more general abstractions.

In the next and final chapter of part 2, we'll look at another domain, *parsing*, with its own unique challenges. We'll take a slightly different approach in that chapter, but once again familiar patterns will emerge.

Parser combinators 9

In this chapter, we'll work through the design of a combinator library for creating *parsers*. We'll use JSON parsing (http://mng.bz/DpNA) as a motivating use case. Like chapters 7 and 8, this chapter is not so much about parsing as it is about providing further insight into the process of functional design.

What is a parser?

A parser is a specialized program that takes unstructured data (such as text, or any kind of stream of symbols, numbers, or tokens) as input, and outputs a structured representation of that data. For example, we can write a parser to turn a comma-separated file into a list of lists, where the elements of the outer list represent the records, and the elements of each inner list represent the comma-separated fields of each record. Another example is a parser that takes an XML or JSON document and turns it into a tree-like data structure.

In a parser combinator library, like the one we'll build in this chapter, a parser doesn't have to be anything quite that complicated, and it doesn't have to parse entire documents. It can do something as elementary as recognizing a single character in the input. We then use combinators to assemble composite parsers from elementary ones, and still more complex parsers from those.

This chapter will introduce a design approach that we'll call *algebraic design*. This is just a natural evolution of what we've already been doing to different degrees in past chapters—designing our interface first, along with associated laws, and letting this guide our choice of data type representations.

At a few key points during this chapter, we'll give more open-ended exercises, intended to mimic the scenarios you might encounter when writing your own

146

libraries from scratch. You'll get the most out of this chapter if you use these opportunities to put the book down and spend some time investigating possible approaches. When you design your own libraries, you won't be handed a nicely chosen sequence of type signatures to fill in with implementations. You'll have to make the decisions about what types and combinators you need, and a goal in part 2 of this book has been to prepare you for doing this on your own. As always, if you get stuck on one of the exercises or want some more ideas, you can keep reading or consult the answers. It may also be a good idea to do these exercises with another person, or compare notes with other readers online.

Parser combinators versus parser generators

You might be familiar with *parser generator* libraries like Yacc (http://mng.bz/w3zZ) or similar libraries in other languages (for instance, ANTLR in Java: http://mng.bz/aj8K). These libraries *generate* code for a parser based on a specification of the grammar. This approach works fine and can be quite efficient, but comes with all the usual problems of code generation—the libraries produce as their output a monolithic chunk of code that's difficult to debug. It's also difficult to reuse fragments of logic, since we can't introduce new combinators or helper functions to abstract over common patterns in our parsers.

In a parser combinator library, parsers are just ordinary first-class values. Reusing parsing logic is trivial, and we don't need any sort of external tool separate from our programming language.

9.1 Designing an algebra, first

Recall that we defined *algebra* to mean a collection of functions operating over some data type(s), *along with a set of laws* specifying relationships between these functions. In past chapters, we moved rather fluidly between inventing functions in our algebra, refining the set of functions, and tweaking our data type representations. Laws were somewhat of an afterthought—we worked out the laws only after we had a representation and an API fleshed out. There's nothing wrong with this style of design,[1] but here we'll take a different approach. We'll *start* with the algebra (including its laws) and decide on a representation later. This approach—let's call it *algebraic design*—can be used for any design problem but works particularly well for parsing, because it's easy to imagine what combinators are required for parsing different kinds of inputs.[2] This lets us keep an eye on the concrete goal even as we defer deciding on a representation.

---

[1] For more about different functional design approaches, see the chapter notes for this chapter.

[2] As we'll see, there's a connection between algebras for parsers and the classes of languages (regular, context-free, context-sensitive) studied by computer science.

There are many different kinds of parsing libraries.[3] Ours will be designed for expressiveness (we'd like to be able to parse arbitrary grammars), speed, and good error reporting. This last point is important. Whenever we run a parser on input that it doesn't expect—which can happen if the input is malformed—it should generate a parse error. If there are parse errors, we want to be able to point out exactly where the error is in the input and accurately indicate its cause. Error reporting is often an afterthought in parsing libraries, but we'll make sure we give careful attention to it.

OK, let's begin. For simplicity and for speed, our library will create parsers that operate on strings as input.[4] We need to pick some parsing tasks to help us discover a good algebra for our parsers. What should we look at first? Something practical like parsing an email address, JSON, or HTML? No! These tasks can come later. A good and simple domain to start with is parsing various combinations of repeated letters and gibberish words like `"abracadabra"` and `"abba"`. As silly as this sounds, we've seen before how simple examples like this help us ignore extraneous details and focus on the essence of the problem.

So let's start with the simplest of parsers, one that recognizes the single character input `'a'`. As in past chapters, we can just *invent* a combinator for the task, `char`:

```
def char(c: Char): Parser[Char]
```

What have we done here? We've conjured up a type, `Parser`, which is parameterized on a single parameter indicating the *result type* of the `Parser`. That is, running a parser shouldn't simply yield a yes/no response—if it succeeds, we want to get a *result* that has some useful type, and if it fails, we expect *information about the failure*. The `char('a')` parser will succeed only if the input is exactly the character `'a'` and it will return that same character `'a'` as its result.

This talk of "running a parser" makes it clear our algebra needs to be extended somehow to support that. Let's invent another function for it:

```
def run[A](p: Parser[A])(input: String): Either[ParseError,A]
```

Wait a minute; what is `ParseError`? It's another type we just conjured into existence! At this point, we don't care about the representation of `ParseError`, or `Parser` for that matter. We're in the process of specifying an *interface* that happens to make use of two types whose representation or implementation details we choose to remain ignorant of for now. Let's make this explicit with a `trait`:

---

[3] There's even a parser combinator library in Scala's standard libraries. As in the previous chapter, we're deriving our own library from first principles partially for pedagogical purposes, and to further encourage the idea that no library is authoritative. The standard library's parser combinators don't really satisfy our goals of providing speed and good error reporting (see the chapter notes for some additional discussion).

[4] This is certainly a simplifying design choice. We can make the parsing library more generic, at some cost. See the chapter notes for more discussion.

```
trait Parsers[ParseError, Parser[+_]] {

    def run[A](p: Parser[A])(input: String): Either[ParseError,A]
    def char(c: Char): Parser[Char]
}
```

Here the **Parser type** constructor is applied to **Char**.

Parser is a type parameter that itself is a covariant type constructor

What's with the funny Parser[+_] type argument? It's not too important for right now, but that's Scala's syntax for a type parameter that is itself a type constructor.[5] Making ParseError a type argument lets the Parsers interface work for any representation of ParseError, and making Parser[+_] a type parameter means that the interface works for any representation of Parser. The underscore just means that whatever Parser is, it expects one type argument to represent the type of the result, as in Parser[Char]. This code will compile as it is. We don't need to pick a representation for ParseError or Parser, and we can continue placing additional combinators in the body of this trait.

Our char function should satisfy an obvious law—for any Char, c,

```
run(char(c))(c.toString) == Right(c)
```

Let's continue. We can recognize the single character 'a', but what if we want to recognize the string "abracadabra"? We don't have a way of recognizing entire strings right now, so let's add that:

```
def string(s: String): Parser[String]
```

Likewise, this should satisfy an obvious law—for any String, s,

```
run(string(s))(s) == Right(s)
```

What if we want to recognize either the string "abra" *or* the string "cadabra"? We could add a very specialized combinator for it:

```
def orString(s1: String, s2: String): Parser[String]
```

But choosing between two parsers seems like something that would be more generally useful, regardless of their result type, so let's go ahead and make this polymorphic:

```
def or[A](s1: Parser[A], s2: Parser[A]): Parser[A]
```

We expect that or(string("abra"),string("cadabra")) will succeed whenever either string parser succeeds:

```
run(or(string("abra"),string("cadabra")))("abra") == Right("abra")
run(or(string("abra"),string("cadabra")))("cadabra") == Right("cadabra")
```

Incidentally, we can give this or combinator nice infix syntax like s1 | s2 or alternately s1 or s2, using implicits like we did in chapter 7.

---

[5] We'll say much more about this in the next few chapters.

Listing 9.1 Adding infix syntax to parsers

```
trait Parsers[ParseError, Parser[+_]] { self =>
  ...
  def or[A](s1: Parser[A], s2: Parser[A]): Parser[A]
  implicit def string(s: String): Parser[String]
  implicit def operators[A](p: Parser[A]) = ParserOps[A](p)
  implicit def asStringParser[A](a: A)(implicit f: A => Parser[String]):
    ParserOps[String] = ParserOps(f(a))



  case class ParserOps[A](p: Parser[A]) {
    def |[B>:A](p2: Parser[B]): Parser[B] = self.or(p,p2)
    def or[B>:A](p2: => Parser[B]): Parser[B] = self.or(p,p2)
  }
}
```

This introduces the name **self** to refer to this **Parsers** instance; it's used later in **ParserOps**.

Use **self** to explicitly disambiguate reference to the **or** method on the **trait**.

We've also made `string` an implicit conversion and added another implicit `asStringParser`. With these two functions, Scala will automatically promote a `String` to a `Parser`, and we get infix operators for any type that can be converted to a `Parser[String]`. So given `val P: Parsers`, we can then `import P._` to let us write expressions like `"abra" | "cadabra"` to create parsers. This will work for *all* implementations of `Parsers`. Other binary operators or methods can be added to the body of `ParserOps`. We'll follow the discipline of keeping the primary definition directly in `Parsers` and delegating in `ParserOps` to this primary definition. See the code for this chapter for more examples. We'll use the a | b syntax liberally throughout the rest of this chapter to mean `or(a,b)`.

We can now recognize various strings, but we don't have a way of talking about repetition. For instance, how would we recognize three repetitions of our `"abra" | "cadabra"` parser? Once again, let's add a combinator for it:[6]

```
def listOfN[A](n: Int, p: Parser[A]): Parser[List[A]]
```

We made `listOfN` parametric in the choice of `A`, since it doesn't seem like it should care whether we have a `Parser[String]`, a `Parser[Char]`, or some other type of parser. Here are some examples of what we expect from `listOfN`:

```
run(listOfN(3, "ab" | "cad"))("ababcad") == Right("ababcad")
run(listOfN(3, "ab" | "cad"))("cadabab") == Right("cadabab")
run(listOfN(3, "ab" | "cad"))("ababab") == Right("ababab")
```

At this point, we've just been collecting up required combinators, but we haven't tried to refine our algebra into a minimal set of primitives, and we haven't talked much about more general laws. We'll start doing this next, but rather than give the game away, we'll ask you to examine a few more simple use cases yourself and try to design a

---

[6] This should remind you of a similar function we wrote in the previous chapter.

minimal algebra with associated laws. This should be a challenging exercise, but enjoy struggling with it and see what you can come up with.

Here are additional parsing tasks to consider, along with some guiding questions:

- A `Parser[Int]` that recognizes zero or more `'a'` characters, and whose result value is the number of `'a'` characters it has seen. For instance, given `"aa"`, the parser results in 2; given `""` or `"b123"` (a string not starting with `'a'`), it results in 0; and so on.
- A `Parser[Int]` that recognizes *one* or more `'a'` characters, and whose result value is the number of `'a'` characters it has seen. (Is this defined somehow in terms of the same combinators as the parser for `'a'` repeated zero or more times?) The parser should fail when given a string without a starting `'a'`. How would you like to handle error reporting in this case? Could the API support giving an explicit message like `"Expected one or more 'a'"` in the case of failure?
- A parser that recognizes zero or more `'a'`, followed by one or more `'b'`, and which results in the pair of counts of characters seen. For instance, given `"bbb"`, we get `(0,3)`, given `"aaaab"`, we get `(4,1)`, and so on.

And additional considerations:

- If we're trying to parse a sequence of zero or more `"a"` and are only interested in the number of characters seen, it seems inefficient to have to build up, say, a `List[Char]` only to throw it away and extract the length. Could something be done about this?
- Are the various forms of repetition primitive in our algebra, or could they be defined in terms of something simpler?
- We introduced a type `ParseError` earlier, but so far we haven't chosen any functions for the API of `ParseError` and our algebra doesn't have any way of letting the programmer control what errors are reported. This seems like a limitation, given that we'd like meaningful error messages from our parsers. Can you do something about it?
- Does a | b mean the same thing as b | a? This is a choice you get to make. What are the consequences if the answer is yes? What about if the answer is no?
- Does a | (b | c) mean the same thing as (a | b) | c? If yes, is this a primitive law for your algebra, or is it implied by something simpler?
- Try to come up with a set of laws to specify your algebra. You don't necessarily need the laws to be complete; just write down some laws that you expect should hold for any `Parsers` implementation.

Spend some time coming up with combinators and possible laws based on this guidance. When you feel stuck or at a good stopping point, then continue by reading the next section, which walks through one possible design.

The advantages of algebraic design

When you design the algebra of a library first, representations for the data types of the algebra don't matter as much. As long as they support the required laws and functions, you don't even need to make your representations public.

There's an idea here that a type is given meaning based on its relationship to other types (which are specified by the set of functions and their laws), rather than its internal representation.[7] This viewpoint is often associated with category theory, a branch of mathematics we've mentioned before. See the chapter notes for more on this connection if you're interested.

9.2   *A possible algebra*

We'll walk through the discovery of a set of combinators for the parsing tasks mentioned earlier. If you worked through this design task yourself, you likely took a different path and may have ended up with a different set of combinators, which is fine.

First, let's consider the parser that recognizes zero or more repetitions of the character `'a'` and returns the number of characters it has seen. We can start by adding a primitive combinator for it; let's call it `many`:

```
def many[A](p: Parser[A]): Parser[List[A]]
```

This isn't exactly what we're after—we need a `Parser[Int]` that counts the number of elements. We could change the `many` combinator to return a `Parser[Int]`, but that feels too specific—undoubtedly there will be occasions where we care about more than just the list length. Better to introduce another combinator that should be familiar by now, `map`:

```
def map[A,B](a: Parser[A])(f: A => B): Parser[B]
```

We can now define our parser like this:

```
map(many(char('a')))(_.size)
```

Let's add map and `many` as methods in `ParserOps`, so we can write the same thing with nicer syntax:

```
val numA: Parser[Int] = char('a').many.map(_.size)
```

We expect that, for instance, `run(numA)("aaa")` gives `Right(3)`, and `run(numA)("b")` gives `Right(0)`.

We have a strong expectation for the behavior of `map`—it should merely transform the result value if the `Parser` was successful. No additional input characters should be examined by `map`, and a failing parser can't become a successful one via `map` or vice

---

[7]   This sort of viewpoint might also be associated with object-oriented design, although OO hasn't traditionally placed much emphasis on algebraic laws. Furthermore, a big reason for encapsulation in OO is that objects often have some mutable state, and making this public would allow client code to violate invariants. That concern isn't relevant in FP.

versa. In general, we expect map to be *structure preserving* much like we required for Par and Gen. Let's formalize this by stipulating the now-familiar law:

```
map(p)(a => a) == p
```

How should we document this law? We could put it in a documentation comment, but in the preceding chapter we developed a way to make our laws *executable*. Let's use that library here.

Listing 9.2 Combining `Parser` with `map`

```
import fpinscala.testing._

trait Parsers[ParseError, Parser[+_]] {
  ...
  object Laws {
    def equal[A](p1: Parser[A], p2: Parser[A])(in: Gen[String]): Prop =
      forAll(in)(s => run(p1)(s) == run(p2)(s))

    def mapLaw[A](p: Parser[A])(in: Gen[String]): Prop =
      equal(p, p.map(a => a))(in)
  }
}
```

This will come in handy later when we test that our implementation of Parsers behaves as we expect. When we discover more laws later on, you're encouraged to write them out as actual properties inside the Laws object.[8]

Incidentally, now that we have map, we can actually implement char in terms of string:

```
def char(c: Char): Parser[Char] =
  string(c.toString) map (_.charAt(0))
```

And similarly another combinator, succeed, can be defined in terms of string and map:

```
def succeed[A](a: A): Parser[A] =
  string("") map (_ => a)
```

This parser always succeeds with the value a, regardless of the input string (since string("") will always succeed, even if the input is empty). Does this combinator seem familiar to you? We can specify its behavior with a law:

```
run(succeed(a))(s) == Right(a)
```

---

[8] Again, see the chapter code for more examples. In the interest of keeping this chapter shorter, we won't give Prop implementations of all the laws, but that doesn't mean you shouldn't write them yourself!

9.2.1 *Slicing and nonempty repetition*

The combination of `many` and `map` certainly lets us express the parsing task of counting the number of `'a'` characters, but it seems inefficient to construct a `List[Char]` only to discard its values and extract its length. It would be nice if we could run a `Parser` purely to see what portion of the input string it examines. Let's conjure up a combinator for that purpose:

```
def slice[A](p: Parser[A]): Parser[String]
```

We call this combinator `slice` since we intend for it to return the portion of the input string examined by the parser if successful. As an example, `run(slice(('a'|'b').many))("aaba")` results in `Right("aaba")`—we ignore the list accumulated by `many` and simply return the portion of the input string matched by the parser.

With `slice`, our parser that counts `'a'` characters can now be written as `char('a').many.slice.map(_.size)` (assuming we add an alias for `slice` to `ParserOps`). The `_.size` function here is now referencing the `size` method on `String`, which takes constant time, rather than the `size` method on `List`, which takes time proportional to the length of the list (and requires us to actually construct the list).

Note that there's no implementation here yet. We're still just coming up with our desired interface. But `slice` does put a constraint on the implementation, namely, that even if the parser `p.many.map(_.size)` will generate an intermediate list when run, `slice(p.many).map(_.size)` will not. This is a strong hint that `slice` is primitive, since it will have to have access to the internal representation of the parser.

Let's consider the next use case. What if we want to recognize *one* or more `'a'` characters? First, we introduce a new combinator for it, `many1`:

```
def many1[A](p: Parser[A]): Parser[List[A]]
```

It feels like `many1` shouldn't have to be primitive, but should be defined somehow in terms of `many`. Really, `many1(p)` is just p *followed by* `many(p)`. So it seems we need some way of running one parser, followed by another, assuming the first is successful. Let's add that:

```
def product[A,B](p: Parser[A], p2: Parser[B]): Parser[(A,B)]
```

We can add `**` and `product` as methods on `ParserOps`, where `a ** b` and `a product b` both delegate to `product(a,b)`.

■── EXERCISE 9.1 ──────────────────────

Using `product`, implement the now-familiar combinator `map2` and then use this to implement `many1` in terms of `many`. Note that we could have chosen to make `map2` primitive and defined `product` in terms of `map2` as we've done in previous chapters. The choice is up to you.

```
def map2[A,B,C](p: Parser[A], p2: Parser[B])(f: (A,B) => C): Parser[C]
```

With `many1`, we can now implement the parser for zero or more `'a'` followed by one or more `'b'` as follows:

```
char('a').many.slice.map(_.size) ** char('b').many1.slice.map(_.size)
```

EXERCISE 9.2

Hard: Try coming up with laws to specify the behavior of `product`.

Now that we have `map2`, is `many` really primitive? Let's think about what `many(p)` will do. It tries running `p`, *followed by* `many(p)` again, and again, and so on until the attempt to parse `p` fails. It'll accumulate the results of all successful runs of `p` into a list. As soon as `p` fails, the parser returns the empty `List`.

EXERCISE 9.3

Hard: Before continuing, see if you can define `many` in terms of `or`, `map2`, and `succeed`.

EXERCISE 9.4

Hard: Using `map2` and `succeed`, implement the `listOfN` combinator from earlier.

```
def listOfN[A](n: Int, p: Parser[A]): Parser[List[A]]
```

Now let's try to implement `many`. Here's an implementation in terms of `or`, `map2`, and `succeed`:

```
def many[A](p: Parser[A]): Parser[List[A]] =
  map2(p, many(p))(_ :: _) or succeed(List())
```

This code looks nice and tidy. We're using `map2` to say that we want `p` followed by `many(p)` again, and that we want to combine their results with `::` to construct a list of results. Or, if that fails, we want to `succeed` with the empty list. But there's a problem with this implementation. Can you spot what it is? We're calling `many` recursively in the second argument to `map2`, which is *strict* in evaluating its second argument. Consider a simplified program trace of the evaluation of `many(p)` for some parser `p`. We're only showing the expansion of the left side of the `or` here:

```
many(p)
map2(p, many(p))(_ :: _)
map2(p, map2(p, many(p))(_ :: _))(_ :: _)
map2(p, map2(p, map2(p, many(p))(_ :: _))(_ :: _))(_ :: _)
...
```

Because a call to map2 always evaluates its second argument, our many function will never terminate! That's no good. This indicates that we need to make product and map2 non-strict in their second argument:

```
def product[A,B](p: Parser[A], p2: => Parser[B]): Parser[(A,B)]

def map2[A,B,C](p: Parser[A], p2: => Parser[B])(
                f: (A,B) => C): Parser[C] =
  product(p, p2) map (f.tupled)
```

EXERCISE 9.5

We could also deal with non-strictness with a separate combinator like we did in chapter 7. Try this here and make the necessary changes to your existing combinators. What do you think of that approach in this instance?

Now our implementation of many should work fine. Conceptually, product should have been non-strict in its second argument anyway, since if the first Parser fails, the second won't even be consulted.

We now have good combinators for parsing one thing followed by another, or multiple things of the same kind in succession. But since we're considering whether combinators should be non-strict, let's revisit the or combinator from earlier:

```
def or[A](p1: Parser[A], p2: Parser[A]): Parser[A]
```

We'll assume that or is left-biased, meaning it tries p1 on the input, and then tries p2 only if p1 fails.[9] In this case, we ought to make it non-strict in its second argument, which may never even be consulted:

```
def or[A](p1: Parser[A], p2: => Parser[A]): Parser[A]
```

9.3   *Handling context sensitivity*

Let's take a step back and look at the primitives we have so far:

- string(s)—Recognizes and returns a single String
- slice(p)—Returns the portion of input inspected by p if successful
- succeed(a)—Always succeeds with the value a
- map(p)(f)—Applies the function f to the result of p, if successful
- product(p1,p2)—Sequences two parsers, running p1 and then p2, and returns the pair of their results if both succeed
- or(p1,p2)—Chooses between two parsers, first attempting p1, and then p2 if p1 fails

---

[9] This is a design choice. You may wish to think about the consequences of having a version of or that always runs both p1 and p2.

Using these primitives, we can express repetition and nonempty repetition (many, listOfN, and many1) as well as combinators like char and map2. Would it surprise you if these primitives were sufficient for parsing *any* context-free grammar, including JSON? Well, they are! We'll get to writing that JSON parser soon, but what *can't* we express yet?

Suppose we want to parse a single digit, like '4', followed by *that many* 'a' characters (this sort of problem should feel familiar from previous chapters). Examples of valid input are "0", "1a", "2aa", "4aaaa", and so on. This is an example of a context-sensitive grammar. It can't be expressed with product because our choice of the second parser *depends on* the result of the first (the second parser depends on its context). We want to run the first parser, and then do a listOfN using the number extracted from the first parser's result. Can you see why product can't express this?

This progression might feel familiar to you. In past chapters, we encountered similar expressiveness limitations and dealt with it by introducing a new primitive, flatMap. Let's introduce that here (and we'll add an alias to ParserOps so we can write parsers using for-comprehensions):

```
def flatMap[A,B](p: Parser[A])(f: A => Parser[B]): Parser[B]
```

Can you see how this signature implies an ability to sequence parsers where each parser in the chain depends on the output of the previous one?

EXERCISE 9.6

Using flatMap and any other combinators, write the context-sensitive parser we couldn't express earlier. To parse the digits, you can make use of a new primitive, regex, which promotes a regular expression to a Parser.[10] In Scala, a string s can be promoted to a Regex object (which has methods for matching) using s.r, for instance, "[a-zA-Z_][a-zA-Z0-9_]*".r.

```
implicit def regex(r: Regex): Parser[String]
```

EXERCISE 9.7

Implement product and map2 in terms of flatMap.

EXERCISE 9.8

map is no longer primitive. Express it in terms of flatMap and/or other combinators.

---

[10] In theory this isn't necessary; we could write out "0" | "1" | ... "9" to recognize a single digit, but this isn't likely to be very efficient.

So it appears we have a new primitive, `flatMap`, which enables context-sensitive parsing and lets us implement `map` and `map2`. This is not the first time `flatMap` has made an appearance.

We now have an even smaller set of just six primitives: `string`, `regex`, `slice`, `succeed`, `or`, and `flatMap`. But we also have more power than before. With `flatMap`, instead of the less-general `map` and `product`, we can parse not just arbitrary context-free grammars like JSON, but context-sensitive grammars as well, including extremely complicated ones like C++ and PERL!

9.4   *Writing a JSON parser*

Let's write that JSON parser now, shall we? We don't have an implementation of our algebra yet, and we've yet to add any combinators for good error reporting, but we can deal with these things later. Our JSON parser doesn't need to know the internal details of how parsers are represented. We can simply write a function that produces a JSON parser using only the set of primitives we've defined and any derived combinators.

That is, for some JSON parse result type (we'll explain the JSON format and the parse result type shortly), we'll write a function like this:

```
def jsonParser[Err,Parser[+_]](P: Parsers[Err,Parser]): Parser[JSON] = {
  import P._                    ←............................ Gives access to all the combinators
  val spaces = char(' ').many.slice
  ...
}
```

This might seem like a peculiar thing to do, since we won't actually be able to run our parser until we have a concrete implementation of the `Parsers` interface. But we'll proceed, because in FP, it's common to define an algebra and explore its expressiveness without having a concrete implementation. A concrete implementation can tie us down and makes changes to the API more difficult. Especially during the design phase of a library, it can be much easier to refine an algebra *without* having to commit to any particular implementation, and part of our goal here is to get you comfortable with this style of working.

After this section, we'll return to the question of adding better error reporting to our parsing API. We can do this without disturbing the overall structure of the API or changing our JSON parser very much. And we'll also come up with a concrete, runnable representation of our `Parser` type. Importantly, the JSON parser we'll implement in this next section will be completely independent of that representation.

9.4.1   *The JSON format*

If you aren't already familiar with the JSON format, you may want to read Wikipedia's description (http://mng.bz/DpNA) and the grammar specification (http://json.org). Here's an example JSON document:

```
{
  "Company name" : "Microsoft Corporation",
  "Ticker"  : "MSFT",
```

```
"Active"   : true,
"Price"    : 30.66,
"Shares outstanding" : 8.38e9,
"Related companies" :
   [ "HPQ", "IBM", "YHOO", "DELL", "GOOG" ]
}
```

A *value* in JSON can be one of several types. An *object* in JSON is a comma-separated sequence of key-value pairs, wrapped in curly braces ({}). The keys must be strings like "Ticker" or "Price", and the values can be either another object, an *array* like ["HPQ", "IBM" ...] that contains further values, or a *literal* like "MSFT", true, null, or 30.66.

We'll write a rather dumb parser that simply parses a syntax tree from the document without doing any further processing.[11] We'll need a representation for a parsed JSON document. Let's introduce a data type for this:

```
trait JSON
object JSON {
  case object JNull extends JSON
  case class JNumber(get: Double) extends JSON
  case class JString(get: String) extends JSON
  case class JBool(get: Boolean) extends JSON
  case class JArray(get: IndexedSeq[JSON]) extends JSON
  case class JObject(get: Map[String, JSON]) extends JSON
}
```

9.4.2 A JSON parser

Recall that we've built up the following set of primitives:

- string(s): Recognizes and returns a single String
- regex(s): Recognizes a regular expression s
- slice(p): Returns the portion of input inspected by p if successful
- succeed(a): Always succeeds with the value a
- flatMap(p)(f): Runs a parser, then uses its result to select a second parser to run in sequence
- or(p1,p2): Chooses between two parsers, first attempting p1, and then p2 if p1 fails

We used these primitives to define a number of combinators like map, map2, many, and many1.

EXERCISE 9.9

Hard: At this point, *you* are going to take over the process. You'll be creating a Parser[JSON] from scratch using the primitives we've defined. You don't need to

---

[11] See the chapter notes for discussion of alternate approaches.

worry (yet) about the representation of `Parser`. As you go, you'll undoubtedly discover additional combinators and idioms, notice and factor out common patterns, and so on. Use the skills you've been developing throughout this book, and have fun! If you get stuck, you can always consult the answers.

Here's some minimal guidance:

- Any general-purpose combinators you discover can be added to the `Parsers` trait directly.
- You'll probably want to introduce combinators that make it easier to parse the tokens of the JSON format (like string literals and numbers). For this you could use the `regex` primitive we introduced earlier. You could also add a few primitives like `letter`, `digit`, `whitespace`, and so on, for building up your token parsers.

Consult the hints if you'd like more guidance. A full JSON parser is given in the file `JSON.scala` in the answers.

9.5   *Error reporting*

So far we haven't discussed error reporting at all. We've focused exclusively on discovering a set of primitives that let us express parsers for different grammars. But besides just parsing a grammar, we want to be able to determine how the parser should respond when given unexpected input.

Even without knowing what an implementation of `Parsers` will look like, we can reason abstractly about what information is being specified by a set of combinators. None of the combinators we've introduced so far say anything about *what error message* should be reported in the event of failure or what other information a `ParseError` should contain. Our existing combinators only specify what the grammar is and what to do with the result if successful. If we were to declare ourselves done and move to implementation at this point, we'd have to make some arbitrary decisions about error reporting and error messages that are unlikely to be universally appropriate.

EXERCISE 9.10

Hard: If you haven't already done so, spend some time discovering a nice set of combinators for expressing what errors get reported by a `Parser`. For each combinator, try to come up with laws specifying what its behavior should be. This is a very open-ended design task. Here are some guiding questions:

- Given the parser `"abra".**(" ".many).**("cadabra")`, what sort of error would you like to report given the input `"abra cAdabra"` (note the capital `'A'`)? Only something like `Expected 'a'`? Or `Expected "cadabra"`? What if you wanted to choose a different error message, like `"Magic word incorrect, try again!"`?

- Given a or b, if a fails on the input, do we *always* want to run b, or are there cases where we might not want to? If there are such cases, can you think of additional combinators that would allow the programmer to specify when or should consider the second parser?
- How do you want to handle reporting the *location* of errors?
- Given a or b, if a and b both fail on the input, might we want to support reporting both errors? And do we *always* want to report both errors, or do we want to give the programmer a way to specify which of the two errors is reported?

We suggest you continue reading once you're satisfied with your design. The next section works through a possible design in detail.

Combinators specify information

In a typical library design scenario, where we have at least some idea of a concrete representation, we often think of functions in terms of how they will affect this representation. By starting with the algebra first, we're forced to think differently—we must think of functions in terms of *what information they specify* to a possible implementation. The signatures determine what information is given to the implementation, and the implementation is free to use this information however it wants as long as it respects any specified laws.

9.5.1 *A possible design*

Now that you've spent some time coming up with some good error-reporting combinators, we'll work through one possible design. Again, you may have arrived at a different design and that's totally fine. This is just another opportunity to see a worked design process.

We'll progressively introduce our error-reporting combinators. To start, let's introduce an obvious one. None of the primitives so far let us assign an error message to a parser. We can introduce a primitive combinator for this, `label`:

```
def label[A](msg: String)(p: Parser[A]): Parser[A]
```

The intended meaning of `label` is that if `p` fails, its `ParseError` will somehow incorporate `msg`. What does this mean exactly? Well, we could just assume type `ParseError = String` and that the returned `ParseError` will *equal* the label. But we'd like our parse error to also tell us *where* the problem occurred. Let's tentatively add this to our algebra:

```
case class Location(input: String, offset: Int = 0) {
  lazy val line = input.slice(0,offset+1).count(_ == '\n') + 1
  lazy val col = input.slice(0,offset+1).lastIndexOf('\n') match {
    case -1 => offset + 1
    case lineStart => offset - lineStart
  }
}

def errorLocation(e: ParseError): Location
def errorMessage(e: ParseError): String
```

We've picked a concrete representation for Location here that includes the full input, an offset into this input, and the line and column numbers, which can be computed lazily from the full input and offset. We can now say more precisely what we expect from label. In the event of failure with Left(e), errorMessage(e) will equal the message set by label. This can be specified with a Prop:

```
def labelLaw[A](p: Parser[A], inputs: SGen[String]): Prop =
  forAll(inputs ** Gen.string) { case (input, msg) =>
    run(label(msg)(p))(input) match {
      case Left(e) => errorMessage(e) == msg
      case _ => true
    }
  }
```

What about the Location? We'd like for this to be filled in by the Parsers implementation with the location where the error occurred. This notion is still a bit fuzzy—if we have a or b and both parsers fail on the input, which location is reported, and which label(s)? We'll discuss this in the next section.

9.5.2 *Error nesting*

Is the label combinator sufficient for all our error-reporting needs? Not quite. Let's look at an example:

```
val p = label("first magic word")("abra") **
        " ".many **                            ←———— Skip whitespace
        label("second magic word")("cadabra")
```

What sort of ParseError would we like to get back from run(p)("abra cAdabra")? (Note the capital A in cAdabra.) The immediate cause is that capital 'A' instead of the expected lowercase 'a'. That error will have a location, and it might be nice to report it somehow. But reporting *only* that low-level error wouldn't be very informative, especially if this were part of a large grammar and we were running the parser on a larger input. We have some more context that would be useful to know—the immediate error occurred in the Parser labeled "second magic word". This is certainly helpful information. Ideally, the error message should tell us that while parsing "second magic word", there was an unexpected capital 'A'. That pinpoints the error and gives us the context needed to understand it. Perhaps the top-level parser (p in this case) might be able to provide an even higher-level description of what the parser was doing when it failed ("parsing magic spell", say), which could also be informative.

So it seems wrong to assume that one level of error reporting will always be sufficient. Let's therefore provide a way to *nest* labels:

```
def scope[A](msg: String)(p: Parser[A]): Parser[A]
```

Unlike label, scope doesn't throw away the label(s) attached to p—it merely adds additional information in the event that p fails. Let's specify what this means exactly. First, we modify the functions that pull information out of a ParseError.

Rather than containing just a single `Location` and `String` message, we should get a `List[(Location,String)]`:

```
case class ParseError(stack: List[(Location,String)])
```

This is a stack of error messages indicating what the `Parser` was doing when it failed. We can now specify what `scope` does—if `run(p)(s)` is `Left(e1)`, then `run(scope(msg)(p))` is `Left(e2)`, where `e2.stack.head` will be `msg` and `e2.stack.tail` will be `e1`.

We can write helper functions later to make constructing and manipulating `ParseError` values more convenient, and to format them nicely for human consumption. For now, we just want to make sure it contains all the relevant information for error reporting, and it seems like `ParseError` will be sufficient for most purposes. Let's pick this as our concrete representation and remove the abstract type parameter from `Parsers`:

```
trait Parsers[Parser[+_]] {
  def run[A](p: Parser[A])(input: String): Either[ParseError,A]
  ...
}
```

Now we're giving the `Parsers` implementation all the information it needs to construct nice, hierarchical errors if it chooses. As users of the `Parsers` library, we'll judiciously sprinkle our grammar with `label` and `scope` calls that the `Parsers` implementation can use when constructing parse errors. Note that it would be perfectly reasonable for implementations of `Parsers` to not use the full power of `ParseError` and retain only basic information about the cause and location of errors.

9.5.3 *Controlling branching and backtracking*

There's one last concern regarding error reporting that we need to address. As we just discussed, when we have an error that occurs inside an `or` combinator, we need some way of determining which error(s) to report. We don't want to *only* have a global convention for this; we sometimes want to allow the programmer to control this choice. Let's look at a more concrete motivating example:

```
val spaces = " ".many
val p1 = scope("magic spell") {
  "abra" ** spaces ** "cadabra"
}
val p2 = scope("gibberish") {
  "abba" ** spaces ** "babba"
}
val p = p1 or p2
```

What `ParseError` would we like to get back from `run(p)("abra cAdabra")`? (Again, note the capital A in cAdabra.) Both branches of the `or` will produce errors on the input. The `"gibberish"`-labeled parser will report an error due to expecting the first word to be `"abba"`, and the `"magic spell"` parser will report an error due to the accidental capitalization in `"cAdabra"`. Which of these errors do we want to report back to the user?

In this instance, we happen to want the `"magic spell"` parse error—after successfully parsing the `"abra"` word, we're *committed* to the `"magic spell"` branch of the or, which means if we encounter a parse error, we don't examine the next branch of the or. In other instances, we may want to allow the parser to consider the next branch of the or.

So it appears we need a primitive for letting the programmer indicate when to commit to a particular parsing branch. Recall that we loosely assigned p1 or p2 to mean *try running p1 on the input, and then try running p2 on the same input if p1 fails*. We can change its meaning to *try running p1 on the input, and if it fails in an uncommitted state, try running p2 on the same input; otherwise, report the failure.* This is useful for more than just providing good error messages—it also improves efficiency by letting the implementation avoid examining lots of possible parsing branches.

One common solution to this problem is to have all parsers *commit by default* if they examine at least one character to produce a result.[12] We then introduce a combinator, `attempt`, which delays committing to a parse:

```
def attempt[A](p: Parser[A]): Parser[A]
```

It should satisfy something like this:[13]

```
attempt(p flatMap (_ => fail)) or p2 == p2
```

Here `fail` is a parser that always fails (we could introduce this as a primitive combinator if we like). That is, even if p fails midway through examining the input, `attempt` reverts the commit to that parse and allows p2 to be run. The `attempt` combinator can be used whenever there's ambiguity in the grammar and multiple tokens may have to be examined before the ambiguity can be resolved and parsing can commit to a single branch. As an example, we might write this:

```
(attempt("abra" ** spaces ** "abra") ** "cadabra") or (
 "abra" ** spaces "cadabra!")
```

Suppose this parser is run on `"abra cadabra!"`—after parsing the first `"abra"`, we don't know whether to expect another `"abra"` (the first branch) or `"cadabra!"` (the second branch). By wrapping an `attempt` around `"abra" ** spaces ** "abra"`, we allow the second branch to be considered up until we've finished parsing the second `"abra"`, at which point we commit to that branch.

---

[12] See the chapter notes for more discussion of this.

[13] This is not quite an equality. Even though we want to run p2 if the attempted parser fails, we may want p2 to somehow incorporate the errors from both branches if it fails.

■ **EXERCISE 9.11**

Can you think of any other primitives that might be useful for letting the programmer specify what error(s) in an `or` chain get reported?

Note that we still haven't written an implementation of our algebra! But this exercise has been more about making sure our combinators provide a way for users of our library to convey the right information to the implementation. It's up to the implementation to figure out how to use this information in a way that satisfies the laws we've stipulated.

9.6 *Implementing the algebra*

By this point, we've fleshed out our algebra and defined a `Parser[JSON]` in terms of it.[14] Aren't you curious to try running it?

Let's again recall our set of primitives:

- `string(s)`—Recognizes and returns a single `String`
- `regex(s)`—Recognizes a regular expression s
- `slice(p)`—Returns the portion of input inspected by p if successful
- `label(e)(p)`—In the event of failure, replaces the assigned message with e
- `scope(e)(p)`—In the event of failure, adds e to the error stack returned by p
- `flatMap(p)(f)`—Runs a parser, and then uses its result to select a second parser to run in sequence
- `attempt(p)`—Delays committing to p until after it succeeds
- `or(p1,p2)`—Chooses between two parsers, first attempting p1, and then p2 if p1 fails in an uncommitted state on the input

□ **EXERCISE 9.12**

Hard: In the next section, we'll work through a representation for `Parser` and implement the `Parsers` interface using this representation. But before we do that, try to come up with some ideas on your own. This is a very open-ended design task, but the algebra we've designed places strong constraints on possible representations. You should be able to come up with a simple, purely functional representation of `Parser` that can be used to implement the `Parsers` interface.[15]

---

[14] You may want to revisit your parser to make use of some of the error-reporting combinators we just discussed in the previous section.

[15] Note that if you try running your JSON parser once you have an implementation of `Parsers`, you may get a stack overflow error. See the end of the next section for a discussion of this.

Your code will likely look something like this:

```
class MyParser[+A](...) { ... }

object MyParsers extends Parsers[MyParser] {
  // implementations of primitives go here
}
```

Replace `MyParser` with whatever data type you use for representing your parsers. When you have something you're satisfied with, get stuck, or want some more ideas, keep reading.

9.6.1   *One possible implementation*

We're now going to discuss an implementation of `Parsers`. Our parsing algebra supports a lot of features. Rather than jumping right to the final representation of `Parser`, we'll build it up gradually by inspecting the primitives of the algebra and reasoning about the information that will be required to support each one.

Let's begin with the `string` combinator:

```
def string(s: String): Parser[A]
```

We know we need to support the function `run`:

```
def run[A](p: Parser[A])(input: String): Either[ParseError,A]
```

As a first guess, we can assume that our `Parser` *is* simply the implementation of the run function:

```
type Parser[+A] = String => Either[ParseError,A]
```

We could use this to implement the `string` primitive:

```
def string(s: String): Parser[A] =
  (input: String) =>
    if (input.startsWith(s))
      Right(s)
    else
      Left(Location(input).toError("Expected: " + s))
```

> Uses `toError`, defined later, to construct a `ParseError`

The `else` branch has to build up a `ParseError`. These are a little inconvenient to construct right now, so we've introduced a helper function, `toError`, on `Location`:

```
def toError(msg: String): ParseError =
  ParseError(List((this, msg)))
```

9.6.2   *Sequencing parsers*

So far, so good. We have a representation for `Parser` that at least supports `string`. Let's move on to sequencing of parsers. Unfortunately, to represent a parser like `"abra" ** "cadabra"`, our existing representation isn't going to suffice. If the parse of `"abra"` is successful, then we want to consider those characters *consumed* and run the "cadabra" parser on the remaining characters. So in order to support sequencing, we require a way of letting a `Parser` indicate how many characters it consumed. Capturing this is pretty easy:[16]

```
type Parser[+A] = Location => Result[A]    ⟵    A parser now returns a Result
                                                that's either a success or a failure.

trait Result[+A]
case class Success[+A](get: A, charsConsumed: Int) extends Result[A]    ⟵
case class Failure(get: ParseError) extends Result[Nothing]
```

In the success case, we return the number of characters consumed by the parser.

We introduced a new type here, `Result`, rather than just using `Either`. In the event of success, we return a value of type `A` as well as the number of characters of input consumed, which the caller can use to update the `Location` state.[17] This type is starting to get at the essence of what a `Parser` is—it's a kind of state action that can fail, similar to what we built in chapter 6. It receives an input state, and if successful, returns a value as well as enough information to control how the state should be updated.

This understanding—that a `Parser` is just a state action—gives us a way of framing a representation that supports all the fancy combinators and laws we've stipulated. We simply consider what each primitive requires our state type to track (just a `Location` may not be sufficient), and work through the details of how each combinator transforms this state.

EXERCISE 9.13

Implement `string`, `regex`, `succeed`, and `slice` for this initial representation of `Parser`. Note that `slice` is less efficient than it could be, since it must still construct a value only to discard it. We'll return to this later.

9.6.3 *Labeling parsers*

Moving down our list of primitives, let's look at `scope` next. In the event of failure, we want to push a new message onto the `ParseError` stack. Let's introduce a helper function for this on `ParseError`. We'll call it push:[18]

```
def push(loc: Location, msg: String): ParseError =
  copy(stack = (loc,msg) :: stack)
```

---

[16] Recall that `Location` contains the full input string and an offset into this string.

[17] Note that returning an `(A,Location)` would give `Parser` the ability to change the `input` stored in the `Location`. That's granting it too much power!

[18] The `copy` method comes for free with any `case class`. It returns a copy of the object, but with one or more attributes modified. If no new value is specified for a field, it will have the same value as in the original object. Behind the scenes, this just uses the ordinary mechanism for default arguments in Scala.

With this we can implement scope:

```
def scope[A](msg: String)(p: Parser[A]): Parser[A] =
  s => p(s).mapError(_.push(s.loc,msg))
```

In the event of failure, push msg *onto the error stack.*

The function mapError is defined on Result—it just applies a function to the failing case:

```
def mapError(f: ParseError => ParseError): Result[A] = this match {
  case Failure(e) => Failure(f(e))
  case _ => this
}
```

Because we push onto the stack after the inner parser has returned, the bottom of the stack will have more detailed messages that occurred later in parsing. For example, if scope(msg1)(a ** scope(msg2)(b)) fails while parsing b, the first error on the stack will be msg1, followed by whatever errors were generated by a, then msg2, and finally errors generated by b.

We can implement label similarly, but instead of pushing onto the error stack, it replaces what's already there. We can write this again using mapError:

```
def label[A](msg: String)(p: Parser[A]): Parser[A] =
  s => p(s).mapError(_.label(msg))
```

Calls a helper method on ParseError, *which is also named* label.

We added a helper function to ParseError, also named label. We'll make a design decision that label trims the error stack, cutting off more detailed messages from inner scopes, using only the most recent location from the bottom of the stack:

```
def label[A](s: String): ParseError =
  ParseError(latestLoc.map((_,s)).toList)

def latestLoc: Option[Location] =
  latest map (_._1)

def latest: Option[(Location,String)] =
  stack.lastOption
```

Gets the last element of the stack or None *if the stack is empty.*

■ **EXERCISE 9.14**

Revise your implementation of string to use scope and/or label to provide a meaningful error message in the event of an error.

9.6.4   *Failover and backtracking*

Let's now consider or and attempt. Recall what we specified for the expected behavior of or: it should run the first parser, and if that fails *in an uncommitted state*, it should run the second parser on the same input. We said that consuming at least one character should result in a committed parse, and that `attempt(p)` converts committed failures of p to uncommitted failures.

We can support the behavior we want by adding one more piece of information to the `Failure` case of `Result`—a `Boolean` value indicating whether the parser failed in a committed state:

```
case class Failure(get: ParseError,
                   isCommitted: Boolean) extends Result[Nothing]
```

The implementation of `attempt` just cancels the commitment of any failures that occur. It uses a helper function, `uncommit`, which we can define on `Result`:

```
def attempt[A](p: Parser[A]): Parser[A] =
  s => p(s).uncommit

def uncommit: Result[A] = this match {
  case Failure(e,true) => Failure(e,false)
  case _ => this
}
```

Now the implementation of `or` can simply check the `isCommitted` flag before running the second parser. In the parser x `or` y, if x succeeds, then the whole thing succeeds. If x fails in a committed state, we fail early and skip running y. Otherwise, if x fails in an uncommitted state, we run y and ignore the result of x:

```
def or[A](x: Parser[A], y: => Parser[A]): Parser[A] =
  s => x(s) match {
    case Failure(e,false) => y(s)          ←——  Committed failure or
    case r => r                                  success skips running y.
  }
```

9.6.5 *Context-sensitive parsing*

Now for the final primitive in our list, `flatMap`. Recall that `flatMap` enables context-sensitive parsers by allowing the selection of a second parser to depend on the result of the first parser. The implementation is simple—we advance the location before calling the second parser. Again we use a helper function, `advanceBy`, on `Location`. There is one subtlety—if the first parser consumes any characters, we ensure that the second parser is committed, using a helper function, `addCommit`, on `ParseError`.

Listing 9.3 Using `addCommit` to make sure our parser is committed

```
def flatMap[A,B](f: Parser[A])(g: A => Parser[B]): Parser[B] =      Advance the source
  s => f(s) match {                                                 location before calling
    case Success(a,n) => g(a)(s.advanceBy(n))    ←——————            the second parser.
                         .addCommit(n != 0)
Commit if the    ————→   .advanceSuccess(n)      ←——  If successful, we increment the
first parser has                                      number of characters consumed
consumed any     case e@Failure(_,_) => e             by n, to account for characters
characters.  }                                        already consumed by f.
```

advanceBy has the obvious implementation. We simply increment the offset:

```
def advanceBy(n: Int): Location =
  copy(offset = offset+n)
```

Likewise, addCommit, defined on ParseError, is straightforward:

```
def addCommit(isCommitted: Boolean): Result[A] = this match {
  case Failure(e,c) => Failure(e, c || isCommitted)
  case _ => this
}
```

And finally, advanceSuccess increments the number of consumed characters of a successful result. We want the total number of characters consumed by flatMap to be the sum of the consumed characters of the parser f and the parser produced by g. We use advanceSuccess on the result of g to ensure this:

```
def advanceSuccess(n: Int): Result[A] = this match {
  case Success(a,m) => Success(a,n+m)
  case _ => this          ←
}                                    If unsuccessful, leave
                                     the result alone.
```

EXERCISE 9.15

Implement the rest of the primitives, including run, using this representation of Parser, and try running your JSON parser on various inputs.[19]

EXERCISE 9.16

Come up with a nice way of formatting a ParseError for human consumption. There are a lot of choices to make, but a key insight is that we typically want to combine or group labels attached to the same location when presenting the error as a String for display.

EXERCISE 9.17

Hard: The slice combinator is still less efficient than it could be. For instance, many(char('a')).slice will still build up a List[Char], only to discard it. Can you think of a way of modifying the Parser representation to make slicing more efficient?

---

[19] You'll find, unfortunately, that it causes stack overflow for large inputs (for instance, [1,2,3,...10000]). One simple solution to this is to provide a specialized implementation of many that avoids using a stack frame for each element of the list being built up. So long as any combinators that do repetition are defined in terms of many (which they all can be), this solves the problem. See the answers for discussion of more general approaches.

EXERCISE 9.18

Some information is lost when we combine parsers with the or combinator. If both parsers fail, we're only keeping the errors from the second parser. But we might want to show both error messages, or choose the error from whichever branch got *furthest* without failing. Change the representation of ParseError to keep track of errors that occurred in other branches of the parser.

9.7 *Summary*

In this chapter, we introduced *algebraic design*, an approach to writing combinator libraries, and we used it to design a parser library and to implement a JSON parser. Along the way, we discovered a number of combinators similar to what we saw in previous chapters, and these were again related by familiar laws. In part 3, we'll finally understand the nature of the connection between these libraries and learn how to abstract over their common structure.

This is the final chapter in part 2. We hope you've come away from these chapters with a basic sense of how functional design can proceed, and more importantly, we hope these chapters have motivated you to try your hand at designing your own functional libraries, for whatever domains interest *you*. Functional design isn't something reserved only for experts—it should be part of the day-to-day work done by functional programmers at all levels of experience. Before you start on part 3, we encourage you to venture beyond this book, write some more functional code, and design some of your own libraries. Have fun, enjoy struggling with design problems that come up, and see what you discover. When you come back, a universe of patterns and abstractions awaits in part 3.

Part 3

Common structures in functional design

We've now written a number of libraries using the principles of functional design. In part 2, we saw these principles applied to a few concrete problem domains. By now you should have a good grasp of how to approach a programming problem in your own work while striving for compositionality and algebraic reasoning.

Part 3 takes a much wider perspective. We'll look at the common patterns that arise in functional programming. In part 2, we experimented with various libraries that provided concrete solutions to real-world problems, and now we want to integrate what we've learned from our experiments into abstract theories that describe the common structure among those libraries.

This kind of abstraction has a direct practical benefit: the elimination of duplicate code. We can capture abstractions as classes, interfaces, and functions that we can refer to in our actual programs. But the primary benefit is *conceptual integration*. When we recognize common structure among different solutions in different contexts, we unite all of those instances of the structure under a single definition and give it a *name*. As you gain experience with this, you can look at the general shape of a problem and say, for example: "That looks like a *monad!*" You're then already far along in finding the shape of the solution. A secondary benefit is that if other people have developed the same kind of vocabulary, you can communicate your designs to them with extraordinary efficiency.

Part 3 won't be a sequence of meandering journeys in the style of part 2. Instead, we'll begin each chapter by introducing an abstract concept, give its definition, and then tie it back to what we've seen already. The primary goal will be to train you in recognizing patterns when designing your own libraries, and to write code that takes advantage of such patterns.

Monoids

10

By the end of part 2, we were getting comfortable with considering data types in terms of their *algebras*—that is, the operations they support and the laws that govern those operations. Hopefully you will have noticed that the algebras of very different data types tend to share certain patterns in common. In this chapter, we'll begin identifying these patterns and taking advantage of them.

This chapter will be our first introduction to *purely algebraic* structures. We'll consider a simple structure, the *monoid*,[1] which is defined *only by its algebra*. Other than satisfying the same laws, instances of the monoid interface may have little or nothing to do with one another. Nonetheless, we'll see how this algebraic structure is often all we need to write useful, polymorphic functions.

We choose to start with monoids because they're simple, ubiquitous, and useful. Monoids come up all the time in everyday programming, whether we're aware of them or not. Working with lists, concatenating strings, or accumulating the results of a loop can often be phrased in terms of monoids. We'll see how monoids are useful in two ways: they facilitate parallel computation by giving us the freedom to break our problem into chunks that can be computed in parallel; and they can be composed to assemble complex calculations from simpler pieces.

10.1 What is a monoid?

Let's consider the algebra of string concatenation. We can add `"foo" + "bar"` to get `"foobar"`, and the empty string is an *identity element* for that operation. That is, if we say `(s + "")` or `("" + s)`, the result is always `s`. Furthermore, if we combine three

---

[1] The name *monoid* comes from mathematics. In category theory, it means a category with one object. This mathematical connection isn't important for our purposes in this chapter, but see the chapter notes for more information.

strings by saying $(r + s + t)$, the operation is *associative*—it doesn't matter whether we parenthesize it: $((r + s) + t)$ or $(r + (s + t))$.

The exact same rules govern integer addition. It's associative, since $(x + y) + z$ is always equal to $x + (y + z)$, and it has an identity element, 0, which "does nothing" when added to another integer. Ditto for multiplication, whose identity element is 1.

The Boolean operators `&&` and `||` are likewise associative, and they have identity elements `true` and `false`, respectively.

These are just a few simple examples, but algebras like this are virtually everywhere. The term for this kind of algebra is *monoid*. The laws of associativity and identity are collectively called the *monoid laws*. A monoid consists of the following:

- Some type `A`
- An associative binary operation, `op`, that takes two values of type `A` and combines them into one: `op(op(x,y), z) == op(x, op(y,z))` for any choice of `x: A`, `y: A, z: A`
- A value, `zero: A`, that is an identity for that operation: `op(x, zero) == x` and `op(zero, x) == x` for any `x: A`

We can express this with a Scala trait:

```
trait Monoid[A] {                           Satisfies
  def op(a1: A, a2: A): A    ←            op(op(x,y), z) == op(x, op(y,z))
  def zero: A  ←          Satisfies op(x, zero) == x
}                          and op(zero, x) == x
```

An example instance of this trait is the `String` monoid:

```
val stringMonoid = new Monoid[String] {
  def op(a1: String, a2: String) = a1 + a2
  val zero = ""
}
```

List concatenation also forms a monoid:

```
def listMonoid[A] = new Monoid[List[A]] {
  def op(a1: List[A], a2: List[A]) = a1 ++ a2
  val zero = Nil
}
```

The purely abstract nature of an algebraic structure

Notice that other than satisfying the monoid laws, the various `Monoid` instances don't have much to do with each other. The answer to the question "What is a monoid?" is simply that a monoid is a type, together with the monoid operations and a set of laws. A monoid is the algebra, and nothing more. Of course, you may build some other intuition by considering the various concrete instances, but this intuition is necessarily imprecise and nothing guarantees that all monoids you encounter will match your intuition!

EXERCISE 10.1

Give `Monoid` instances for integer addition and multiplication as well as the Boolean operators.

```
val intAddition: Monoid[Int]
val intMultiplication: Monoid[Int]
val booleanOr: Monoid[Boolean]
val booleanAnd: Monoid[Boolean]
```

EXERCISE 10.2

Give a `Monoid` instance for combining `Option` values.

```
def optionMonoid[A]: Monoid[Option[A]]
```

EXERCISE 10.3

A function having the same argument and return type is sometimes called an *endofunction*.[2] Write a monoid for endofunctions.

```
def endoMonoid[A]: Monoid[A => A]
```

EXERCISE 10.4

Use the property-based testing framework we developed in part 2 to implement a property for the monoid laws. Use your property to test the monoids we've written.

```
def monoidLaws[A](m: Monoid[A], gen: Gen[A]): Prop
```

Having versus being a monoid

There is a slight terminology mismatch between programmers and mathematicians when they talk about a type *being* a monoid versus *having* a monoid instance. As a programmer, it's tempting to think of the instance of type `Monoid[A]` as *being* a monoid. But that's not accurate terminology. The monoid is actually both things—the type together with the instance satisfying the laws. It's more accurate to say that the

---

[2] The Greek prefix *endo-* means *within*, in the sense that an endofunction's codomain is within its domain.

> **(continued)**
>
> type A *forms* a monoid under the operations defined by the `Monoid[A]` instance. Less precisely, we might say that "type A *is* a monoid," or even that "type A is *monoidal.*" In any case, the `Monoid[A]` instance is simply evidence of this fact.
>
> This is much the same as saying that the page or screen you're reading "forms a rectangle" or "is rectangular." It's less accurate to say that it "is a rectangle" (although that still makes sense), but to say that it "has a rectangle" would be strange.

Just what *is* a monoid, then? It's simply a type A and an implementation of `Monoid[A]` that satisfies the laws. Stated tersely, *a monoid is a type together with a binary operation* (op) *over that type, satisfying associativity and having an identity element* (zero).

What does this buy us? Just like any abstraction, a monoid is useful to the extent that we can write useful generic code assuming only the capabilities provided by the abstraction. Can we write any interesting programs, knowing nothing about a type other than that it forms a monoid? Absolutely! Let's look at some examples.

10.2 *Folding lists with monoids*

Monoids have an intimate connection with lists. If you look at the signatures of `fold-Left` and `foldRight` on `List`, you might notice something about the argument types:

```
def foldRight[B](z: B)(f: (A, B) => B): B
def foldLeft[B](z: B)(f: (B, A) => B): B
```

What happens when A and B are the same type?

```
def foldRight(z: A)(f: (A, A) => A): A
def foldLeft(z: A)(f: (A, A) => A): A
```

The components of a monoid fit these argument types like a glove. So if we had a list of `Strings`, we could simply pass the `op` and `zero` of the `stringMonoid` in order to reduce the list with the monoid and concatenate all the strings:

```
scala> val words = List("Hic", "Est", "Index")
words: List[String] = List(Hic, Est, Index)

scala> val s = words.foldRight(stringMonoid.zero)(stringMonoid.op)
s: String = "HicEstIndex"

scala> val t = words.foldLeft(stringMonoid.zero)(stringMonoid.op)
t: String = "HicEstIndex"
```

Note that it doesn't matter if we choose `foldLeft` or `foldRight` when folding with a monoid;[3] we should get the same result. This is precisely because the laws of associativity and identity hold. A left fold associates operations to the left, whereas a right fold associates to the right, with the identity element on the left and right respectively:

---

[3] Given that both `foldLeft` and `foldRight` have tail-recursive implementations.

```
words.foldLeft("")(_ + _)   == (("" + "Hic") + "Est") + "Index"
```

```
words.foldRight("")(_ + _) == "Hic" + ("Est" + ("Index" + ""))
```

We can write a general function concatenate that folds a list with a monoid:

```
def concatenate[A](as: List[A], m: Monoid[A]): A =
  as.foldLeft(m.zero)(m.op)
```

But what if our list has an element type that doesn't have a Monoid instance? Well, we can always map over the list to turn it into a type that does:

```
def foldMap[A,B](as: List[A], m: Monoid[B])(f: A => B): B
```

EXERCISE 10.5

Implement foldMap.

EXERCISE 10.6

Hard: The foldMap function can be implemented using either foldLeft or fold-Right. But you can also write foldLeft and foldRight using foldMap! Try it.

10.3 *Associativity and parallelism*

The fact that a monoid's operation is associative means we can choose how we fold a data structure like a list. We've already seen that operations can be associated to the left or right to reduce a list sequentially with foldLeft or foldRight. But if we have a monoid, we can reduce a list using a *balanced fold*, which can be more efficient for some operations and also allows for parallelism.

As an example, suppose we have a sequence a, b, c, d that we'd like to reduce using some monoid. Folding to the right, the combination of a, b, c, and d would look like this:

```
op(a, op(b, op(c, d)))
```

Folding to the left would look like this:

```
op(op(op(a, b), c), d)
```

But a balanced fold looks like this:

```
op(op(a, b), op(c, d))
```

Note that the balanced fold allows for parallelism, because the two inner op calls are independent and can be run simultaneously. But beyond that, the more balanced tree structure can be more efficient in cases where the cost of each op is proportional to the size of its arguments. For instance, consider the runtime performance of this expression:

```
List("lorem", "ipsum", "dolor", "sit").foldLeft("")(_ + _)
```

At every step of the fold, we're allocating the full intermediate `String` only to discard it and allocate a larger string in the next step. Recall that `String` values are immutable, and that evaluating a + b for strings a and b requires allocating a fresh character array and copying both a and b into this new array. It takes time proportional to `a.length + b.length`.

Here's a trace of the preceding expression being evaluated:

```
List("lorem", ipsum", "dolor", "sit").foldLeft("")(_ + _)
List("ipsum", "dolor", "sit").foldLeft("lorem")(_ + _)
List("dolor", "sit").foldLeft("loremipsum")(_ + _)
List("sit").foldLeft("loremipsumdolor")(_ + _)
List().foldLeft("loremipsumdolorsit")(_ + _)
"loremipsumdolorsit"
```

Note the intermediate strings being created and then immediately discarded. A more efficient strategy would be to combine the sequence by halves, which we call a *balanced fold*—we first construct `"loremipsum"` and `"dolorsit"`, and then add those together.

EXERCISE 10.7

Implement a `foldMap` for `IndexedSeq`.[4] Your implementation should use the strategy of splitting the sequence in two, recursively processing each half, and then adding the answers together with the monoid.

```
def foldMapV[A,B](v: IndexedSeq[A], m: Monoid[B])(f: A => B): B
```

EXERCISE 10.8

Hard: Also implement a *parallel* version of `foldMap` using the library we developed in chapter 7. Hint: Implement par, a combinator to promote `Monoid[A]` to a `Monoid[Par[A]]`,[5] and then use this to implement parFoldMap.

```
import fpinscala.parallelism.Nonblocking._

def par[A](m: Monoid[A]): Monoid[Par[A]]
def parFoldMap[A,B](v: IndexedSeq[A], m: Monoid[B])(f: A => B): Par[B]
```

---

[4] Recall that `IndexedSeq` is the interface for immutable data structures supporting efficient random access. It also has efficient `splitAt` and `length` methods.

[5] The ability to "lift" a `Monoid` into the `Par` context is something we'll discuss more generally in chapters 11 and 12.

■ **EXERCISE 10.9**

Hard: Use `foldMap` to detect whether a given `IndexedSeq[Int]` is ordered. You'll need to come up with a creative `Monoid`.

10.4 *Example: Parallel parsing*

As a nontrivial use case, let's say that we wanted to count the number of words in a `String`. This is a fairly simple parsing problem. We could scan the string character by character, looking for whitespace and counting up the number of runs of consecutive nonwhitespace characters. Parsing sequentially like that, the parser state could be as simple as tracking whether the last character seen was a whitespace.

But imagine doing this not for just a short string, but an enormous text file, possibly too big to fit in memory on a single machine. It would be nice if we could work with chunks of the file in parallel. The strategy would be to split the file into manageable chunks, process several chunks in parallel, and then combine the results. In that case, the parser state needs to be slightly more complicated, and we need to be able to combine intermediate results regardless of whether the section we're looking at is at the beginning, middle, or end of the file. In other words, we want the combining operation to be associative.

To keep things simple and concrete, let's consider a short string and pretend it's a large file:

```
"lorem ipsum dolor sit amet, "
```

If we split this string roughly in half, we might split it in the middle of a word. In the case of our string, that would yield `"lorem ipsum do"` and `"lor sit amet, "`. When we add up the results of counting the words in these strings, we want to avoid double-counting the word `dolor`. Clearly, just counting the words as an `Int` isn't sufficient. We need to find a data structure that can handle partial results like the half words `do` and `lor`, and can track the complete words seen so far, like `ipsum`, `sit`, and `amet`.

The partial result of the word count could be represented by an algebraic data type:

```
sealed trait WC
case class Stub(chars: String) extends WC
case class Part(lStub: String, words: Int, rStub: String) extends WC
```

A `Stub` is the simplest case, where we haven't seen any complete words yet. But a `Part` keeps the number of complete words we've seen so far, in `words`. The value `lStub` holds any partial word we've seen to the left of those words, and `rStub` holds any partial word on the right.

For example, counting over the string `"lorem ipsum do"` would result in `Part` `("lorem", 1, "do")` since there's one certainly complete word, `"ipsum"`. And since there's no whitespace to the left of `lorem` or right of `do`, we can't be sure if they're complete words, so we don't count them yet. Counting over `"lor sit amet, "` would result in `Part("lor", 2, "")`.

■   **EXERCISE 10.10**

Write a monoid instance for `WC` and make sure that it meets the monoid laws.

val wcMonoid: Monoid[WC]

■   **EXERCISE 10.11**

Use the `WC` monoid to implement a function that counts words in a `String` by recursively splitting it into substrings and counting the words in those substrings.

Monoid homomorphisms

If you have your law-discovering cap on while reading this chapter, you may notice that there's a law that holds for some functions *between* monoids. Take the `String` concatenation monoid and the integer addition monoid. If you take the lengths of two strings and add them up, it's the same as taking the length of the concatenation of those two strings:

```
"foo".length + "bar".length == ("foo" + "bar").length
```

Here, `length` is a function from `String` to `Int` that *preserves the monoid structure*. Such a function is called a *monoid homomorphism*.[6] A monoid homomorphism `f` between monoids `M` and `N` obeys the following general law for all values `x` and `y`:

```
M.op(f(x), f(y)) == f(N.op(x, y))
```

The same law should hold for the homomorphism from `String` to `WC` in the present exercise.

This property can be useful when designing your own libraries. If two types that your library uses are monoids, and there exist functions between them, it's a good idea to think about whether those functions are expected to preserve the monoid structure and to check the monoid homomorphism law with automated tests.

---

[6] *Homomorphism* comes from Greek, *homo* meaning "same" and *morphe* meaning "shape."

Sometimes there will be a homomorphism in both directions between two monoids. If they satisfy a *monoid isomorphism* (*iso-* meaning *equal*), we say that the two monoids are isomorphic. A monoid isomorphism between M and N has two homomorphisms f and g, where both f andThen g and g andThen f are an identity function.

For example, the String and List[Char] monoids with concatenation are isomorphic. The two Boolean monoids (false, ||) and (true, &&) are also isomorphic, via the ! (negation) function.

10.5 *Foldable data structures*

In chapter 3, we implemented the data structures List and Tree, both of which could be folded. In chapter 5, we wrote Stream, a lazy structure that also can be folded much like a List can, and now we've just written a fold for IndexedSeq.

When we're writing code that needs to process data contained in one of these structures, we often don't care about the shape of the structure (whether it's a tree or a list), or whether it's lazy or not, or provides efficient random access, and so forth.

For example, if we have a structure full of integers and want to calculate their sum, we can use foldRight:

```
ints.foldRight(0)(_ + _)
```

Looking at just this code snippet, we shouldn't have to care about the type of ints. It could be a Vector, a Stream, or a List, or anything at all with a foldRight method. We can capture this commonality in a trait:

```
trait Foldable[F[_]] {
  def foldRight[A,B](as: F[A])(z: B)(f: (A,B) => B): B
  def foldLeft[A,B](as: F[A])(z: B)(f: (B,A) => B): B
  def foldMap[A,B](as: F[A])(f: A => B)(mb: Monoid[B]): B
  def concatenate[A](as: F[A])(m: Monoid[A]): A =
    foldLeft(as)(m.zero)(m.op)
}
```

Here we're abstracting over a type constructor F, much like we did with the Parser type in the previous chapter. We write it as F[_], where the underscore indicates that F is not a type but a *type constructor* that takes one type argument. Just like functions that take other functions as arguments are called higher-order functions, something like Foldable is a *higher-order type constructor* or a *higher-kinded type*.[7]

---

[7] Just like values and functions have types, types and type constructors have *kinds*. Scala uses kinds to track how many type arguments a type constructor takes, whether it's co- or contravariant in those arguments, and what the kinds of those arguments are.

■—(**EXERCISE 10.12**)————————————————————————————

Implement Foldable[List], Foldable[IndexedSeq], and Foldable[Stream]. Remember that foldRight, foldLeft, and foldMap can all be implemented in terms of each other, but that might not be the most efficient implementation.

■—(**EXERCISE 10.13**)————————————————————————————

Recall the binary Tree data type from chapter 3. Implement a Foldable instance for it.

```
sealed trait Tree[+A]
case object Leaf[A](value: A) extends Tree[A]
case class Branch[A](left: Tree[A], right: Tree[A]) extends Tree[A]
```

■—(**EXERCISE 10.14**)————————————————————————————

Write a Foldable[Option] instance.

■—(**EXERCISE 10.15**)————————————————————————————

Any Foldable structure can be turned into a List. Write this conversion in a generic way:

```
def toList[A](fa: F[A]): List[A]
```

10.6   *Composing monoids*

The Monoid abstraction in itself is not all that compelling, and with the generalized foldMap it's only slightly more interesting. The real power of monoids comes from the fact that they *compose*.

This means, for example, that if types A and B are monoids, then the tuple type (A, B) is also a monoid (called their *product*).

■—(**EXERCISE 10.16**)————————————————————————————

Prove it. Notice that your implementation of op is obviously associative so long as A.op and B.op are both associative.

```
def productMonoid[A,B](A: Monoid[A], B: Monoid[B]): Monoid[(A,B)]
```

10.6.1 *Assembling more complex monoids*

Some data structures form interesting monoids as long as the types of the elements they contain also form monoids. For instance, there's a monoid for merging key-value Maps, as long as the value type is a monoid.

Listing 10.1   Merging key-value Maps

```
def mapMergeMonoid[K,V](V: Monoid[V]): Monoid[Map[K, V]] =
  new Monoid[Map[K, V]] {
    def zero = Map[K,V]()
    def op(a: Map[K, V], b: Map[K, V]) =
      (a.keySet ++ b.keySet).foldLeft(zero) { (acc,k) =>
        acc.updated(k, V.op(a.getOrElse(k, V.zero),
                            b.getOrElse(k, V.zero)))
      }
  }
```

Using this simple combinator, we can assemble more complex monoids fairly easily:

```
scala> val M: Monoid[Map[String, Map[String, Int]]] =
     | mapMergeMonoid(mapMergeMonoid(intAddition))
M: Monoid[Map[String, Map[String, Int]]] = $anon$1@21dfac82
```

This allows us to combine nested expressions using the monoid, with no additional programming:

```
scala> val m1 = Map("o1" -> Map("i1" -> 1, "i2" -> 2))
m1: Map[String,Map[String,Int]] = Map(o1 -> Map(i1 -> 1, i2 -> 2))

scala> val m2 = Map("o1" -> Map("i2" -> 3))
m2: Map[String,Map[String,Int]] = Map(o1 -> Map(i2 -> 3))

scala> val m3 = M.op(m1, m2)
m3: Map[String,Map[String,Int]] = Map(o1 -> Map(i1 -> 1, i2 -> 5))
```

■ **EXERCISE 10.17** ───

Write a monoid instance for functions whose results are monoids.

```
def functionMonoid[A,B](B: Monoid[B]): Monoid[A => B]
```

■ **EXERCISE 10.18** ───

A bag is like a set, except that it's represented by a map that contains one entry per element with that element as the key, and the value under that key is the number of times the element appears in the bag. For example:

```
scala> bag(Vector("a", "rose", "is", "a", "rose"))
res0: Map[String,Int] = Map(a -> 2, rose -> 2, is -> 1)
```

Use monoids to compute a "bag" from an `IndexedSeq`.

```
def bag[A](as: IndexedSeq[A]): Map[A, Int]
```

10.6.2 *Using composed monoids to fuse traversals*

The fact that multiple monoids can be composed into one means that we can perform multiple calculations simultaneously when folding a data structure. For example, we can take the length and sum of a list at the same time in order to calculate the mean:

```
scala> val m = productMonoid(intAddition, intAddition)
m: Monoid[(Int, Int)] = $anon$1@8ff557a

scala> val p = listFoldable.foldMap(List(1,2,3,4))(a => (1, a))(m)
p: (Int, Int) = (4, 10)

scala> val mean = p._1 / p._2.toDouble
mean: Double = 2.5
```

It can be tedious to assemble monoids by hand using `productMonoid` and `foldMap`. Part of the problem is that we're building up the `Monoid` separately from the mapping function of `foldMap`, and we must manually keep these "aligned" as we did here. But we can create a combinator library that makes it much more convenient to assemble these composed monoids and define complex computations that may be parallelized and run in a single pass. Such a library is beyond the scope of this chapter, but see the chapter notes for a brief discussion and links to further material.

10.7 *Summary*

Our goal in part 3 is to get you accustomed to working with more abstract structures, and to develop the ability to recognize them. In this chapter, we introduced one of the simplest purely algebraic abstractions, the monoid. When you start looking for it, you'll find ample opportunity to exploit the monoidal structure of your own libraries. The associative property enables folding any `Foldable` data type and gives the flexibility of doing so in parallel. Monoids are also compositional, and you can use them to assemble folds in a declarative and reusable way.

`Monoid` has been our first purely abstract algebra, defined only in terms of its abstract operations and the laws that govern them. We saw how we can still write useful functions that know nothing about their arguments except that their type forms a monoid. This more abstract mode of thinking is something we'll develop further in the rest of part 3. We'll consider other purely algebraic interfaces and show how they encapsulate common patterns that we've repeated throughout this book.

Monads

In the previous chapter, we introduced a simple algebraic structure, the monoid. This was our first instance of a completely abstract, purely algebraic interface, and it led us to think about interfaces in a new way. A useful interface may be defined only by a collection of operations related by laws.

In this chapter, we'll continue this mode of thinking and apply it to the problem of factoring out code duplication across some of the libraries we wrote in parts 1 and 2. We'll discover two new abstract interfaces, Functor and Monad, and get more general experience with spotting these sorts of abstract structures in our code.[1]

11.1 Functors: generalizing the map function

In parts 1 and 2, we implemented several different combinator libraries. In each case, we proceeded by writing a small set of primitives and then a number of combinators defined purely in terms of those primitives. We noted some similarities between derived combinators across the libraries we wrote. For instance, we implemented a map function for each data type, to lift a function taking one argument "into the context of" some data type. For Gen, Parser, and Option, the type signatures were as follows:

```
def map[A,B](ga: Gen[A])(f: A => B): Gen[B]

def map[A,B](pa: Parser[A])(f: A => B): Parser[B]

def map[A,B](oa: Option[A])(f: A => B): Option[A]
```

---

[1] The names *functor* and *monad* come from the branch of mathematics called *category theory*, but it isn't necessary to have any category theory background to follow the content in this chapter. You may be interested in following some of the references in the chapter notes for more information.

These type signatures differ only in the concrete data type (Gen, Parser, or Option). We can capture as a Scala trait the idea of "a data type that implements map":

```
trait Functor[F[_]] {
  def map[A,B](fa: F[A])(f: A => B): F[B]
}
```

Here we've parameterized map on the type constructor, F[_], much like we did with Foldable in the previous chapter.[2] Instead of picking a particular F[_], like Gen or Parser, the Functor trait is parametric in the choice of F. Here's an instance for List:

```
val listFunctor = new Functor[List] {
  def map[A,B](as: List[A])(f: A => B): List[B] = as map f
}
```

We say that a type constructor like List (or Option, or F) is a functor, and the Functor[F] instance constitutes proof that F is in fact a functor.

What can we do with this abstraction? As we did in several places throughout this book, we can discover useful functions just by *playing* with the operations of the interface, in a purely algebraic way. You may want to pause here to see what (if any) useful operations you can define only in terms of map.

Let's look at one example. If we have F[(A, B)] where F is a functor, we can "distribute" the F over the pair to get (F[A], F[B]):

```
trait Functor[F[_]] {
  ...
  def distribute[A,B](fab: F[(A, B)]): (F[A], F[B]) =
    (map(fab)(_._1), map(fab)(_._2))
}
```

We wrote this just by following the types, but let's think about what it *means* for concrete data types like List, Gen, Option, and so on. For example, if we distribute a List[(A, B)], we get two lists of the same length, one with all the As and the other with all the Bs. That operation is sometimes called *unzip*. So we just wrote a generic unzip function that works not just for lists, but for any functor!

And when we have an operation on a product like this, we should see if we can construct the opposite operation over a sum or coproduct:

```
def codistribute[A,B](e: Either[F[A], F[B]]): F[Either[A, B]] =
  e match {
    case Left(fa) => map(fa)(Left(_))
    case Right(fb) => map(fb)(Right(_))
  }
```

What does codistribute mean for Gen? If we have either a generator for A or a generator for B, we can construct a generator that produces either A or B depending on which generator we actually have.

---

[2] Recall that a *type constructor* is applied to a type to produce a type. For example, List is a type constructor, not a type. There are no values of type List, but we can apply it to the type Int to produce the type List[Int]. Likewise, Parser can be applied to String to yield Parser[String].

We just came up with two really general and potentially useful combinators based purely on the abstract interface of `Functor`, and we can reuse them for any type that allows an implementation of `map`.

11.1.1 Functor laws

Whenever we create an abstraction like `Functor`, we should consider not only what abstract methods it should have, but which *laws* we expect to hold for the implementations. The laws you stipulate for an abstraction are entirely up to you,[3] and of course Scala won't enforce any of these laws. But laws are important for two reasons:

- Laws help an interface form a new semantic level whose algebra may be reasoned about *independently* of the instances. For example, when we take the product of a `Monoid[A]` and a `Monoid[B]` to form a `Monoid[(A,B)]`, the monoid laws let us conclude that the "fused" monoid operation is also associative. We don't need to know anything about A and B to conclude this.
- More concretely, we often rely on laws when writing various combinators derived from the functions of some abstract interface like `Functor`. We'll see examples of this later.

For `Functor`, we'll stipulate the familiar law we first introduced in chapter 7 for our `Par` data type:[4]

```
map(x)(a => a) == x
```

In other words, mapping over a structure x with the identity function should itself be an identity. This law is quite natural, and we noticed later in part 2 that this law was satisfied by the `map` functions of other types besides `Par`. This law (and its corollaries given by parametricity) capture the requirement that `map(x)` "preserves the structure" of x. Implementations satisfying this law are restricted from doing strange things like throwing exceptions, removing the first element of a `List`, converting a `Some` to `None`, and so on. Only the elements of the structure are modified by `map`; the shape or structure itself is left intact. Note that this law holds for `List`, `Option`, `Par`, `Gen`, and most other data types that define `map`!

To give a concrete example of this preservation of structure, we can consider `distribute` and `codistribute`, defined earlier. Here are their signatures again:

```
def distribute[A,B](fab: F[(A, B)]): (F[A], F[B])
```

```
def codistribute[A,B](e: Either[F[A], F[B]]): F[Either[A, B]]
```

Since we know nothing about F other than that it's a functor, the law assures us that the returned values will have the same shape as the arguments. If the input to `distribute` is a list of pairs, the returned pair of lists will be of the same length as the

---

[3] Though if you're going to borrow the name of some existing mathematical abstraction like functor or monoid, we recommend using the laws already specified by mathematics.

[4] This law also comes from the mathematical definition of functor.

input, and corresponding elements will appear in the same order. This kind of algebraic reasoning can potentially save us a lot of work, since we don't have to write separate tests for these properties.

11.2 *Monads: generalizing the flatMap and unit functions*

Functor is just one of many abstractions that we can factor out of our libraries. But Functor isn't too compelling, as there aren't many useful operations that can be defined purely in terms of map. Next, we'll look at a more interesting interface, Monad. Using this interface, we can implement a number of useful operations, once and for all, factoring out what would otherwise be duplicated code. And it comes with laws with which we can reason that our libraries work the way we expect.

Recall that for several of the data types in this book so far, we implemented map2 to "lift" a function taking two arguments. For Gen, Parser, and Option, the map2 function could be implemented as follows.

Listing 11.1   Implementing map2 for Gen, Parser, and Option

Makes a generator of a random C that runs random generators fa and fb, combining their results with the function f.

```
def map2[A,B,C](
    fa: Gen[A], fb: Gen[B])(f: (A,B) => C): Gen[C] =
  fa flatMap (a => fb map (b => f(a,b)))
```

Makes a parser that produces C by combining the results of parsers fa and fb with the function f.

```
def map2[A,B,C](
    fa: Parser[A], fb: Parser[B])(f: (A,B) => C): Parser[C] =
  fa flatMap (a => fb map (b => f(a,b)))
```

Combines two Options with the function f, if both have a value; otherwise returns None.

```
def map2[A,B,C](
    fa: Option[A], fb: Option[B])(f: (A,B) => C): Option[C] =
  fa flatMap (a => fb map (b => f(a,b)))
```

These functions have more in common than just the name. In spite of operating on data types that seemingly have nothing to do with one another, the implementations are identical! The only thing that differs is the particular data type being operated on. This confirms what we've suspected all along—that these are particular instances of some more general pattern. We should be able to exploit that fact to avoid repeating ourselves. For example, we should be able to write map2 once and for all in such a way that it can be reused for all of these data types.

We've made the code duplication particularly obvious here by choosing uniform names for our functions, taking the arguments in the same order, and so on. It may be more difficult to spot in your everyday work. But the more libraries you write, the better you'll get at identifying patterns that you can factor out into common abstractions.

11.2.1 The Monad trait

What unites `Parser`, `Gen`, `Par`, `Option`, and many of the other data types we've looked at is that they're *monads*. Much like we did with `Functor` and `Foldable`, we can come up with a Scala trait for `Monad` that defines `map2` and numerous other functions once and for all, rather than having to duplicate their definitions for every concrete data type.

In part 2 of this book, we concerned ourselves with individual data types, finding a minimal set of primitive operations from which we could derive a large number of useful combinators. We'll do the same kind of thing here to refine an *abstract* interface to a small set of primitives.

Let's start by introducing a new trait, called `Mon` for now. Since we know we want to eventually define `map2`, let's go ahead and add that.

Listing 11.2 Creating a `Mon` trait for `map2`

```
trait Mon[F[_]] {
  def map2[A,B,C](fa: F[A], fb: F[B])(f: (A,B) => C): F[C] =
    fa flatMap (a => fb map (b => f(a,b)))
}
```

> This won't compile, since `map` and `flatMap` are undefined in this context.

Here we've just taken the implementation of `map2` and changed `Parser`, `Gen`, and `Option` to the polymorphic F of the `Mon[F]` interface in the signature.[5] But in this polymorphic context, this won't compile! We don't know *anything* about F here, so we certainly don't know how to `flatMap` or `map` over an `F[A]`.

What we can do is simply *add* `map` and `flatMap` to the `Mon` interface and keep them abstract. The syntax for calling these functions changes a bit (we can't use infix syntax anymore), but the structure is otherwise the same.

Listing 11.3 Adding `map` and `flatMap` to our trait

```
trait Mon[F[_]] {
  def map[A,B](fa: F[A])(f: A => B): F[B]
  def flatMap[A,B](fa: F[A])(f: A => F[B]): F[B]

  def map2[A,B,C](
      fa: F[A], fb: F[B])(f: (A,B) => C): F[C] =
    flatMap(fa)(a => map(fb)(b => f(a,b)))
}
```

> We're calling the (abstract) functions `map` and `flatMap` in the `Mon` interface.

This translation was rather mechanical. We just inspected the implementation of `map2`, and added all the functions it called, `map` and `flatMap`, as suitably abstract methods on our interface. This trait will now compile, but before we declare victory and move on to defining instances of `Mon[List]`, `Mon[Parser]`, `Mon[Option]`, and so on,

---

[5] Our decision to call the type constructor argument F here was arbitrary. We could have called this argument `Foo`, `w00t`, or `Blah2`, though by convention, we usually give type constructor arguments one-letter uppercase names, such as F, G, and H, or sometimes M and N, or P and Q.

let's see if we can refine our set of primitives. Our current set of primitives is `map` and `flatMap`, from which we can derive `map2`. Is `flatMap` and `map` a minimal set of primitives? Well, the data types that implemented `map2` all had a `unit`, and we know that `map` can be implemented in terms of `flatMap` and `unit`. For example, on `Gen`:

```
def map[A,B](f: A => B): Gen[B] =
  flatMap(a => unit(f(a)))
```

So let's pick `unit` and `flatMap` as our minimal set. We'll unify under a single concept all data types that have these functions defined. The trait is called `Monad`, it has `flatMap` and `unit` abstract, and it provides default implementations for `map` and `map2`.

Listing 11.4   Creating our `Monad` trait

```
trait Monad[F[_]] extends Functor[F] {
  def unit[A](a: => A): F[A]
  def flatMap[A,B](ma: F[A])(f: A => F[B]): F[B]

  def map[A,B](ma: F[A])(f: A => B): F[B] =
    flatMap(ma)(a => unit(f(a)))
  def map2[A,B,C](ma: F[A], mb: F[B])(f: (A, B) => C): F[C] =
    flatMap(ma)(a => map(mb)(b => f(a, b)))
}
```

Since `Monad` provides a default implementation of `map`, it can extend `Functor`. All monads are functors, but not all functors are monads.

The name *monad*

We could have called `Monad` anything at all, like `FlatMappable`, `Unicorn`, or `Bicycle`. But *monad* is already a perfectly good name in common use. The name comes from category theory, a branch of mathematics that has inspired a lot of functional programming concepts. The name *monad* is intentionally similar to *monoid*, and the two concepts are related in a deep way. See the chapter notes for more information.

To tie this back to a concrete data type, we can implement the `Monad` instance for `Gen`.

Listing 11.5   Implementing `Monad` for `Gen`

```
object Monad {
  val genMonad = new Monad[Gen] {
    def unit[A](a: => A): Gen[A] = Gen.unit(a)
    def flatMap[A,B](ma: Gen[A])(f: A => Gen[B]): Gen[B] =
      ma flatMap f
  }
}
```

We only need to implement `unit` and `flatMap`, and we get `map` and `map2` at no additional cost. We've implemented them once and for all, for any data type for which it's possible to supply an instance of `Monad`! But we're just getting started. There are many more functions that we can implement once and for all in this manner.

EXERCISE 11.1

Write monad instances for `Par`, `Parser`, `Option`, `Stream`, and `List`.

EXERCISE 11.2

Hard: `State` looks like it would be a monad too, but it takes two type arguments and you need a type constructor of one argument to implement `Monad`. Try to implement a `State` monad, see what issues you run into, and think about possible solutions. We'll discuss the solution later in this chapter.

11.3 *Monadic combinators*

Now that we have our primitives for monads, we can look back at previous chapters and see if there were some other functions that we implemented for each of our monadic data types. Many of them can be implemented once for all monads, so let's do that now.

EXERCISE 11.3

The `sequence` and `traverse` combinators should be pretty familiar to you by now, and your implementations of them from various prior chapters are probably all very similar. Implement them once and for all on `Monad[F]`.

```
def sequence[A](lma: List[F[A]]): F[List[A]]
def traverse[A,B](la: List[A])(f: A => F[B]): F[List[B]]
```

One combinator we saw for `Gen` and `Parser` was `listOfN`, which allowed us to replicate a parser or generator n times to get a parser or generator of lists of that length. We can implement this combinator for all monads F by adding it to our `Monad` trait. We should also give it a more generic name such as `replicateM` (meaning "replicate in a monad").

EXERCISE 11.4

Implement `replicateM`.

```
def replicateM[A](n: Int, ma: F[A]): F[List[A]]
```

■ ── **EXERCISE 11.5** ──

Think about how `replicateM` will behave for various choices of F. For example, how does it behave in the `List` monad? What about `Option`? Describe in your own words the general meaning of `replicateM`.

There was also a combinator for our `Gen` data type, `product`, to take two generators and turn them into a generator of pairs, and we did the same thing for `Par` computations. In both cases, we implemented `product` in terms of map2. So we can definitely write it generically for any monad F:

```
def product[A,B](ma: F[A], mb: F[B]): F[(A, B)] = map2(ma, mb)((_, _))
```

We don't have to restrict ourselves to combinators that we've seen already. It's important to *play around* and see what we find.

■ ── **EXERCISE 11.6** ──

Hard: Here's an example of a function we haven't seen before. Implement the function `filterM`. It's a bit like `filter`, except that instead of a function from A => Boolean, we have an A => F[Boolean]. (Replacing various ordinary functions like this with the monadic equivalent often yields interesting results.) Implement this function, and then think about what it means for various data types.

```
def filterM[A](ms: List[A])(f: A => F[Boolean]): F[List[A]]
```

The combinators we've seen here are only a small sample of the full library that `Monad` lets us implement once and for all. We'll see some more examples in chapter 13.

11.4 *Monad laws*

In this section, we'll introduce laws to govern our `Monad` interface.[6] Certainly we'd expect the functor laws to also hold for `Monad`, since a `Monad[F]` *is* a `Functor[F]`, but what else do we expect? What laws should constrain `flatMap` and `unit`?

11.4.1 *The associative law*

For example, if we wanted to combine three monadic values into one, which two should we combine first? Should it matter? To answer this question, let's for a moment

───

[6] These laws, once again, come from the concept of monads from category theory, but a background in category theory isn't necessary to understand this section.

take a step down from the abstract level and look at a simple concrete example using the `Gen` monad.

Say we're testing a product order system and we need to mock up some orders. We might have an `Order` case class and a generator for that class.

Listing 11.6 Defining our `Order` class

```
case class Order(item: Item, quantity: Int)
case class Item(name: String, price: Double)

val genOrder: Gen[Order] = for {
  name <- Gen.stringN(3)            ←————————— A random string of length 3
  price <- Gen.uniform.map(_ * 10)  ←————————— A uniform random Double
  quantity <- Gen.choose(1,100)     ←—————————   between 0 and 10
} yield Order(Item(name, price), quantity)       A random Int between 0 and 100
```

Here we're generating the `Item` inline (from `name` and `price`), but there might be places where we want to generate an `Item` separately. So we could pull that into its own generator:

```
val genItem: Gen[Item] = for {
  name <- Gen.stringN(3)
  price <- Gen.uniform.map(_ * 10)
} yield Item(name, price)
```

Then we can use that in `genOrder`:

```
val genOrder: Gen[Order] = for {
  item <- genItem
  quantity <- Gen.choose(1,100)
} yield Order(item, quantity)
```

And that should do exactly the same thing, right? It seems safe to assume that. But not so fast. How can we be sure? It's not exactly the same code.

Let's expand both implementations of `genOrder` into calls to `map` and `flatMap` to better see what's going on. In the former case, the translation is straightforward:

```
Gen.nextString.flatMap(name =>
Gen.nextDouble.flatMap(price =>
Gen.nextInt.map(quantity =>
  Order(Item(name, price), quantity))))
```

But the second case looks like this (inlining the call to `genItem`):

```
Gen.nextString.flatMap(name =>
Gen.nextInt.map(price =>
  Item(name, price))).flatMap(item =>
Gen.nextInt.map(quantity =>
  Order(item, quantity)
```

Once we expand them, it's clear that those two implementations aren't identical. And yet when we look at the for-comprehension, it seems perfectly reasonable to assume that the two implementations do exactly the same thing. In fact, it would be surprising and weird if they didn't. It's because we're assuming that `flatMap` obeys an *associative law*.

```
x.flatMap(f).flatMap(g) == x.flatMap(a => f(a).flatMap(g))
```

And this law should hold for all values x, f, and g of the appropriate types—not just for `Gen` but for `Parser`, `Option`, and any other monad.

11.4.2 *Proving the associative law for a specific monad*

Let's *prove* that this law holds for `Option`. All we have to do is substitute `None` or `Some(v)` for x in the preceding equation and expand both sides of it.

We start with the case where x is `None`, and then both sides of the equal sign are `None`:

```
None.flatMap(f).flatMap(g) == None.flatMap(a => f(a).flatMap(g))
```

Since `None.flatMap(f)` is `None` for all f, this simplifies to

```
None == None
```

Thus, the law holds if x is `None`. What about if x is `Some(v)` for an arbitrary choice of v? In that case, we have

Original law

Apply definition of `Some(v).flatMap(...)`

```
x.flatMap(f).flatMap(g)            == x.flatMap(a => f(a).flatMap(g))
Some(v).flatMap(f).flatMap(g) == Some(v).flatMap(a => f(a).flatMap(g))
f(v).flatMap(g)                    == (a => f(a).flatMap(g))(v)
f(v).flatMap(g)                    == f(v).flatMap(g)
```

Substitute Some(v) for x on both sides

Simplify function application (a => ..)(v)

Thus, the law also holds when x is `Some(v)` for any v. We're now done, as we've shown that the law holds when x is `None` or when x is `Some`, and these are the only two possibilities for `Option`.

KLEISLI COMPOSITION: A CLEARER VIEW ON THE ASSOCIATIVE LAW

It's not so easy to see that the law we just discussed is an *associative* law. Remember the associative law for monoids? That was clear:

```
op(op(x,y), z) == op(x, op(y,z))
```

But our associative law for monads doesn't look anything like that! Fortunately, there's a way we can make the law clearer if we consider not the monadic values of types like `F[A]`, but monadic *functions* of types like `A => F[B]`. Functions like that are called *Kleisli arrows,*[7] and they can be composed with one another:

```
def compose[A,B,C](f: A => F[B], g: B => F[C]): A => F[C]
```

---

[7] *Kleisli arrow* comes from category theory and is named after the Swiss mathematician Heinrich Kleisli.

■ EXERCISE 11.7

Implement the Kleisli composition function `compose`.

We can now state the associative law for monads in a much more symmetric way:

```
compose(compose(f, g), h) == compose(f, compose(g, h))
```

■ EXERCISE 11.8

Hard: Implement `flatMap` in terms of `compose`. It seems that we've found another minimal set of monad combinators: `compose` and `unit`.

□ EXERCISE 11.9

Show that the two formulations of the associative law, the one in terms of `flatMap` and the one in terms of `compose`, are equivalent.

11.4.3 *The identity laws*

The other monad law is now pretty easy to see. Just like `zero` was an *identity element* for `append` in a monoid, there's an identity element for `compose` in a monad. Indeed, that's exactly what `unit` is, and that's why we chose this name for this operation:[8]

```
def unit[A](a: => A): F[A]
```

This function has the right type to be passed as an argument to `compose`.[9] The effect should be that anything composed with `unit` is that same thing. This usually takes the form of two laws, *left identity* and *right identity*:

```
compose(f, unit) == f
compose(unit, f) == f
```

We can also state these laws in terms of `flatMap`, but they're less clear that way:

```
flatMap(x)(unit) == x
flatMap(unit(y))(f) == f(y)
```

---

[8] The name *unit* is often used in mathematics to mean an identity for some operation.

[9] Not quite, since it takes a non-strict A to F[A] (it's an (=> A) => F[A]), and in Scala this type is different from an ordinary A => F[A]. We'll ignore this distinction for now, though.

■ **EXERCISE 11.10**

Prove that these two statements of the identity laws are equivalent.

■ **EXERCISE 11.11**

Prove that the identity laws hold for a monad of your choice.

■ **EXERCISE 11.12**

There's a third minimal set of monadic combinators: map, unit, and join. Implement join in terms of flatMap.

```
def join[A](mma: F[F[A]]): F[A]
```

■ **EXERCISE 11.13**

Implement either flatMap or compose in terms of join and map.

□ **EXERCISE 11.14**

Restate the monad laws to mention only join, map, and unit.

□ **EXERCISE 11.15**

Write down an explanation, in your own words, of what the associative law means for Par and Parser.

□ **EXERCISE 11.16**

Explain in your own words what the identity laws are stating in concrete terms for Gen and List.

11.5   *Just what is a monad?*

Let's now take a wider perspective. There's something unusual about the Monad interface. The data types for which we've given monad instances don't seem to have much to do with each other. Yes, Monad factors out code duplication among them, but what *is* a monad exactly? What does "monad" *mean*?

You may be used to thinking of interfaces as providing a relatively complete API for an abstract data type, merely abstracting over the specific representation. After all, a singly linked list and an array-based list may be implemented differently behind the scenes, but they'll share a common interface in terms of which a lot of useful and concrete application code can be written. Monad, like Monoid, is a more abstract, purely algebraic interface. The Monad combinators are often just a small fragment of the full API for a given data type that happens to be a monad. So Monad doesn't generalize one type or another; rather, many vastly different data types can satisfy the Monad interface and laws.

We've seen three minimal sets of primitive Monad combinators, and instances of Monad will have to provide implementations of one of these sets:

- unit and flatMap
- unit and compose
- unit, map, and join

And we know that there are two monad laws to be satisfied, associativity and identity, that can be formulated in various ways. So we can state plainly what a monad *is*:

> A monad is an implementation of one of the minimal sets of monadic combinators, satisfying the laws of associativity and identity.

That's a perfectly respectable, precise, and terse definition. And if we're being precise, this is the *only* correct definition. A monad is precisely defined by its operations and laws; no more, no less. But it's a little unsatisfying. It doesn't say much about what it implies—what a monad *means*. The problem is that it's a *self-contained* definition. Even if you're a beginning programmer, you have by now obtained a vast amount of knowledge related to programming, and this definition integrates with none of that.

In order to really *understand* what's going on with monads, try to think about monads in terms of things you already know and connect them to a wider context. To develop some intuition for what monads *mean*, let's look at another couple of monads and compare their behavior.

11.5.1 *The identity monad*

To distill monads to their essentials, let's look at the simplest interesting specimen, the identity monad, given by the following type:

```
case class Id[A](value: A)
```

EXERCISE 11.17

Implement map and flatMap as methods on this class, and give an implementation for Monad[Id].

Now, `Id` is just a simple wrapper. It doesn't really add anything. Applying `Id` to `A` is an identity since the wrapped type and the unwrapped type are totally isomorphic (we can go from one to the other and back again without any loss of information). But what is the meaning of the identity *monad*? Let's try using it in the REPL:

```
scala> Id("Hello, ") flatMap (a =>
     |   Id("monad!") flatMap (b =>
     |     Id(a + b)))
res0: Id[java.lang.String] = Id(Hello, monad!)
```

When we write the exact same thing with a for-comprehension, it might be clearer:

```
scala> for {
     |   a <- Id("Hello, ")
     |   b <- Id("monad!")
     | } yield a + b
res1: Id[java.lang.String] = Id(Hello, monad!)
```

So what is the *action* of `flatMap` for the identity monad? It's simply variable substitution. The variables `a` and `b` get bound to `"Hello, "` and `"monad!"`, respectively, and then substituted into the expression `a + b`. We could have written the same thing without the `Id` wrapper, using just Scala's own variables:

```
scala> val a = "Hello, "
a: java.lang.String = "Hello, "

scala> val b = "monad!"
b: java.lang.String = monad!

scala> a + b
res2: java.lang.String = Hello, monad!
```

Besides the `Id` wrapper, there's no difference. So now we have at least a partial answer to the question of what monads mean. We could say that monads provide a context for introducing and binding variables, and performing variable substitution.

Let's see if we can get the rest of the answer.

11.5.2 *The State monad and partial type application*

Look back at the discussion of the `State` data type in chapter 6. Recall that we implemented some combinators for `State`, including `map` and `flatMap`.

Listing 11.7   Revisiting our `State` data type

```
case class State[S, A](run: S => (A, S)) {
  def map[B](f: A => B): State[S, B] =
    State(s => {
      val (a, s1) = run(s)
      (f(a), s1)
    })
  def flatMap[B](f: A => State[S, B]): State[S, B] =
    State(s => {
```

```
    val (a, s1) = run(s)
    f(a).run(s1)
  })
}
```

It looks like `State` definitely fits the profile for being a monad. But its type constructor takes two type arguments, and `Monad` requires a type constructor of one argument, so we can't just say `Monad[State]`. But if we choose some particular `S`, then we have something like `State[S, _]`, which is the kind of thing expected by `Monad`. So `State` doesn't just have one monad instance but a whole family of them, one for each choice of `S`. We'd like to be able to partially apply `State` to where the `S` type argument is fixed to be some concrete type.

This is much like how we might partially apply a function, except at the type level. For example, we can create an `IntState` type constructor, which is an alias for `State` with its first type argument fixed to be `Int`:

```
type IntState[A] = State[Int, A]
```

And `IntState` is exactly the kind of thing that we can build a `Monad` for:

```
object IntStateMonad extends Monad[IntState] {
  def unit[A](a: => A): IntState[A] = State(s => (a, s))
  def flatMap[A,B](st: IntState[A])(f: A => IntState[B]): IntState[B] =
    st flatMap f
}
```

Of course, it would be really repetitive if we had to manually write a separate `Monad` instance for each specific state type. Unfortunately, Scala doesn't allow us to use underscore syntax to simply say `State[Int, _]` to create an anonymous type constructor like we create anonymous functions. But instead we can use something similar to lambda syntax at the type level. For example, we could have declared `IntState` directly inline like this:

```
object IntStateMonad extends
  Monad[({type IntState[A] = State[Int, A]})#IntState] {
  ...
}
```

This syntax can be jarring when you first see it. But all we're doing is declaring an anonymous type within parentheses. This anonymous type has, as one of its members, the type alias `IntState`, which looks just like before. Outside the parentheses we're then accessing its `IntState` member with the `#` syntax. Just like we can use a dot (`.`) to access a member of an object at the value level, we can use the `#` symbol to access a type member (see the "Type Projection" section of the Scala Language Specification: http://mng.bz/u70U).

A type constructor declared inline like this is often called a *type lambda* in Scala. We can use this trick to partially apply the `State` type constructor and declare a `State`-`Monad` trait. An instance of `StateMonad[S]` is then a monad instance for the given state type `S`:

```
def stateMonad[S] = new Monad[({type f[x] = State[S,x]})#f] {
  def unit[A](a: => A): State[S,A] = State(s => (a, s))
  def flatMap[A,B](st: State[S,A])(f: A => State[S,B]): State[S,B] =
    st flatMap f
}
```

The choice of the name f here is arbitrary.

Again, just by giving implementations of unit and flatMap, we get implementations of all the other monadic combinators for free.

■ **EXERCISE 11.18**

Now that we have a State monad, you should try it out to see how it behaves. What is the meaning of replicateM in the State monad? How does map2 behave? What about sequence?

Let's now look at the difference between the Id monad and the State monad. Remember that the primitive operations on State (besides the monadic operations unit and flatMap) are that we can read the current state with getState and we can set a new state with setState:

```
def getState[S]: State[S, S]
def setState[S](s: => S): State[S, Unit]
```

Remember that we also discovered that these combinators constitute a minimal set of primitive operations for State. So together with the monadic primitives (unit and flatMap) they *completely specify* everything that we can do with the State data type. This is true in general for monads—they all have unit and flatMap, and each monad brings its own set of additional primitive operations that are specific to it.

■ **EXERCISE 11.19**

What laws do you expect to mutually hold for getState, setState, unit, and flatMap?

What does this tell us about the meaning of the State *monad*? Let's study a simple example. The details of this code aren't too important, but notice the use of getState and setState in the for block.

Listing 11.8   Getting and setting state with a for-comprehension

```
val F = stateMonad[Int]

def zipWithIndex[A](as: List[A]): List[(Int,A)] =
  as.foldLeft(F.unit(List[(Int, A)]()))((acc,a) => for {
```

```
      xs <- acc
      n  <- getState
      _  <- setState(n + 1)
} yield (n, a) :: xs).run(0)._1.reverse
```

This function numbers all the elements in a list using a `State` action. It keeps a state that's an `Int`, which is incremented at each step. We run the whole composite state action starting from 0. We then reverse the result since we constructed it in reverse order.[10]

Note what's going on with `getState` and `setState` in the for-comprehension. We're obviously getting variable binding just like in the `Id` monad—we're binding the value of each successive state action (`getState`, `acc`, and then `setState`) to variables. But there's more going on, literally *between the lines*. At each line in the for-comprehension, the implementation of `flatMap` is making sure that the current state is available to `getState`, and that the new state gets propagated to all actions that follow a `setState`.

What does the difference between the action of `Id` and the action of `State` tell us about monads in general? We can see that a chain of `flatMap` calls (or an equivalent for-comprehension) is like an imperative program with statements that assign to variables, and *the monad specifies what occurs at statement boundaries.* For example, with `Id`, nothing at all occurs except unwrapping and rewrapping in the `Id` constructor. With `State`, the most current state gets passed from one statement to the next. With the `Option` monad, a statement may return `None` and terminate the program. With the `List` monad, a statement may return many results, which causes statements that follow it to potentially run multiple times, once for each result.

The `Monad` contract doesn't specify *what* is happening between the lines, only that whatever *is* happening satisfies the laws of associativity and identity.

■ EXERCISE 11.20

Hard: To cement your understanding of monads, give a monad instance for the following type, and explain what it means. What are its primitive operations? What is the action of `flatMap`? What meaning does it give to monadic functions like `sequence`, `join`, and `replicateM`? What meaning does it give to the monad laws?[11]

```
case class Reader[R, A](run: R => A)

object Reader {
  def readerMonad[R] = new Monad[({type f[x] = Reader[R,x]})#f] {
    def unit[A](a: => A): Reader[R,A]
    def flatMap[A,B](st: Reader[R,A])(f: A => Reader[R,B]): Reader[R,B]
  }
}
```

---

[10] This is asymptotically faster than appending to the list in the loop.
[11] See the chapter notes for further discussion of this data type.

11.6 *Summary*

In this chapter, we took a pattern that we've seen repeated throughout the book and we unified it under a single concept: monad. This allowed us to write a number of combinators once and for all, for many different data types that at first glance don't seem to have anything in common. We discussed laws that they all satisfy, the monad laws, from various perspectives, and we developed some insight into what it all means.

An abstract topic like this can't be fully understood all at once. It requires an iterative approach where you keep revisiting the topic from different perspectives. When you discover new monads or new applications of them, or see them appear in a new context, you'll inevitably gain new insight. And each time it happens, you might think to yourself, "OK, I thought I understood monads before, but now I *really* get it."

Applicative and
traversable functors

In the previous chapter on monads, we saw how a lot of the functions we've been writing for different combinator libraries can be expressed in terms of a single interface, Monad. Monads provide a powerful interface, as evidenced by the fact that we can use flatMap to essentially write imperative programs in a purely functional way.

In this chapter, we'll learn about a related abstraction, *applicative functors*, which are less powerful than monads, but more general (and hence more common). The process of arriving at applicative functors will also provide some insight into *how to discover such abstractions*, and we'll use some of these ideas to uncover another useful abstraction, *traversable functors*. It may take some time for the full significance and usefulness of these abstractions to sink in, but you'll see them popping up again and again in your daily work with FP if you pay attention.

12.1 Generalizing monads

By now we've seen various operations, like sequence and traverse, implemented many times for different monads, and in the last chapter we generalized the implementations to work for *any* monad F:

```
def sequence[A](lfa: List[F[A]]): F[List[A]]
  traverse(lfa)(fa => fa)

def traverse[A,B](as: List[A])(f: A => F[B]): F[List[B]]
  as.foldRight(unit(List[B]()))((a, mbs) => map2(f(a), mbs)(_ :: _))
```

Here, the implementation of traverse is using map2 and unit, and we've seen that map2 can be implemented in terms of flatMap:

```
def map2[A,B,C](ma: F[A], mb: F[B])(f: (A,B) => C): F[C] =
  flatMap(ma)(a => map(mb)(b => f(a,b)))
```

What you may not have noticed is that a large number of the useful combinators on Monad can be defined using only unit and map2. The traverse combinator is one example—it doesn't call flatMap directly and is therefore agnostic to whether map2 is primitive or derived. Furthermore, for many data types, map2 can be implemented directly, without using flatMap.

All this suggests a variation on Monad—the Monad interface has flatMap and unit as primitives, and derives map2, but we can obtain a *different* abstraction by letting unit and map2 be the primitives. We'll see that this new abstraction, called an *applicative functor*, is less powerful than a monad, but we'll also see that limitations come with benefits.

12.2 The Applicative trait

Applicative functors can be captured by a new interface, Applicative, in which map2 and unit are primitives.

Listing 12.1 Creating the `Applicative` interface

We can
implement
map in terms
of unit and
map2.

Definition of
traverse
is identical.

```
trait Applicative[F[_]] extends Functor[F] {
  // primitive combinators
  def map2[A,B,C](fa: F[A], fb: F[B])(f: (A, B) => C): F[C]
  def unit[A](a: => A): F[A]

  // derived combinators
  def map[B](fa: F[A])(f: A => B): F[B] =
    map2(fa, unit(()))((a, _) => f(a))

  def traverse[A,B](as: List[A])(f: A => F[B]): F[List[B]]
    as.foldRight(unit(List[B]()))((a, fbs) => map2(f(a), fbs)(_ :: _))

}
```

Recall () is the sole
value of type Unit,
so unit(()) is
calling unit with
the dummy value ().

This establishes that *all applicatives are functors*. We implement map in terms of map2 and unit, as we've done before for particular data types. The implementation is suggestive of laws for Applicative that we'll examine later, since we expect this implementation of map to preserve structure as dictated by the Functor laws.

Note that the implementation of traverse is unchanged. We can similarly move other combinators into Applicative that don't depend directly on flatMap or join.

■ **EXERCISE 12.1** ──────────────────────────────────────

Transplant the implementations of as many combinators as you can from Monad to Applicative, using only map2 and unit, or methods implemented in terms of them.

```
def sequence[A](fas: List[F[A]]): F[List[A]]
def replicateM[A](n: Int, fa: F[A]): F[List[A]]
def product[A,B](fa: F[A], fb: F[A]): F[(A,B)]
```

■ **EXERCISE 12.2**

Hard: The name *applicative* comes from the fact that we can formulate the Applicative interface using an alternate set of primitives, unit and the function apply, rather than unit and map2. Show that this formulation is equivalent in expressiveness by defining map2 and map in terms of unit and apply. Also establish that apply can be implemented in terms of map2 and unit.

```
trait Applicative[F[_]] extends Functor[F] {                    Define in terms of
                                                                map2 and unit.
  def apply[A,B](fab: F[A => B])(fa: F[A]): F[B]        ←
  def unit[A](a: => A): F[A]
                                                                Define in terms
  def map[A,B](fa: F[A])(f: A => B): F[B]               ←      of apply and
  def map2[A,B,C](fa: F[A], fb: F[B])(f: (A,B) => C): F[A]  ←  unit.
}
```

■ **EXERCISE 12.3**

The apply method is useful for implementing map3, map4, and so on, and the pattern is straightforward. Implement map3 and map4 using only unit, apply, and the curried method available on functions.[1]

```
def map3[A,B,C,D](fa: F[A],
                  fb: F[B],
                  fc: F[C])(f: (A, B, C) => D): F[D]

def map4[A,B,C,D,E](fa: F[A],
                    fb: F[B],
                    fc: F[C],
                    fd: F[D])(f: (A, B, C, D) => E): F[E]
```

Furthermore, we can now make Monad[F] a subtype of Applicative[F] by providing the default implementation of map2 in terms of flatMap. This tells us that *all monads are applicative functors*, and we don't need to provide separate Applicative instances for all our data types that are already monads.

---

[1] Recall that given f: (A,B) => C, f.curried has type A => B => C. A curried method exists for functions of any arity in Scala.

Listing 12.2 Making Monad a subtype of Applicative

```
trait Monad[F[_]] extends Applicative[F] {
  def flatMap[A,B](fa: F[A])(f: A => F[B]): F[B] = join(map(fa)(f))

  def join[A](ffa: F[F[A]]): F[A] = flatMap(ffa)(fa => fa)

  def compose[A,B,C](f: A => F[B], g: B => F[C]): A => F[C] =
    a => flatMap(f(a))(g)

  def map[B](fa: F[A])(f: A => B): F[B] =
    flatMap(fa)((a: A) => unit(f(a)))

  def map2[A,B,C](fa: F[A], fb: F[B])(f: (A, B) => C): F[C] =
    flatMap(fa)(a => map(fb)(b => f(a,b)))
}
```

A minimal implementation of Monad must implement unit and override either flatMap or join and map.

So far, we've been just rearranging the functions of our API and following the type signatures. Let's take a step back to understand the difference in expressiveness between Monad and Applicative and what it all means.

12.3 *The difference between monads and applicative functors*

In the last chapter, we noted there were several minimal sets of operations that defined a Monad:

- unit and flatMap
- unit and compose
- unit, map, and join

Are the Applicative operations unit and map2 yet another minimal set of operations for monads? No. There are monadic combinators such as join and flatMap that can't be implemented with just map2 and unit. To see convincing proof of this, take a look at join:

```
def join[A](f: F[F[A]]): F[A]
```

Just reasoning algebraically, we can see that unit and map2 have no hope of implementing this function. The join function "removes a layer" of F. But the unit function only lets us *add* an F layer, and map2 lets us apply a function *within* F but does no flattening of layers. By the same argument, we can see that Applicative has no means of implementing flatMap either.

So Monad is clearly adding some extra capabilities beyond Applicative. But what exactly? Let's look at some concrete examples.

12.3.1 *The Option applicative versus the Option monad*

Suppose we're using `Option` to work with the results of lookups in two `Map` objects. If we simply need to combine the results from two (independent) lookups, map2 is fine.

> **Listing 12.3   Combining results with the `Option` applicative**

Salaries, indexed by employee name.

Department, indexed by employee name.

String interpolation substitutes values for dept and salary.

```
val F: Applicative[Option] = ...

val depts: Map[String,String] = ...
val salaries: Map[String,Double] = ...
val o: Option[String] =
  F.map2(depts.get("Alice"), salaries.get("Alice"))(
    (dept, salary) => s"Alice in $dept makes $salary per year"
  )
```

Here we're doing two lookups, but they're independent and we merely want to combine their results within the `Option` context. If we want *the result of one lookup to affect what lookup we do next*, then we need `flatMap` or `join`, as the following listing shows.

> **Listing 12.4   Combining results with the `Option` monad**

Employee ID, indexed by employee name.

Department, indexed by employee ID.

Salaries, indexed by employee ID.

Look up Bob's ID; then use result to do further lookups.

```
val idsByName: Map[String,Int]

val depts: Map[Int,String] = ...
val salaries: Map[Int,Double] = ...
val o: Option[String] =
  idsByName.get("Bob").flatMap { id =>
    F.map2(depts.get(id), salaries.get(id))(
      (dept, salary) => s"Bob in $dept makes $salary per year"
    )
  }
```

Here depts is a `Map[Int,String]` indexed by employee *ID*, which is an `Int`. If we want to print out Bob's department and salary, we need to first resolve Bob's name to his ID, and then *use this ID* to do lookups in depts and salaries. We might say that with `Applicative`, the structure of our computation is fixed; with `Monad`, the results of previous computations may influence what computations to run next.

> **"Effects" in FP**
>
> Functional programmers often informally call type constructors like `Par`, `Option`, `List`, `Parser`, `Gen`, and so on *effects*. This usage is distinct from the term *side effect*, which implies some violation of referential transparency. These types are called *effects* because they augment ordinary values with "extra" capabilities. (`Par` adds the ability to define parallel computation, `Option` adds the possibility of failure, and so on.) Related to this usage of effects, we sometimes use the terms *monadic effects* or *applicative effects* to mean types with an associated `Monad` or `Applicative` instance.

12.3.2 *The Parser applicative versus the Parser monad*

Let's look at one more example. Suppose we're parsing a file of comma-separated values with two columns: *date* and *temperature*. Here's an example file:

```
1/1/2010, 25
2/1/2010, 28
3/1/2010, 42
4/1/2010, 53
...
```

If we know ahead of time the file will have the *date* and *temperature* columns in that order, we can just encode this order in the `Parser` we construct:

```
case class Row(date: Date, temperature: Double)

val F: Applicative[Parser] = ...
val d: Parser[Date] = ...
val temp: Parser[Double] = ...

val row: Parser[Row] = F.map2(d, temp)(Row(_, _))
val rows: Parser[List[Row]] = row.sep("\n")
```

If we don't know the order of the columns and need to extract this information from the header, then we need `flatMap`. Here's an example file where the columns happen to be in the opposite order:

```
# Temperature, Date
25, 1/1/2010
28, 2/1/2010
42, 3/1/2010
53, 4/1/2010
...
```

To parse this format, where we must dynamically choose our `Row` parser based on first parsing the header (the first line starting with #), we need `flatMap`:

```
case class Row(date: Date, temperature: Double)

val F: Monad[Parser] = ...
val d: Parser[Date] = ...
val temp: Parser[Double] = ...

val header: Parser[Parser[Row]] = ...
val rows: Parser[List[Row]] =
  F.flatMap (header) { row => row.sep("\n") }
```

Here we're parsing the header, which gives us a `Parser[Row]` as its result. We then use this parser to parse the subsequent rows. Since we don't know the order of the columns up front, we're selecting our `Row` parser *dynamically*, based on the result of parsing the header.

There are many ways to state the distinction between `Applicative` and `Monad`. Of course, the type signatures tell us all we really need to know and we can understand the difference between the interfaces algebraically. But here are a few other common ways of stating the difference:

- Applicative computations have fixed structure and simply *sequence* effects, whereas monadic computations may choose structure dynamically, based on the result of previous effects.
- Applicative constructs *context-free* computations, while Monad allows for *context sensitivity*.[2]
- Monad makes effects first class; they may be generated at "interpretation" time, rather than chosen ahead of time by the program. We saw this in our Parser example, where we generated our Parser[Row] *as part of* the act of parsing, and used this Parser[Row] for subsequent parsing.

12.4 *The advantages of applicative functors*

The Applicative interface is important for a few reasons:

- In general, it's preferable to implement combinators like traverse using as few assumptions as possible. It's better to assume that a data type can provide map2 than flatMap. Otherwise we'd have to write a new traverse every time we encountered a type that's Applicative but not a Monad! We'll look at examples of such types next.
- Because Applicative is "weaker" than Monad, this gives the *interpreter* of applicative effects more flexibility. To take just one example, consider parsing. If we describe a parser without resorting to flatMap, this implies that the structure of our grammar is determined before we begin parsing. Therefore, our interpreter or runner of parsers has *more information* about what it'll be doing up front and is free to make additional assumptions and possibly use a more efficient implementation strategy for running the parser, based on this known structure. Adding flatMap is powerful, but it means we're generating our parsers dynamically, so the interpreter may be more limited in what it can do. Power comes at a cost. See the chapter notes for more discussion of this issue.
- Applicative functors compose, whereas monads (in general) don't. We'll see how this works later.

12.4.1 *Not all applicative functors are monads*

Let's look at two examples of data types that are applicative functors but not monads. These are certainly not the only examples. If you do more functional programming, you'll undoubtedly discover or create lots of data types that are applicative but not monadic.[3]

---

[2] For example, a monadic parser allows for context-sensitive grammars while an applicative parser can only handle context-free grammars.

[3] *Monadic* is the adjective form of *monad*.

THE APPLICATIVE FOR STREAMS

The first example we'll look at is (possibly infinite) streams. We can define `map2` and unit for these streams, but not `flatMap`:

```
val streamApplicative = new Applicative[Stream] {

  def unit[A](a: => A): Stream[A] =                    The infinite, constant stream.
    Stream.continually(a)           <──────────

  def map2[A,B,C](a: Stream[A], b: Stream[B])(  <──────
               f: (A,B) => C): Stream[C] =
    a zip b map f.tupled                          Combine elements pointwise.
}
```

The idea behind this `Applicative` is to combine corresponding elements via zipping.

EXERCISE 12.4

Hard: What is the meaning of `streamApplicative.sequence`? Specializing the signature of `sequence` to `Stream`, we have this:

```
def sequence[A](a: List[Stream[A]]): Stream[List[A]]
```

VALIDATION: AN EITHER VARIANT THAT ACCUMULATES ERRORS

In chapter 4, we looked at the `Either` data type and considered the question of how such a data type would have to be modified to allow us to report multiple errors. For a concrete example, think of validating a web form submission. Only reporting the first error means the user would have to repeatedly submit the form and fix one error at a time.

This is the situation with `Either` if we use it monadically. First, let's actually write the monad for the partially applied `Either` type.

EXERCISE 12.5

Write a monad instance for `Either`.

```
def eitherMonad[E]: Monad[({type f[x] = Either[E, x]})#f]
```

Now consider what happens in a sequence of `flatMap` calls like the following, where each of the functions `validName`, `validBirthdate`, and `validPhone` has type `Either[String, T]` for a given type `T`:

```
validName(field1) flatMap (f1 =>
validBirthdate(field2) flatMap (f2 =>
validPhone(field3) map (f3 => WebForm(f1, f2, f3))
```

If `validName` fails with an error, then `validBirthdate` and `validPhone` won't even run. The computation with `flatMap` inherently establishes a linear chain of dependencies. The variable `f1` will never be bound to anything unless `validName` succeeds.

Now think of doing the same thing with `map3`:

```
map3(
  validName(field1),
  validBirthdate(field2),
  validPhone(field3))(
  WebForm(_,_,_))
```

Here, no dependency is implied between the three expressions passed to `map3`, and in principle we can imagine collecting any errors from each `Either` into a `List`. But if we use the `Either` monad, its implementation of `map3` in terms of `flatMap` will halt after the first error.

Let's invent a new data type, `Validation`, that is much like `Either` except that it can explicitly handle more than one error:

```
sealed trait Validation[+E, +A]

case class Failure[E](head: E, tail: Vector[E] = Vector())
  extends Validation[E, Nothing]

case class Success[A](a: A) extends Validation[Nothing, A]
```

■ **EXERCISE 12.6**

Write an `Applicative` instance for `Validation` that accumulates errors in `Failure`. Note that in the case of `Failure` there's always at least one error, stored in `head`. The rest of the errors accumulate in the `tail`.

To continue the example, consider a web form that requires a name, a birth date, and a phone number:

```
case class WebForm(name: String, birthdate: Date, phoneNumber: String)
```

This data will likely be collected from the user as strings, and we must make sure that the data meets a certain specification. If it doesn't, we must give a list of errors to the user indicating how to fix the problem. The specification might say that `name` can't be empty, that `birthdate` must be in the form `"yyyy-MM-dd"`, and that `phoneNumber` must contain exactly 10 digits.

> **Listing 12.5   Validating user input in a web form**
>
> ```
> def validName(name: String): Validation[String, String] =
>   if (name != "") Success(name)
>   else Failure("Name cannot be empty")
>
> def validBirthdate(birthdate: String): Validation[String, Date] =
>   try {
>     import java.text._
>     Success((new SimpleDateFormat("yyyy-MM-dd")).parse(birthdate))
>   } catch {
>     Failure("Birthdate must be in the form yyyy-MM-dd")
>   }
>
> def validPhone(phoneNumber: String): Validation[String, String] =
>   if (phoneNumber.matches("[0-9]{10}"))
>       Success(phoneNumber)
>   else Failure("Phone number must be 10 digits")
> ```

And to validate an entire web form, we can simply lift the `WebForm` constructor with map3:

```
def validWebForm(name: String,
                 birthdate: String,
                 phone: String): Validation[String, WebForm] =
  map3(
    validName(name),
    validBirthdate(birthdate),
    validPhone(phone))(
    WebForm(_,_,_))
```

If any or all of the functions produce `Failure`, the whole `validWebForm` method will return all of those failures combined.

12.5   *The applicative laws*

This section walks through the laws for applicative functors.[4] For each of these laws, you may want to verify that they're satisfied by some of the data types we've been working with so far (an easy one to verify is `Option`).

12.5.1   *Left and right identity*

What sort of laws should we expect applicative functors to obey? Well, we should definitely expect them to obey the functor laws:

```
map(v)(id) == v
map(map(v)(g))(f) == map(v)(f compose g)
```

This implies some other laws for applicative functors because of how we've implemented map in terms of map2 and unit. Recall the definition of map:

---

[4] There are various other ways of presenting the laws for `Applicative`. See the chapter notes for more information.

```
def map[B](fa: F[A])(f: A => B): F[B] =
  map2(fa, unit(()))((a, _) => f(a))
```

Of course, there's something rather arbitrary about this definition—we could have just as easily put the unit on the *left* side of the call to map2:

```
def map[B](fa: F[A])(f: A => B): F[B] =
  map2(unit(()), fa)((_, a) => f(a))
```

The first two laws for Applicative might be summarized by saying that *both* these implementations of map respect the functor laws. In other words, map2 of some fa: F[A] with unit preserves the structure of fa. We'll call these the left and right identity laws (shown here in the first and second lines of code, respectively):

```
map2(unit(()), fa)((_,a) => a) == fa
map2(fa, unit(()))((a,_) => a) == fa
```

12.5.2 Associativity

To see the next law, *associativity*, let's look at the signature of map3:

```
def map3[A,B,C,D](fa: F[A],
                  fb: F[B],
                  fc: F[C])(f: (A, B, C) => D): F[D]
```

We can implement map3 using apply and unit, but let's think about how we might define it in terms of map2. We have to combine our effects two at a time, and we seem to have two choices—we can combine fa and fb, and then combine the result with fc. Or we could associate the operation the other way, grouping fb and fc together and combining the result with fa. The associativity law for applicative functors tells us that we should get the same result either way. This should remind you of the associativity laws for monoids and monads:

```
op(a, op(b, c)) == op(op(a, b), c)
compose(f, op(g, h)) == compose(compose(f, g), h)
```

The associativity law for applicative functors is the same general idea. If we didn't have this law, we'd need *two* versions of map3, perhaps map3L and map3R, depending on the grouping, and we'd get an explosion of other combinators based on having to distinguish between different groupings.

We can state the associativity law in terms of product.[5] Recall that product just combines two effects into a pair, using map2:

```
def product[A,B](fa: F[A], fb: F[B]): F[(A,B)] =
  map2(fa, fb)((_,_))
```

And if we have pairs nested on the right, we can always turn those into pairs nested on the left:

---

[5] product, map, and unit are an alternate formulation of Applicative. Can you see how map2 can be implemented using product and map?

```
def assoc[A,B,C](p: (A,(B,C))): ((A,B), C) =
  p match { case (a, (b, c)) => ((a,b), c) }
```

Using these combinators, `product` and `assoc`, the law of associativity for applicative functors is as follows:

```
product(product(fa,fb),fc) == map(product(fa, product(fb,fc)))(assoc)
```

Note that the calls to `product` are associated to the left on one side and to the right on the other side of the `==` sign. On the right side we're then mapping the `assoc` function to make the resulting tuples line up.

12.5.3 *Naturality of product*

Our final law for applicative functors is *naturality*. To illustrate, let's look at a simple example using `Option`.

Listing 12.6 Retrieving employee names and annual pay

```
val F: Applicative[Option] = ...

case class Employee(name: String, id: Int)
case class Pay(rate: Double, hoursPerYear: Double)

def format(e: Option[Employee], pay: Option[Pay]): Option[String] =
  F.map2(e, pay) { (e, pay) =>
    s"${e.name} makes ${pay.rate * pay.hoursPerYear}"
  }

val e: Option[Employee] = ...
val pay: Option[Pay] = ...
format(e, pay)
```

Here we're applying a transformation to the *result* of map2—from `Employee` we extract the name, and from `Pay` we extract the yearly wage. But we could just as easily apply these transformations separately, before calling `format`, giving `format` an `Option [String]` and `Option[Double]` rather than an `Option[Employee]` and `Option[Pay]`. This might be a reasonable refactoring, so that `format` doesn't need to know the details of how the `Employee` and `Pay` data types are represented.

Listing 12.7 Refactoring `format`

```
val F: Applicative[Option] = ...

def format(name: Option[String], pay: Option[Double]): Option[String] =
  F.map2(e, pay) { (e, pay) => s"$e makes $pay" }

val e: Option[Employee] = ...
val pay: Option[Pay] = ...

format(
  F.map(e)(_.name),
  F.map(pay)(pay => pay.rate * pay.hoursPerYear))
```

> `format` now takes the employee name as a `Option[String]`, rather than extracting the name from an `Option[Employee]`. Similarly for pay.

We're applying the transformation to extract the name and pay fields before calling map2. We expect this program to have the same meaning as before, and this sort of pattern comes up frequently. When working with Applicative effects, we generally have the option of applying transformations *before* or *after* combining values with map2. The naturality law states that it doesn't matter; we get the same result either way. Stated more formally,

```
map2(a,b)(productF(f,g)) == product(map(a)(f), map(b)(g))
```

Where productF combines two functions into one function that takes both their arguments and returns the pair of their results:

```
def productF[I,O,I2,O2](f: I => O, g: I2 => O2): (I,I2) => (O,O2) =
  (i,i2) => (f(i), g(i2))
```

The applicative laws are not surprising or profound. Just like the monad laws, these are simple sanity checks that the applicative functor works in the way that we'd expect. They ensure that unit, map, and map2 behave in a consistent and reasonable manner.

EXERCISE 12.7

Hard: Prove that all monads are applicative functors by showing that if the monad laws hold, the Monad implementations of map2 and map satisfy the applicative laws.

EXERCISE 12.8

Just like we can take the product of two monoids A and B to give the monoid (A, B), we can take the product of two applicative functors. Implement this function:

```
def product[G[_]](G: Applicative[G]):
  Applicative[({type f[x] = (F[x], G[x])})#f]
```

EXERCISE 12.9

Hard: Applicative functors also compose another way! If F[_] and G[_] are applicative functors, then so is F[G[_]]. Implement this function:

```
def compose[G[_]](G: Applicative[G]):
  Applicative[({type f[x] = F[G[x]]})#f]
```

EXERCISE 12.10

Hard: Prove that this composite applicative functor meets the applicative laws. This is an extremely challenging exercise.

Try to write compose on Monad. It's not possible, but it is instructive to attempt it and understand why this is the case.

```
def compose[G[_]](G: Monad[G]): Monad[({type f[x] = F[G[x]]})#f]
```

12.6 *Traversable functors*

We discovered applicative functors by noticing that our traverse and sequence functions (and several other operations) didn't depend directly on flatMap. We can spot another abstraction by generalizing traverse and sequence once again. Look again at the signatures of traverse and sequence:

```
def traverse[F[_],A,B](as: List[A])(f: A => F[B]): F[List[B]]
def sequence[F[_],A](fas: List[F[A]]): F[List[A]]
```

Any time you see a concrete type constructor like List showing up in an abstract interface like Applicative, you may want to ask the question, "What happens if I abstract over this type constructor?" Recall from chapter 10 that a number of data types other than List are Foldable. Are there data types other than List that are *traversable?* Of course!

On the Applicative trait, implement sequence over a Map rather than a List:

```
def sequenceMap[K,V](ofa: Map[K,F[V]]): F[Map[K,V]]
```

But traversable data types are too numerous for us to write specialized sequence and traverse methods for each of them. What we need is a new interface. We'll call it Traverse:[6]

```
trait Traverse[F[_]] {
  def traverse[G[_]:Applicative,A,B](fa: F[A])(f: A => G[B]): G[F[B]] =
    sequence(map(fa)(f))
  def sequence[G[_]:Applicative,A](fga: F[G[A]]): G[F[A]] =
    traverse(fga)(ga => ga)
}
```

---

[6] The name Traversable is already taken by an unrelated trait in the Scala standard library.

The interesting operation here is `sequence`. Look at its signature closely. It takes `F[G[A]]` and swaps the order of `F` and `G`, so long as `G` is an applicative functor. Now, this is a rather abstract, algebraic notion. We'll get to what it all means in a minute, but first, let's look at a few instances of `Traverse`.

■ **EXERCISE 12.13** ────────────────────────────────

Write `Traverse` instances for `List`, `Option`, and `Tree`.

```
case class Tree[+A](head: A, tail: List[Tree[A]])
```

─────────────────────────────────────

We now have instances for `List`, `Option`, `Map`, and `Tree`. What does this generalized traverse/sequence mean? Let's just try plugging in some concrete type signatures for calls to `sequence`. We can speculate about what these functions do, just based on their signatures:

- `List[Option[A]] => Option[List[A]]` (a call to `Traverse[List].sequence` with `Option` as the `Applicative`) returns `None` if any of the input `List` is `None`; otherwise it returns the original `List` wrapped in `Some`.
- `Tree[Option[A]] => Option[Tree[A]]` (a call to `Traverse[Tree].sequence` with `Option` as the `Applicative`) returns `None` if any of the input `Tree` is `None`; otherwise it returns the original `Tree` wrapped in `Some`.
- `Map[K, Par[A]] => Par[Map[K,A]]` (a call to `Traverse[Map[K,_]].sequence` with `Par` as the `Applicative`) produces a parallel computation that evaluates all values of the map in parallel.

There turns out to be a startling number of operations that can be defined in the most general possible way in terms of `sequence` and/or `traverse`. We'll explore these in the next section.

A traversal is similar to a fold in that both take some data structure and apply a function to the data within in order to produce a result. The difference is that `traverse` *preserves the original structure*, whereas `foldMap` discards the structure and replaces it with the operations of a monoid. Look at the signature `Tree[Option[A]] => Option[Tree[A]]`, for instance. We're preserving the `Tree` structure, not merely collapsing the values using some monoid.

12.7 *Uses of Traverse*

Let's now explore the large set of operations that can be implemented quite generally using `Traverse`. We'll only scratch the surface here. If you're interested, follow some of the references in the chapter notes to learn more, and do some exploring on your own.

Hard: Implement `map` in terms of `traverse` as a method on `Traverse[F]`. This establishes that `Traverse` is an extension of `Functor` and that the `traverse` function is a generalization of `map` (for this reason we sometimes call these *traversable functors*). Note that in implementing `map`, you can call `traverse` with *your choice* of `Applicative[G]`.

```
trait Traverse[F[_]] extends Functor[F] {

  def traverse[G[_],A,B](fa: F[A])(f: A => G[B])(
                        implicit G: Applicative[G]): G[F[B]] =
    sequence(map(fa)(f))

  def sequence[G[_],A](fga: F[G[A]])(
                        implicit G: Applicative[G]): G[F[A]] =
    traverse(fga)(ga => ga)

  def map[A,B](fa: F[A])(f: A => B): F[B] = ???
}
```

But what is the relationship between `Traverse` and `Foldable`? The answer involves a connection between `Applicative` and `Monoid`.

12.7.1 *From monoids to applicative functors*

We've just learned that `traverse` is more general than `map`. Next we'll learn that `traverse` can also express `foldMap` and by extension `foldLeft` and `foldRight`! Take another look at the signature of `traverse`:

```
def traverse[G[_]:Applicative,A,B](fa: F[A])(f: A => G[B]): G[F[B]]
```

Suppose that our `G` were a type constructor `ConstInt` that takes any type to `Int`, so that `ConstInt[A]` throws away its type argument `A` and just gives us `Int`:

```
type ConstInt[A] = Int
```

Then in the type signature for `traverse`, if we instantiate `G` to be `ConstInt`, it becomes

```
def traverse[A,B](fa: F[A])(f: A => Int): Int
```

This looks a lot like `foldMap` from `Foldable`. Indeed, if `F` is something like `List`, then what we need to implement this signature is a way of combining the `Int` values returned by `f` for each element of the list, and a "starting" value for handling the empty list. In other words, we only need a `Monoid[Int]`. And that's easy to come by.

In fact, given a constant functor like we have here, we can turn any `Monoid` into an `Applicative`.

Listing 12.8 Turning a `Monoid` into an `Applicative`

```
type Const[M, B] = M                    ←
                                                        This is ConstInt
                                                        generalized to any
implicit def monoidApplicative[M](M: Monoid[M]) =       M, not just Int.
  new Applicative[({ type f[x] = Const[M, x] })#f] {
    def unit[A](a: => A): M = M.zero
    def map2[A,B,C](m1: M, m2: M)(f: (A,B) => C): M = M.op(m1,m2)
  }
```

This means that `Traverse` can extend `Foldable` and we can give a default implementation of `foldMap` in terms of `traverse`:

A `trait` may list multiple supertraits, separated by the keyword `with`.

```
trait Traverse[F[_]] extends Functor[F] with Foldable[F] {  ←
  ...
  def foldMap[A,M](as: F[A])(f: A => M)(mb: Monoid[M]): M =
    traverse[({type f[x] = Const[M,x]})#f,A,Nothing](  ←
      as)(f)(monoidApplicative(mb))
}
```

Scala can't infer the partially applied `Const` type alias here, so we have to provide an annotation.

Note that `Traverse` now extends both `Foldable` *and* `Functor`! Importantly, `Foldable` itself can't extend `Functor`. Even though it's possible to write `map` in terms of a fold for most foldable data structures like `List`, it's not possible *in general*.

■   **EXERCISE 12.15**
_____

Answer, to your own satisfaction, the question of why it's not possible for `Foldable` to extend `Functor`. Can you think of a `Foldable` that isn't a functor?

_____

So what is `Traverse` really for? We've already seen practical applications of particular instances, such as turning a list of parsers into a parser that produces a list. But in what kinds of cases do we want the *generalization*? What sort of generalized library does `Traverse` allow us to write?

12.7.2 *Traversals with State*

The `State` applicative functor is a particularly powerful one. Using a `State` action to traverse a collection, we can implement complex traversals that keep some kind of internal state.

   An unfortunate amount of type annotation is necessary in order to partially apply `State` in the proper way, but traversing with `State` is common enough that we can create a special method for it and write those type annotations once and for all:

```
def traverseS[S,A,B](fa: F[A])(f: A => State[S, B]): State[S, F[B]] =
  traverse[({type f[x] = State[S,x]})#f,A,B](fa)(f)(Monad.stateMonad)
```

To demonstrate this, here's a State traversal that labels every element with its position. We keep an integer state, starting with 0, and add 1 at each step.

Listing 12.9   Numbering the elements in a traversable

```
def zipWithIndex[A](ta: F[A]): F[(A,Int)] =
  traverseS(ta)((a: A) => (for {
    i <- get[Int]
    _ <- set(i + 1)
  } yield (a, i))).run(0)._1
```

This definition works for List, Tree, or any other traversable.

Continuing along these lines, we can keep a state of type List[A], to turn any traversable functor into a List.

Listing 12.10   Turning traversable functors into lists

```
def toList[A](fa: F[A]): List[A] =
  traverseS(fa)((a: A) => (for {
    as <- get[List[A]]
    _  <- set(a :: as)
  } yield ())).run(Nil)._2.reverse
```

Get the current state, the accumulated list.

Add the current element and set the new list as the new state.

We begin with the empty list Nil as the initial state, and at every element in the traversal, we add it to the front of the accumulated list. This will of course construct the list in the reverse order of the traversal, so we end by reversing the list that we get from running the completed state action. Note that we yield () because in this instance we don't want to return any value other than the state.

Of course, the code for toList and zipWithIndex is nearly identical. And in fact most traversals with State will follow this exact pattern: we get the current state, compute the next state, set it, and yield some value. We should capture that in a function.

Listing 12.11   Factoring out our `mapAccum` function

```
def mapAccum[S,A,B](fa: F[A], s: S)(f: (A, S) => (B, S)): (F[B], S) =
  traverseS(fa)((a: A) => (for {
    s1 <- get[S]
    (b, s2) = f(a, s1)
    _  <- set(s2)
  } yield b)).run(s)

override def toList[A](fa: F[A]): List[A] =
  mapAccum(fa, List[A]())((a, s) => ((), a :: s))._2.reverse

def zipWithIndex[A](fa: F[A]): F[(A, Int)] =
  mapAccum(fa, 0)((a, s) => ((a, s), s + 1))._1
```

■ **EXERCISE 12.16**

There's an interesting consequence of being able to turn any traversable functor into a *reversed* list—we can write, once and for all, a function to reverse any traversable functor! Write this function, and think about what it means for List, Tree, and other traversable functors.

```
def reverse[A](fa: F[A]): F[A]
```

It should obey the following law, for all x and y of the appropriate types:

```
toList(reverse(x)) ++ toList(reverse(y)) ==
  reverse(toList(y) ++ toList(x))
```

■ **EXERCISE 12.17**

Use mapAccum to give a default implementation of foldLeft for the Traverse trait.

12.7.3 *Combining traversable structures*

It's the nature of a traversal that it must preserve the shape of its argument. This is both its strength and its weakness. This is well demonstrated when we try to combine two structures into one.

Given Traverse[F], can we combine a value of some type F[A] and another of some type F[B] into an F[C]? We could try using mapAccum to write a generic version of zip.

Listing 12.12 Combining two different structure types

```
def zip[A,B](fa: F[A], fb: F[B]): F[(A, B)] =
  (mapAccum(fa, toList(fb)) {
    case (a, Nil) => sys.error("zip: Incompatible shapes.")
    case (a, b :: bs) => ((a, b), bs)
  })._1
```

Note that this version of zip is unable to handle arguments of different "shapes." For example, if F is List, then it can't handle lists of different lengths. In this implementation, the list fb must be at least as long as fa. If F is Tree, then fb must have at least the same number of branches as fa at every level.

We can change the generic zip slightly and provide two versions so that the shape of one side or the other is dominant.

Listing 12.13   A more flexible implementation of `zip`

```
def zipL[A,B](fa: F[A], fb: F[B]): F[(A, Option[B])] =
  (mapAccum(fa, toList(fb)) {
    case (a, Nil) => ((a, None), Nil)
    case (a, b :: bs) => ((a, Some(b)), bs)
  })._1

def zipR[A,B](fa: F[A], fb: F[B]): F[(Option[A], B)] =
  (mapAccum(fb, toList(fa)) {
    case (b, Nil) => ((None, b), Nil)
    case (b, a :: as) => ((Some(a), b), as)
  })._1
```

These implementations work out nicely for `List` and other sequence types. In the case of `List`, for example, the result of `zipR` will have the shape of the `fb` argument, and it will be padded with `None` on the left if `fb` is longer than `fa`.

For types with more interesting structures, like `Tree`, these implementations may not be what we want. Note that in `zipL`, we're simply flattening the right argument to a `List[B]` and discarding its structure. For `Tree`, this will amount to a preorder traversal of the labels at each node. We're then "zipping" this sequence of labels with the values of our left `Tree`, `fa`; we aren't skipping over nonmatching subtrees. For trees, `zipL` and `zipR` are most useful if we happen to know that both trees share the same shape.

12.7.4 *Traversal fusion*

In chapter 5, we talked about how multiple passes over a structure can be fused into one. In chapter 10, we looked at how we can use monoid products to carry out multiple computations over a foldable structure in a single pass. Using products of applicative functors, we can likewise fuse multiple traversals of a traversable structure.

EXERCISE 12.18

Use applicative functor products to write the fusion of two traversals. This function will, given two functions `f` and `g`, traverse `fa` a single time, collecting the results of both functions at once.

```
def fuse[G[_],H[_],A,B](fa: F[A])(f: A => G[B], g: A => H[B])
                       (G: Applicative[G], H: Applicative[H]):
                       (G[F[B]], H[F[B]])
```

12.7.5 *Nested traversals*

Not only can we use composed applicative functors to fuse traversals, traversable functors themselves compose. If we have a nested structure like `Map[K,Option[List[V]]]`, then we can traverse the map, the option, and the list at the same time and easily get to the V value inside, because `Map`, `Option`, and `List` are all traversable.

■ **EXERCISE 12.19**

Implement the composition of two `Traverse` instances.

```
def compose[G[_]](implicit G: Traverse[G]):
    Traverse[({type f[x] = F[G[x]]})#f]
```

12.7.6 *Monad composition*

Let's now return to the issue of composing monads. As we saw earlier in this chapter, `Applicative` instances always compose, but `Monad` instances do not. If you tried before to implement general monad composition, then you would have found that in order to implement `join` for nested monads F and G, you'd have to write something of a type like `F[G[F[G[A]]]] => F[G[A]]`. And that can't be written generally. But if G also happens to have a `Traverse` instance, we can `sequence` to turn `G[F[_]]` into `F[G[_]]`, leading to `F[F[G[G[A]]]]`. Then we can join the adjacent F layers as well as the adjacent G layers using their respective `Monad` instances.

□ **EXERCISE 12.20**

Hard: Implement the composition of two monads where one of them is traversable.

```
def composeM[F[_],G[_]](F: Monad[F], G: Monad[G], T: Traverse[G]):
    Monad[({type f[x] = F[G[x]]})#f]
```

Expressivity and power sometimes come at the price of compositionality and modularity. The issue of composing monads is often addressed with a custom-written version of each monad that's specifically constructed for composition. This kind of thing is called a *monad transformer.* For example, the `OptionT` monad transformer composes `Option` with any other monad:

```
case class OptionT[M[_],A](value: M[Option[A]])(implicit M: Monad[M]) {
  def flatMap[B](f: A => OptionT[M, B]): OptionT[M, B] =
    OptionT(value flatMap {
      case None => M.unit(None)
      case Some(a) => f(a).value
    })
}
```

Option is added to the inside of the monad M.

The flatMap definition here maps over both M and Option, and flattens structures like M[Option[M[Option[A]]]] to just M[Option[A]]. But this particular implementation is specific to Option. And the general strategy of taking advantage of Traverse works only with traversable functors. To compose with State (which can't be traversed), for example, a specialized StateT monad transformer has to be written. There's no generic composition strategy that works for every monad.

See the chapter notes for more information about monad transformers.

12.8 *Summary*

In this chapter, we discovered two new useful abstractions, Applicative and Traverse, simply by playing with the signatures of our existing Monad interface. Applicative functors are a less expressive but more compositional generalization of monads. The functions unit and map allow us to lift values and functions, whereas map2 and apply give us the power to lift functions of higher arities. Traversable functors are the result of generalizing the sequence and traverse functions we've seen many times. Together, Applicative and Traverse let us construct complex nested and parallel traversals out of simple elements that need only be written once. As you write more functional code, you'll learn to spot instances of these abstractions and how to make better use of them in your programs.

This is the final chapter in part 3, but there are many abstractions beyond Monad, Applicative, and Traverse, and you can apply the techniques we've developed here to discover new structures yourself. Functional programmers have of course been discovering and cataloguing for a while, and there is by now a whole zoo of such abstractions that captures various common patterns (*arrows*, *categories*, and *comonads*, just to name a few). Our hope is that these chapters have given you enough of an introduction to start exploring this wide world on your own. The material linked in the chapter notes is a good place to start.

In part 4 we'll complete the functional programming story. So far we've been writing libraries that might constitute the core of a practical application, but such applications will ultimately need to interface with the outside world. In part 4 we'll see that referential transparency can be made to apply even to programs that perform I/O operations or make use of mutable state. Even there, the principles and patterns we've learned so far allow us to write such programs in a compositional and reusable way.

Part 4

Effects and I/O

Functional programming is a complete programming paradigm. All programs that we can imagine can be expressed functionally, including those that mutate data in place and interact with the external world by writing to files or reading from databases. In this part, we'll apply what we covered in parts 1–3 of this book to show how FP can express these effectful programs.

We'll begin in the next chapter by examining the most straightforward handling of external effects, using an I/O monad. This is a simplistic embedding of an imperative programming language into a functional language. The same general approach can be used for handling local effects and mutation, which we'll introduce in chapter 14. Both of these chapters will motivate the development of more composable ways to deal with effects. In chapter 15, our final chapter, we'll develop a library for streaming I/O, and discuss how to write compositional and modular programs that incrementally process I/O streams.

Our goal in this part of the book is not to cover absolutely every technique relevant to handling I/O and mutation, but to introduce the essential ideas and equip you with a conceptual framework for future learning. You'll undoubtedly encounter problems that don't look exactly like those discussed here. But along with parts 1–3, after finishing this part you'll be in good position to apply FP to whatever programming tasks you may face.

External effects and I/O

13

In this chapter, we'll take what we've learned so far about monads and algebraic data types and extend it to handle *external effects* like reading from databases and writing to files. We'll develop a monad for I/O, aptly called IO, that will allow us to handle such external effects in a purely functional way.

We'll make an important distinction in this chapter between *effects* and *side effects*. The IO monad provides a straightforward way of embedding *imperative programming with I/O effects* in a pure program while preserving referential transparency. It clearly separates *effectful* code—code that needs to have some effect on the outside world—from the rest of our program.

This will also illustrate a key technique for dealing with external effects—using pure functions to compute a *description* of an effectful computation, which is then executed by a separate *interpreter* that actually performs those effects. Essentially we're crafting an embedded domain-specific language (EDSL) for imperative programming. This is a powerful technique that we'll use throughout the rest of part 4. Our goal is to equip you with the skills needed to craft your own EDSLs for describing effectful programs.

13.1 *Factoring effects*

We'll work our way up to the IO monad by first considering a simple example of a program with side effects.

Listing 13.1 Program with side effects

```
case class Player(name: String, score: Int)

def contest(p1: Player, p2: Player): Unit =
  if (p1.score > p2.score)
```

```
  println(s"${p1.name} is the winner!")
else if (p2.score > p1.score)
  println(s"${p2.name} is the winner!")
else
  println("It's a draw.")
```

The contest function couples the I/O code for displaying the result to the pure logic for computing the winner. We can factor the logic into its own pure function, winner:

```
def winner(p1: Player, p2: Player): Option[Player] =          Contains the logic for
  if (p1.score > p2.score) Some(p1)                           computing the winner,
  else if (p1.score < p2.score) Some(p2)                      or the fact that there
  else None                                                   is a draw

def contest(p1: Player, p2: Player): Unit = winner(p1, p2) match {
  case Some(Player(name, _)) => println(s"$name is the winner!")
  case None => println("It's a draw.")
}                                                   Has the responsibility of
                                                    declaring the winner on the console
```

It is *always* possible to factor an impure procedure into a pure "core" function and two procedures with side effects: one that supplies the pure function's input and one that does something with the pure function's output. In listing 13.1, we factored the pure function winner out of contest. Conceptually, contest had two responsibilities—it was *computing* the result of the contest, and it was *displaying* the result that was computed. With the refactored code, winner has a single responsibility: to compute the winner. The contest method retains the responsibility of printing the result of winner to the console.

We can refactor this even further. The contest function *still* has two responsibilities: it's computing which message to display and then printing that message to the console. We could factor out a pure function here as well, which might be beneficial if we later decide to display the result in some sort of UI or write it to a file instead. Let's perform this refactoring now:

```
def winnerMsg(p: Option[Player]): String = p map {       Has the responsibility of
  case Player(name, _) => s"$name is the winner!"         determining which
} getOrElse "It's a draw."                                message is appropriate

def contest(p1: Player, p2: Player): Unit =
  println(winnerMsg(winner(p1, p2)))
                                              Has the responsibility of printing
                                              the message to the console
```

Note how the side effect, println, is now only in the *outermost* layer of the program, and what's inside the call to println is a pure expression.

This might seem like a simplistic example, but the same principle applies in larger, more complex programs, and we hope you can see how this sort of refactoring is quite natural. We aren't changing what our program does, just the internal details of how it's factored into smaller functions. The insight here is that *inside every function with side effects is a pure function waiting to get out.*

We can formalize this insight a bit. Given an impure function f of type A => B, we can split f into two functions:

- A *pure* function of type A => D, where D is some *description* of the result of f.
- An *impure* function of type D => B, which can be thought of as an *interpreter* of these descriptions.

We'll extend this to handle "input" effects shortly. For now, let's consider applying this strategy repeatedly to a program. Each time we apply it, we make more functions pure and push side effects to the outer layers. We could call these impure functions the "imperative shell" around the pure "core" of the program. Eventually, we reach functions that seem to necessitate side effects like the built-in println, which has type String => Unit. What do we do then?

13.2 *A simple IO type*

It turns out that even procedures like println are doing more than one thing. And they can be factored in much the same way, by introducing a new data type that we'll call IO:

```
trait IO { def run: Unit }

def PrintLine(msg: String): IO =
  new IO { def run = println(msg) }

def contest(p1: Player, p2: Player): IO =
  PrintLine(winnerMsg(winner(p1, p2)))
```

Our contest function is now pure—it returns an IO value, which simply describes an action that needs to take place, but doesn't actually execute it. We say that contest has (or produces) an *effect* or is *effectful*, but it's only the interpreter of IO (its run method) that actually has a *side* effect. Now contest only has one responsibility, which is to compose the parts of the program together: winner to compute who the winner is, winnerMsg to compute what the resulting message should be, and Print-Line to indicate that the message should be printed to the console. But the responsibility of *interpreting* the effect and actually manipulating the console is held by the run method on IO.

Other than technically satisfying the requirements of referential transparency, has the IO type actually bought us anything? That's a personal value judgement. As with any other data type, we can assess the merits of IO by considering what sort of algebra it provides—is it something interesting, from which we can define a large number of useful operations and programs, with nice laws that give us the ability to reason about what these larger programs will do? Not really. Let's look at the operations we can define:

```
trait IO { self =>              ← The self argument lets us refer to
  def run: Unit                   this object as self instead of this.
  def ++(io: IO): IO = new IO {
    def run = { self.run; io.run }  ← self refers to the outer IO.
```

```
    }
  }
  object IO {
    def empty: IO = new IO { def run = () }
  }
```

The only thing we can perhaps say about IO as it stands right now is that it forms a Monoid (empty is the identity, and ++ is the associative operation). So if we have, for example, a List[IO], we can reduce that to a single IO, and the associativity of ++ means that we can do this either by folding left or folding right. On its own, this isn't very interesting. All it seems to have given us is the ability to delay when a side effect actually happens.

Now we'll let you in on a secret: you, as the programmer, get to invent whatever API you wish to represent your computations, including those that interact with the universe external to your program. This process of crafting pleasing, useful, and composable descriptions of what you want your programs to do is at its core *language design*. You're crafting a little language, and an associated *interpreter*, that will allow you to express various programs. If you don't like something about this language you've created, change it! You should approach this like any other design task.

13.2.1 *Handling input effects*

As you've seen before, sometimes when building up a little language you'll encounter a program that it can't express. So far our IO type can represent only "output" effects. There's no way to express IO computations that must, at various points, wait for input from some external source. Suppose we wanted to write a program that prompts the user for a temperature in degrees Fahrenheit, and then converts this value to Celsius and echoes it to the user. A typical imperative program might look something like this.[1]

Listing 13.2   Imperative program that converts Fahrenheit to Celsius

```
def fahrenheitToCelsius(f: Double): Double =
  (f - 32) * 5.0/9.0

def converter: Unit = {
  println("Enter a temperature in degrees Fahrenheit: ")
  val d = readLine.toDouble
  println(fahrenheitToCelsius(d))
}
```

Unfortunately, we run into problems if we want to make converter into a pure function that returns an IO:

```
def fahrenheitToCelsius(f: Double): Double =
  (f - 32) * 5.0/9.0

def converter: IO = {
  val prompt: IO = PrintLine(
```

---

[1] We're not doing any sort of error handling here. This is just meant to be an illustrative example.

```
    "Enter a temperature in degrees Fahrenheit: ")
  // now what ???
}
```

In Scala, readLine is a def with the side effect of capturing a line of input from the console. It returns a String. We could wrap a call to readLine in IO, but we have nowhere to put the result! We don't yet have a way of representing this sort of effect. The problem is that our current IO type can't express computations that *yield a value* of some meaningful type—our interpreter of IO just produces Unit as its output. Should we give up on our IO type and resort to using side effects? Of course not! We extend our IO type to allow *input*, by adding a type parameter:

```scala
sealed trait IO[A] { self =>
  def run: A
  def map[B](f: A => B): IO[B] =
    new IO[B] { def run = f(self.run) }
  def flatMap[B](f: A => IO[B]): IO[B] =
    new IO[B] { def run = f(self.run).run }
}
```

An IO computation can now return a meaningful value. Note that we've added map and flatMap functions so IO can be used in for-comprehensions. And IO now forms a Monad:

```scala
object IO extends Monad[IO] {
  def unit[A](a: => A): IO[A] = new IO[A] { def run = a }
  def flatMap[A,B](fa: IO[A])(f: A => IO[B]) = fa flatMap f
  def apply[A](a: => A): IO[A] = unit(a)
}
```

> This method lets us use the function application syntax to construct IO blocks, as in IO { ... }.

We can now write our converter example:

```scala
def ReadLine: IO[String] = IO { readLine }
def PrintLine(msg: String): IO[Unit] = IO { println(msg) }

def converter: IO[Unit] = for {
  _ <- PrintLine("Enter a temperature in degrees Fahrenheit: ")
  d <- ReadLine.map(_.toDouble)
  _ <- PrintLine(fahrenheitToCelsius(d).toString)
} yield ()
```

Our converter definition no longer has side effects—it's a referentially transparent description of a computation with effects, and converter.run is the interpreter that will actually execute those effects. And because IO forms a Monad, we can use all the monadic combinators we wrote previously. Here are some other example usages of IO:

- val echo = ReadLine.flatMap(PrintLine)—An IO[Unit] that reads a line from the console and echoes it back
- val readInt = ReadLine.map(_.toInt)—An IO[Int] that parses an Int by reading a line from the console

- val readInts = readInt ** readInt—An IO[(Int,Int)] that parses an (Int,Int) by reading two lines from the console[2]
- replicateM(10)(ReadLine)—An IO[List[String]] that will read 10 lines from the console and return the list of results[3]

Let's do a larger example—an interactive program that prompts the user for input in a loop and then computes the factorial of the input. Here's an example run:

```
The Amazing Factorial REPL, v2.0
q - quit
<number> - compute the factorial of the given number
<anything else> - crash spectacularly
3
factorial: 6
7
factorial: 5040
q
```

The code for this is shown in listing 13.3. It uses a few Monad functions we haven't seen yet: when, foreachM, and sequence_, discussed in the sidebar. For the full listing, see the associated chapter code. The details of this code aren't too important; the point here is just to demonstrate how we can embed an imperative programming language into the purely functional subset of Scala. All the usual imperative programming tools are here—we can write loops, perform I/O, and so on.

> **Listing 13.3   An imperative program with a doWhile loop**

Allocation of a mutable reference.

Dereference to obtain the value inside a reference.

Imperative factorial using a mutable IO reference.

Modify reference in a loop.

See sidebar for definition of doWhile.

```
def factorial(n: Int): IO[Int] = for {
  acc <- ref(1)
  _ <- foreachM (1 to n toStream) (i => acc.modify(_ * i).skip)
  result <- acc.get
} yield result

val factorialREPL: IO[Unit] = sequence_(
  IO { println(helpstring) },
  doWhile { IO { readLine } } { line =>
    when (line != "q") { for {
      n <- factorial(line.toInt)
      _ <- IO { println("factorial: " + n) }
    } yield () }
  })
```

---

[2] Recall that a ** b is the same as map2(a,b)((_,_)); it combines two effects into a pair of their results.
[3] Recall that replicateM(3)(fa) is the same as sequence(List(fa,fa,fa)).

Additional monad combinators

Listing 13.3 makes use of some monad combinators we haven't seen before, although they can be defined for any `Monad`. You may want to think about what these combinators mean for types other than `IO`. Note that not all of them make sense for every monadic type. (For instance, what does `forever` mean for `Option`? For `Stream`?)

```
def doWhile[A](a: F[A])(cond: A => F[Boolean]): F[Unit] = for {
  a1 <- a
  ok <- cond(a1)
  _ <- if (ok) doWhile(a)(cond) else unit(())
} yield ()
```

Repeats the effect of the first argument as long as the `cond` function yields `true`

```
def forever[A,B](a: F[A]): F[B] = {
  lazy val t: F[B] = forever(a)
  a flatMap (_ => t)
}
```

Repeats the effect of its argument infinitely

Folds the stream with the function `f`, combining the effects and returning the result

```
def foldM[A,B](l: Stream[A])(z: B)(f: (B,A) => F[B]): F[B] =
  l match {
    case h #:: t => f(z,h) flatMap (z2 => foldM(t)(z2)(f))
    case _ => unit(z)
  }
```

The same as the `foldM` function above except ignores the result

```
def foldM_[A,B](l: Stream[A])(z: B)(f: (B,A) => F[B]): F[Unit] =
  skip { foldM(l)(z)(f) }
```

```
def foreachM[A](l: Stream[A])(f: A => F[Unit]): F[Unit] =
  foldM_(l)(())((u,a) => skip(f(a)))
```

Calls the function `f` for each element of the stream and combines the effects

We don't necessarily endorse writing code this way in Scala.[4] But it does demonstrate that FP is not in any way limited in its expressiveness—every program can be expressed in a purely functional way, even if that functional program is a straightforward embedding of an imperative program into the `IO` monad.

13.2.2 Benefits and drawbacks of the simple IO type

An `IO` monad like what we have so far is a kind of least common denominator for expressing programs with external effects. Its usage is important mainly because it

---

[4] If you have a monolithic block of impure code like this, you can always just write a definition that performs actual side effects and then wrap it in `IO`—this will be more efficient, and the syntax is nicer than what's provided using a combination of for-comprehension syntax and the various `Monad` combinators.

clearly separates pure code from impure code, forcing us to be honest about where interactions with the outside world are occurring. It also encourages the beneficial factoring of effects that we discussed earlier. But when programming *within* the IO monad, we have many of the same difficulties as we would in ordinary imperative programming, which has motivated functional programmers to look for more composable ways of describing effectful programs.[5] Nonetheless, our IO monad does provide some real benefits:

- IO computations are ordinary *values*. We can store them in lists, pass them to functions, create them dynamically, and so on. Any common pattern can be wrapped up in a function and reused.

- Reifying IO computations as values means we can craft a more interesting interpreter than the simple run method baked into the IO type itself. Later in this chapter, we'll build a more refined IO type and sketch out an interpreter that uses non-blocking I/O in its implementation. What's more, as we vary the interpreter, client code like the converter example remains identical—we don't expose the representation of IO to the programmer at all! It's entirely an implementation detail of our IO interpreter.

Our naive IO monad also has a few problems:

- Many IO programs will overflow the runtime call stack and throw a StackOverflowError. If you haven't encountered this problem yet in your own experimenting, you'd certainly run into it if you were to write larger programs using our current IO type. For example, if you keep typing numbers into the factorialREPL program from earlier, it eventually overflows the stack.

- A value of type IO[A] is completely opaque. It's really just a lazy identity—a function that takes no arguments. When we call run, we hope that it will eventually produce a value of type A, but there's no way for us to inspect such a program and see what it might do. It might hang forever and do nothing, or it might eventually do something productive. There's no way to tell. We could say that it's *too general,* and as a result there's little reasoning that we can do with IO values. We can compose them with the monadic combinators, or we can run them, but that's all we can do.

- Our simple IO type has nothing at all to say about concurrency or asynchronous operations. The primitives we have so far only allow us to sequence opaque blocking IO actions one after another. Many I/O libraries, such as the java.nio package that comes with the standard libraries, allow non-blocking and asynchronous I/O. Our IO type is incapable of making use of such operations. We'll rectify that by the end of this chapter when we develop a more practical IO monad.

Let's start by solving the first problem (overflowing the call stack), since it will inform our solution for the other two.

---

[5] We'll see an example of this in chapter 15 when we develop a data type for composable streaming I/O.

13.3 Avoiding the StackOverflowError

To better understand the StackOverflowError, consider this very simple program that demonstrates the problem:

```
val p = IO.forever(PrintLine("Still going..."))
```

If we evaluate p.run, it will crash with a StackOverflowError after printing a few thousand lines. If you look at the stack trace, you'll see that run is calling itself over and over. The problem is in the definition of flatMap:

```
def flatMap[B](f: A => IO[B]): IO[B] =
  new IO[B] { def run = f(self.run).run }
```

This method creates a new IO object whose run definition calls run again *before* calling f. This will keep building up nested run calls on the stack and eventually overflow it. What can be done about this?

13.3.1 Reifying control flow as data constructors

The answer is surprisingly simple. Instead of letting program control just flow through with function calls, we explicitly bake into our data type the control flow that we want to support. For example, instead of making flatMap a method that constructs a new IO in terms of run, we can just make it a data constructor of the IO data type. Then the interpreter can be a tail-recursive loop. Whenever it encounters a constructor like FlatMap(x,k), it will simply interpret x and then call k on the result. Here's a new IO type that implements that idea.

Listing 13.4 Creating a new IO type

```
sealed trait IO[A] {
  def flatMap[B](f: A => IO[B]): IO[B] =
    FlatMap(this, f)
  def map[B](f: A => B): IO[B] =
    flatMap(f andThen (Return(_)))
}
case class Return[A](a: A) extends IO[A]
case class Suspend[A](resume: () => A) extends IO[A]
case class FlatMap[A,B](sub: IO[A], k: A => IO[B]) extends IO[B]
```

A pure computation that immediately returns an A without any further steps. When run sees this constructor, it knows the computation has finished.

A suspension of the computation where resume is a function that takes no arguments, but has some effect and yields a result.

A composition of two steps. Reifies flatMap as a data constructor rather than a function. When run sees this, it should first process the subcomputation sub and then continue with k once sub produces a result.

This new IO type has three data constructors, representing the three different kinds of control flow that we want the interpreter of this data type to support. Return represents an IO action that has finished, meaning that we want to return the value a without any further steps. Suspend means that we want to execute some effect to produce a result. And the `FlatMap` data constructor lets us *extend* or *continue* an existing computation by using the result of the first computation to produce a second computation. The `flatMap` method's implementation can now simply call the `FlatMap` data constructor and return immediately. When the interpreter encounters `FlatMap(sub, k)`, it can interpret the subcomputation `sub` and then remember to call the continuation `k` on the result. Then `k` will continue executing the program.

We'll get to the interpreter shortly, but first let's rewrite our `printLine` example to use this new `IO` type:

```
def printLine(s: String): IO[Unit] =
  Suspend(() => Return(println(s)))
```

```
val p = IO.forever(printLine("Still going..."))
```

What this actually creates is an infinite nested structure, much like a `Stream`. The "head" of the stream is a `Function0`, and the rest of the computation is like the "tail":

```
FlatMap(Suspend(() => println(s)),
       _ => FlatMap(Suspend(() => println(s)),
                   _ => FlatMap(...)))
```

And here's the tail-recursive interpreter that traverses the structure and performs the effects:

Here x is a
Suspend(r),
so we force
the r thunk
and call f on
the result.

```
@annotation.tailrec def run[A](io: IO[A]): A = io match {
  case Return(a) => a
  case Suspend(r) => r()
  case FlatMap(x, f) => x match {
    case Return(a) => run(f(a))
    case Suspend(r) => run(f(r()))
    case FlatMap(y, g) => run(y flatMap (a => g(a) flatMap f))
  }
}
```

We could just say
`run(f(run(x)))`
here, but then the inner
call to `run` wouldn't be
in tail position. Instead,
we match on `x` to see
what it is.

In this case, `io` is an expression like
`FlatMap(FlatMap(y, g), f)`. We reassociate
this to the right in order to be able to call `run` in tail
position, and the next iteration will match on `y`.

Note that instead of saying `run(f(run(x)))` in the `FlatMap(x, f)` case (thereby losing tail recursion), we instead pattern match on `x`, since it can only be one of three things. If it's a `Return`, we can just call `f` on the pure value inside. If it's a `Suspend`, then we can just execute its resumption, call `FlatMap` with `f` on its result, and recurse. But if `x` is itself a `FlatMap` constructor, then we know that `io` consists of two `FlatMap` constructors nested on the left like this: `FlatMap(FlatMap(y,g),f)`.

In order to continue running the program in that case, the next thing we naturally want to do is look at `y` to see if *it* is another `FlatMap` constructor, but the expression may be arbitrarily deep and we want to remain tail-recursive. We reassociate this to the right, effectively turning `(y flatMap g) flatMap f` into `y flatMap (a => g(a) flatMap f)`. We're just taking advantage of the monad associativity law! Then we call `run` on the rewritten expression, letting us remain tail-recursive. Thus, when we actually interpret our program, it will be incrementally rewritten to be a right-associated sequence of `FlatMap` constructors:

```
FlatMap(a1, a1 =>
  FlatMap(a2, a2 =>
    FlatMap(a3, a3 =>
      ...
        FlatMap(aN, aN => Return(aN)))))
```

If we now pass our example program `p` to `run`, it'll continue running indefinitely without a stack overflow, which is what we want. Our `run` function won't overflow the stack, even for infinitely recursive `IO` programs.

What have we done here? When a program running on the JVM makes a function call, it'll push a frame onto the call stack in order to remember where to return after the call has finished so that the execution can continue. We've made this program control explicit in our `IO` data type. When `run` interprets an `IO` program, it'll determine whether the program is requesting to execute some effect with a `Suspend(s)`, or whether it wants to call a subroutine with `FlatMap(x,f)`. Instead of the program making use of the call stack, `run` will call `x()` and then continue by calling `f` on the result of that. And `f` will immediately return either a `Suspend`, a `FlatMap`, or a `Return`, transferring control to `run` again. Our `IO` program is therefore a kind of *coroutine*[6] that executes cooperatively with `run`. It continually makes either `Suspend` or `FlatMap` requests, and every time it does so, it suspends its own execution and returns control to `run`. And it's actually `run` that drives the execution of the program forward, one such suspension at a time. A function like `run` is sometimes called a *trampoline*, and the overall technique of returning control to a single loop to eliminate the stack is called *trampolining*.

13.3.2 Trampolining: a general solution to stack overflow

Nothing says that the `resume` functions in our `IO` monad have to perform side effects. The `IO` type we have so far is in fact a general data structure for trampolining computations—even *pure* computations that don't do any I/O at all!

The `StackOverflowError` problem manifests itself in Scala wherever we have a composite function that consists of more function calls than there's space for on the call stack. This problem is easy to demonstrate:

```
scala> val f = (x: Int) => x
f: Int => Int = <function1>

scala> val g = List.fill(100000)(f).foldLeft(f)(_ compose _)
g: Int => Int = <function1>

scala> g(42)
java.lang.StackOverflowError
```

We construct a composite function g that consists of 100,000 functions where each one calls the next.

---

[6] If you aren't familiar with the term *coroutine*, you may want to check out the Wikipedia page (http://mng.bz/ALiI), but it's not essential to following the rest of this chapter.

And it'll likely fail for much smaller compositions. Fortunately, we can solve this with our IO monad:

```scala
scala> val f: Int => IO[Int] = (x: Int) => Return(x)
f: Int => IO[Int] = <function1>

scala> val g = List.fill(100000)(f).foldLeft(f) {
     |     (a, b) => x => Suspend(() => a(x).flatMap(b))
     | }
g: Int => IO[Int] = <function1>

scala> val x1 = run(g(0))
x1: Int = 0

scala> val x2 = run(g(42))
x2: Int = 42
```

Create a large, left-nested chain of `flatMap` calls.

But there's no I/O going on here at all. So IO is a bit of a misnomer. It really gets that name from the fact that Suspend can contain a side-effecting function. But what we have is not really a monad for I/O—it's actually a monad for tail-call elimination! Let's change its name to reflect that:

```scala
sealed trait TailRec[A] {
  def flatMap[B](f: A => TailRec[B]): TailRec[B] =
    FlatMap(this, f)
  def map[B](f: A => B): TailRec[B] =
    flatMap(f andThen (Return(_)))
}
case class Return[A](a: A) extends TailRec[A]
case class Suspend[A](resume: () => A) extends TailRec[A]
case class FlatMap[A,B](sub: TailRec[A],
                        k: A => TailRec[B]) extends TailRec[B]
```

We can use the TailRec data type to add trampolining to any function type A => B by modifying the return type B to TailRec[B] instead. We just saw an example where we changed a program that used Int => Int to use Int => TailRec[Int]. The program just had to be modified to use flatMap in function composition[7] and to Suspend before every function call.

Using TailRec can be slower than direct function calls, but its advantage is that we gain predictable stack usage.[8]

---

[7] This is just Kleisli composition from chapter 11. In other words, the trampolined function uses Kleisli composition in the TailRec monad instead of ordinary function composition.

[8] When we use TailRec to implement tail calls that wouldn't be otherwise optimized, it's faster than using direct calls (not to mention stack-safe). It seems that the overhead of building and tearing down stack frames is greater than the overhead of having all calls be wrapped in a Suspend. There are variations on TailRec that we haven't investigated in detail—it isn't necessary to transfer control to the central loop after every function call, only periodically to avoid stack overflows. We can, for example, implement the same basic idea using exceptions. See Throw.scala in the chapter code.

13.4   *A more nuanced IO type*

If we use `TrailRec` as our `IO` type, this solves the stack overflow problem, but the other two problems with the monad still remain—it's inexplicit about what kinds of effects may occur, and it has no concurrency mechanism or means of performing I/O without blocking the current thread of execution.

During execution, the `run` interpreter will look at a `TailRec` program such as `FlatMap(Suspend(s),k)`, in which case the next thing to do is to call `s()`. The program is returning control to `run`, requesting that it execute some effect `s`, wait for the result, and respond by passing the resulting value to `k` (which may subsequently return a further request). At the moment, the interpreter can't know anything about *what kind of effects* the program is going to have. It's completely opaque. So the only thing it can do is call `s()`. Not only can that have an arbitrary and unknowable side effect, there's no way that the interpreter could allow asynchronous calls if it wanted to. Since the suspension is a `Function0`, all we can do is call it and wait for it to complete.

What if we used `Par` from chapter 7 for the suspension instead of `Function0`? Let's call this type `Async`, since the interpreter can now support asynchronous execution.

Listing 13.5   Defining our `Async` type

```
sealed trait Async[A] {
  def flatMap[B](f: A => Async[B]): Async[B] =
    FlatMap(this, f)
  def map[B](f: A => B): Async[B] =
    flatMap(f andThen (Return(_)))
}
case class Return[A](a: A) extends Async[A]
case class Suspend[A](resume: Par[A]) extends Async[A]
case class FlatMap[A,B](sub: Async[A],
                        k: A => Async[B]) extends Async[B]
```

Note that the `resume` argument to `Suspend` is now a `Par[A]` rather than a `() => A` (or a `Function0[A]`). The implementation of `run` changes accordingly—it now returns a `Par[A]` rather than an `A`, and we rely on a separate tail-recursive `step` function to reassociate the `FlatMap` constructors:

```
@annotation.tailrec
def step[A](async: Async[A]): Async[A] = async match {
  case FlatMap(FlatMap(x,f), g) => step(x flatMap (a => f(a) flatMap g))
  case FlatMap(Return(x), f) => step(f(x))
  case _ => async
}

def run[A](async: Async[A]): Par[A] = step(async) match {
  case Return(a) => Par.unit(a)
  case Suspend(r) => Par.flatMap(r)(a => run(a))
  case FlatMap(x, f) => x match {
    case Suspend(r) => Par.flatMap(r)(a => run(f(a)))
    case _ => sys.error("Impossible; `step` eliminates these cases")
  }
}
```

Our `Async` data type now supports asynchronous computations—we can embed them using the `Suspend` constructor, which takes an arbitrary `Par`. This works, but we take this idea one step further and abstract over the choice of type constructor used in `Suspend`. To do that, we'll generalize `TailRec` / `Async` and parameterize it on some type constructor F rather than use `Function0` or `Par` specifically. We'll name this more abstract data type `Free`:

> The difference between `Free` and `TailRec` is that `Free` is parameterized with a type constructor F. `TailRec` is a special case of `Free` where F is fixed to be `Function0`.

```scala
sealed trait Free[F[_],A]
case class Return[F[_],A](a: A) extends Free[F,A]
case class Suspend[F[_],A](s: F[A]) extends Free[F,A]
case class FlatMap[F[_],A,B](s: Free[F,A],
                             f: A => Free[F,B]) extends Free[F,B]
```

> The suspension is now of some arbitrary type F rather than `Function0`.

Then `TailRec` and `Async` are simply type aliases:

```scala
type TailRec[A] = Free[Function0,A]
type Async[A] = Free[Par,A]
```

13.4.1 Reasonably priced monads

The `Return` and `FlatMap` constructors witness that this data type is a monad *for any choice of* F, and since they're exactly the operations required to generate a monad, we say that it's a *free* monad.[9]

EXERCISE 13.1

Free is a monad for any choice of F. Implement `map` and `flatMap` methods on the Free trait, and give the `Monad` instance for `Free[F,_]`.[10]

```scala
def freeMonad[F[_]]: Monad[({type f[a] = Free[F,a]})#f]
```

EXERCISE 13.2

Implement a specialized tail-recursive interpreter, `runTrampoline`, for running a `Free[Function0,A]`.

```scala
@annotation.tailrec
def runTrampoline[A](a: Free[Function0,A]): A
```

---

[9] "Free" in this context means *generated freely* in the sense that F itself doesn't need to have any monadic structure of its own. See the chapter notes for a more formal statement of what "free" means.

[10] Note that we must use the "type lambda" trick discussed in chapter 10 to partially apply the Free type constructor.

■ **EXERCISE 13.3**

Hard: Implement a generic interpreter for `Free[F,A]`, given a `Monad[F]`. You can pattern your implementation after the `Async` interpreter given previously, including use of a tail-recursive `step` function.

```
def run[F[_],A](a: Free[F,A])(implicit F: Monad[F]): F[A]
```

What is the *meaning* of `Free[F,A]`? Essentially, it's a recursive structure that contains a value of type `A` wrapped in zero or more layers of `F`.[11] It's a monad because `flatMap` lets us take the `A` and from it generate *more* layers of `F`. Before getting at the result, an interpreter of the structure must be able to process all of those `F` layers. We can view the structure and its interpreter as coroutines that are interacting, and the type `F` *defines the protocol of this interaction.* By choosing our `F` carefully, we can precisely control what kinds of interactions are allowed.

13.4.2 *A monad that supports only console I/O*

`Function0` is not just the simplest possible choice for the type parameter `F`, but also one of the least restrictive in terms of what's allowed. This lack of restriction gives us no ability to reason about what a value of type `Function0[A]` might do. A more restrictive choice for `F` in `Free[F,A]` might be an algebraic data type that only models interaction with the console.

Listing 13.6 Creating our `Console` type

```
sealed trait Console[A] {
  def toPar: Par[A]            ← Interpret this Console[A] as a Par[A].
  def toThunk: () => A         ←
}                                        Interpret this
case object ReadLine extends Console[Option[String]] {    Console[A] as a
  def toPar = Par.lazyUnit(run)                           Function0[A].
  def toThunk = () => run

  def run: Option[String] =    ←
    try Some(readLine())                      Helper function used
    catch { case e: Exception => None }       by both interpreters
}                                             of ReadLine.
case class PrintLine(line: String) extends Console[Unit] {
  def toPar = Par.lazyUnit(println(line))
  def toThunk = () => println(line)
}
```

---

[11] Put another way, it's a tree with data of type A at the leaves, where the branching is described by F. Put yet another way, it's an abstract syntax tree for a program in a language whose instructions are given by F, with free variables in A.

A Console[A] represents a computation that yields an A, but it's restricted to one of two possible forms: ReadLine (having type Console[Option[String]]) or PrintLine. We bake two interpreters into Console, one that converts to a Par, and another that converts to a Function0. The implementations of these interpreters are straightforward.

We can now embed this data type into Free to obtain a restricted IO type allowing for only console I/O. We just use the Suspend constructor of Free:

```
object Console {
  type ConsoleIO[A] = Free[Console, A]

  def readLn: ConsoleIO[Option[String]] =
    Suspend(ReadLine)

  def printLn(line: String): ConsoleIO[Unit] =
    Suspend(PrintLine(line))
}
```

Using the Free[Console,A] type, or equivalently ConsoleIO[A], we can write programs that interact with the console, and we reasonably expect that they don't perform other kinds of I/O:[12]

```
val f1: Free[Console, Option[String]] = for {
  _  <- printLn("I can only interact with the console.")
  ln <- readLn
} yield ln
```

Note that these aren't Scala's standard readLine and println, but the monadic methods we defined earlier.

This sounds good, but how do we actually run a ConsoleIO? Recall our signature for run:

```
def run[F[_],A](a: Free[F,A])(implicit F: Monad[F]): F[A]
```

In order to run a Free[Console,A], we seem to need a Monad[Console], which we don't have. Note that it's not possible to implement flatMap for Console:

```
sealed trait Console[A] {
  def flatMap[B](f: A => Console[B]): Console[B] = this match {
    case ReadLine => ???
    case PrintLine(s) => ???
  }
}
```

Translate between any 'F[A]' to 'G[A]'.

We must *translate* our Console type, which doesn't form a monad, to some other type (like Function0 or Par) that does. We'll make use of the following type to do this translation:

This gives us infix syntax F ~> G for Translate[F,G].

```
trait Translate[F[_], G[_]] { def apply[A](f: F[A]): G[A] }
type ~>[F[_], G[_]] = Translate[F,G]
```

---

[12] Of course, a Scala program could always technically have side effects but we're assuming that the programmer has adopted the discipline of programming without side effects, since Scala can't guarantee this for us.

```
val consoleToFunction0 =
  new (Console ~> Function0) { def apply[A](a: Console[A]) = a.toThunk }
val consoleToPar =
  new (Console ~> Par) { def apply[A](a: Console[A]) = a.toPar }
```

Using this type, we can generalize our earlier implementation of run slightly:

```
def runFree[F[_],G[_],A](free: Free[F,A])(t: F ~> G)(
                         implicit G: Monad[G]): G[A] =
  step(free) match {
    case Return(a) => G.unit(a)
    case Suspend(r) => t(r)
    case FlatMap(Suspend(r),f) => G.flatMap(t(r))(a => runFree(f(a))(t))
    case _ => sys.error("Impossible; `step` eliminates these cases")
  }
```

We accept a value of type `F ~> G` and perform the translation as we interpret the `Free[F,A]` program. Now we can implement the convenience functions `runConsoleFunction0` and `runConsolePar` to convert a `Free[Console,A]` to either `Function0[A]` or `Par[A]`:

```
def runConsoleFunction0[A](a: Free[Console,A]): () => A =
  runFree[Console,Function0,A](a)(consoleToFunction0)
```

```
def runConsolePar[A](a: Free[Console,A]): Par[A] =
  runFree[Console,Par,A](a)(consoleToPar)
```

This relies on having `Monad[Function0]` and `Monad[Par]` instances:

```
implicit val function0Monad = new Monad[Function0] {
  def unit[A](a: => A) = () => a
  def flatMap[A,B](a: Function0[A])(f: A => Function0[B]) =
    () => f(a())()
}
implicit val parMonad = new Monad[Par] {
  def unit[A](a: => A) = Par.unit(a)
  def flatMap[A,B](a: Par[A])(f: A => Par[B]) =
    Par.fork { Par.flatMap(a)(f) }
}
```

EXERCISE 13.4

Hard: It turns out that `runConsoleFunction0` isn't stack-safe, since `flatMap` isn't stack-safe for `Function0` (it has the same problem as our original, naive IO type in which run called itself in the implementation of `flatMap`). Implement `translate` using `runFree`, and then use it to implement `runConsole` in a stack-safe way.

```
def translate[F[_],G[_],A](f: Free[F,A])(fg: F ~> G): Free[G,A]
def runConsole[A](a: Free[Console,A]): A
```

A value of type Free[F,A] is like a program written in an instruction set provided by F. In the case of Console, the two instructions are PrintLine and ReadLine. The recursive scaffolding (Suspend) and monadic variable substitution (FlatMap and Return) are provided by Free itself. We can introduce other choices of F for different instruction sets, for example, different I/O capabilities—a file system F granting read/write access (or even just read access) to the file system. Or we could have a network F granting the ability to open network connections and read from them, and so on.

13.4.3 Pure interpreters

Note that nothing about the ConsoleIO type implies that any effects must actually occur! That decision is the responsibility of the interpreter. We could choose to translate our Console actions into pure values that perform no I/O at all! For example, an interpreter for testing purposes could just ignore PrintLine requests and always return a constant string in response to ReadLine requests. We do this by translating our Console requests to a String => A, which forms a monad in A, as we saw in chapter 11, exercise 11.20 (readerMonad).

Listing 13.7 Creating our ConsoleReader class

```
case class ConsoleReader[A](run: String => A) {          ←——————  A specialized
  def map[B](f: A => B): ConsoleReader[B] =                        reader monad
    ConsoleReader(r => f(run(r)))
  def flatMap[B](f: A => ConsoleReader[B]): ConsoleReader[B] =
    ConsoleReader(r => f(run(r)).run(r))
}
object ConsoleReader {
  implicit val monad = new Monad[ConsoleReader] {
    def unit[A](a: => A) = ConsoleReader(_ => a)
    def flatMap[A,B](ra: ConsoleReader[A])(f: A => ConsoleReader[B]) =
      ra flatMap f
  }
}
```

We introduce another function on Console, toReader, and then use that to implement runConsoleReader:

```
sealed trait Console[A] {
  ...
  def toReader: ConsoleReader[A]
}
val consoleToReader = new (Console ~> ConsoleReader) {
  def apply[A](a: Console[A]) = a.toReader
}

@annotation.tailrec
def runConsoleReader[A](io: ConsoleIO[A]): ConsoleReader[A] =
  runFree[Console,ConsoleReader,A](io)(consoleToReader)
```

Or for a more complete simulation of console I/O, we could write an interpreter that uses two lists—one to represent the input buffer and another to represent the output buffer. When the interpreter encounters a `ReadLine`, it can pop an element off the input buffer, and when it encounters a `PrintLine(s)`, it can push s onto the output buffer:

```scala
sealed trait Console[A] {
  ...
  def toState: ConsoleState[A]
}
case class Buffers(in: List[String], out: List[String])

case class ConsoleState[A](run: Buffers => (A, Buffers)) { ... }

object ConsoleState {
  implicit val monad: Monad[ConsoleState] = ...
}

val consoleToState = new (Console ~> ConsoleState) {
  def apply[A](a: Console[A]) = a.toState
}

def runConsoleState[A](io: ConsoleIO[A]): ConsoleState[A] =
  runFree[Console,ConsoleState,A](io)(consoleToState)
```

> Represents a pair of buffers. The `in` buffer will be fed to `ReadLine` requests, and the `out` buffer will receive strings contained in `PrintLine` requests.

> A specialized state action.

> Converts to a pure state action.

This will allow us to have multiple interpreters for our little languages! We could, for example, use `runConsoleState` for testing console applications with our property-based testing library from chapter 8, and then use `runConsole` to run our program for real.[13]

The fact that we can write a generic `runFree` that turns `Free` programs into `State` or `Reader` values demonstrates something amazing—there's nothing about our `Free` type that requires side effects of any kind. For example, from the perspective of our `ConsoleIO` programs, we can't know (and don't care) whether they're going to be run with an interpreter that uses "real" side effects like `runConsole`, or one like `runConsoleState` that doesn't. As far as we're concerned, *a program is just a referentially transparent expression*—a pure computation that may occasionally make requests of some interpreter. The interpreter is free to use side effects or not. That's now an entirely separate concern.

13.5 *Non-blocking and asynchronous I/O*

Let's turn our attention now to the last remaining problem with our original `IO` monad—that of performing non-blocking or asynchronous I/O. When performing I/O, we frequently need to invoke operations that take a long time to complete and don't occupy the CPU. These include accepting a network connection from a server socket, reading a chunk of bytes from an input stream, writing a large number of bytes to a file,

---

[13] Note that `runConsoleReader` and `runConsoleState` aren't stack-safe as implemented, for the same reason that `runConsoleFunction0` wasn't stack-safe. We can fix this by changing the representations to `String => TailRec[A]` for `ConsoleReader` and `Buffers => TailRec[(A,Buffers)]` for `ConsoleState`.

and so on. Let's think about what this means in terms of the implementation of our Free interpreter.

When runConsole, for example, encounters a Suspend(s), s will be of type Console and we'll have a translation f from Console to the target monad. To allow for non-blocking asynchronous I/O, we simply change the target monad from Function0 to Par or another concurrency monad such as scala.concurrent.Future. So just like we were able to write both pure and effectful interpreters for Console, we can write both blocking and non-blocking interpreters as well, just by varying the target monad.[14]

Let's look at an example. Here, runConsolePar will turn the Console requests into Par actions and then combine them all into one Par[A]. We can think of it as a kind of compilation—we're replacing the abstract Console requests with more concrete Par requests that will actually read from and write to the standard input and output streams when the resulting Par value is run:

```
scala> def p: ConsoleIO[Unit] = for {
     |   _ <- printLn("What's your name?")
     |   n <- readLn
     |   _ <- n match {
     |     case Some(n) => printLn(s"Hello, $n!")
     |     case None => printLn(s"Fine, be that way.")
     |   }
     | } yield ()
p: ConsoleIO[Unit] =
FlatMap(Suspend(PrintLine(What's your name?)),<function1>)

scala> val q = runConsolePar(p)
q: Par[Unit] = <function1>
```

Although this simple example runs in Par, which in principle permits asynchronous actions, it doesn't make use of any asynchronous actions—readLine and println are both *blocking* I/O operations. But there are I/O libraries that support *non-blocking* I/O directly and Par will let us bind to such libraries. The details of these libraries vary, but to give the general idea, a non-blocking source of bytes might have an interface like this:

```
trait Source {
  def readBytes(
    numBytes: Int,
    callback: Either[Throwable, Array[Byte]] => Unit): Unit
}
```

Here it's assumed that readBytes returns immediately. We give readBytes a callback function indicating what to do when the result becomes available or the I/O subsystem encounters an error.

---

[14] Our Par monad from chapter 7 doesn't do any handling of exceptions. See the file Task.scala in the answer source code accompanying this chapter for an example of an asynchronous I/O monad with proper exception handling.

Obviously, using this sort of library directly is painful.[15] We want to program against a compositional monadic interface and abstract over the details of the underlying non-blocking I/O library. Luckily, the Par type lets us wrap these callbacks:

```
trait Future[+A] {
  private def apply(k: A => Unit): Unit
}

type Par[+A] = ExecutorService => Future[A]
```

The internal representation of Future is remarkably similar to that of Source. It's a single method that returns immediately, but takes a callback or continuation k that it will invoke once the value of type A becomes available. It's straightforward to wrap Source.readBytes in a Future, but we'll need to add a primitive to our Par algebra:[16]

```
def async[A](run: (A => Unit) => Unit): Par[A] = es => new Future {
  def apply(k: A => Unit) = run(k)
}
```

With this in place, we can now wrap the asynchronous readBytes function in the nice monadic interface of Par:

```
def nonblockingRead(source: Source, numBytes: Int):
    Par[Either[Throwable,Array[Byte]]] =
  async { (cb: Either[Throwable,Array[Byte]] => Unit) =>
    source.readBytes(numBytes, cb)
  }

def readPar(source: Source, numBytes: Int):
    Free[Par,Either[Throwable,Array[Byte]]] =
  Suspend(nonblockingRead(source, numBytes))
```

And we can now use regular for-comprehensions to construct chains of non-blocking computations:

```
val src: Source = ...
val prog: Free[Par,Unit] = for {
  chunk1 <- readPar(src, 1024)
  chunk2 <- readPar(src, 1024)
  ...
}
```

EXERCISE 13.5

Hard: We're not going to work through a full-fledged implementation of a non-blocking I/O library here, but you may be interested to explore this on your own by building off the

---

[15] Even this API is rather nicer than what's offered directly by the nio package in Java (API at http://mng.bz/uojM), which supports non-blocking I/O.

[16] This may in fact be the most primitive Par operation. The other primitives we developed for Par in chapter 7 could be implemented in terms of this one.

java.nio library (API at http://mng.bz/uojM). As a start, try implementing an asynchronous read from an AsynchronousFileChannel (API at http://mng.bz/X30L).[17]

```
def read(file: AsynchronousFileChannel,
         fromPosition: Long,
         numBytes: Int): Par[Either[Throwable, Array[Byte]]]
```

13.6 *A general-purpose IO type*

We can now formulate a general methodology of writing programs that perform I/O. For any given set of I/O operations that we want to support, we can write an algebraic data type whose case classes represent the individual operations. For example, we could have a Files data type for file I/O, a DB data type for database access, and use something like Console for interacting with standard input and output. For any such data type F, we can generate a free monad Free[F,A] in which to write our programs. These can be tested individually and then finally "compiled" down to a lower-level I/O type, what we earlier called Async:

```
type IO[A] = Free[Par, A]
```

This IO type supports both trampolined sequential execution (because of Free) and asynchronous execution (because of Par). In our main program, we bring all of the individual effect types together under this most general type. All we need is a translation from any given F to Par.

13.6.1 *The main program at the end of the universe*

When the JVM calls into our main program, it expects a main method with a specific signature. The return type of this method is Unit, meaning that it's expected to have some side effects. But we can delegate to a pureMain program that's entirely pure! The only thing the main method does in that case is interpret our pure program, actually performing the effects.

> **Listing 13.8 Turning side effects into just effects**

All that the main method does is interpret our pureMain.

```
abstract class App {
  import java.util.concurrent._
```

Interprets the IO action and actually performs the effect by turning IO[A] into Par[A] and then A. The name of this method reflects that it's unsafe to call (because it has side effects).

```
  def unsafePerformIO[A](a: IO[A])(pool: ExecutorService): A =
    Par.run(pool)(run(a)(parMonad))

  def main(args: Array[String]): Unit = {
```

---

[17] This requires Java 7 or better.

```
    val pool = Executors.fixedThreadPool(8)
    unsafePerformIO(pureMain(args))(pool)
  }

  def pureMain(args: IndexedSeq[String]): IO[Unit]
}
```

Our actual program goes here, as an implementation of `pureMain` in a subclass of `App`. It also takes the arguments as an immutable `IndexedSeq` rather than a mutable `Array`.

We want to make a distinction here between effects and *side* effects. The `pureMain` program itself isn't going to have any side effects. It should be a referentially transparent expression of type `IO[Unit]`. The performing of effects is entirely contained within `main`, which is *outside the universe of our actual program*, `pureMain`. Since our program can't observe these effects occurring, but they nevertheless occur, we say that our program has effects but not side effects.

13.7 *Why the IO type is insufficient for streaming I/O*

Despite the flexibility of the `IO` monad and the advantage of having I/O actions as first-class values, the `IO` type fundamentally provides us with the same level of abstraction as ordinary imperative programming. This means that writing efficient, streaming I/O will generally involve monolithic loops.

Let's look at an example. Suppose we wanted to write a program to convert a file, `fahrenheit.txt`, containing a sequence of temperatures in degrees Fahrenheit, separated by line breaks, to a new file, `celsius.txt`, containing the same temperatures in degrees Celsius. An algebra for this might look something like this:[18]

```
trait Files[A]
case class ReadLines(file: String) extends Files[List[String]]
case class WriteLines(file: String, lines: List[String])
  extends Files[Unit]
```

Using this as our `F` type in `Free[F,A]`, we might try to write the program we want in the following way:

```
val p: Free[Files,Unit] = for {
  lines <- Suspend { (ReadLines("fahrenheit.txt")) }
  cs = lines.map(s => fahrenheitToCelsius(s.toDouble).toString)
  _ <- Suspend { WriteLines("celsius.txt", cs) }
} yield ()
```

This works, although it requires loading the contents of `fahrenheit.txt` entirely into memory to work on it, which could be problematic if the file is very large. We'd prefer to perform this task using roughly constant memory—read a line or a fixed-size buffer full of lines from `farenheit.txt`, convert to Celsius, dump to `celsius.txt`, and repeat. To achieve this efficiency we could expose a lower-level file API that gives access to I/O handles:

---

[18] We're ignoring exception handling in this API.

```
trait Files[A]
case class OpenRead(file: String) extends Files[HandleR]
case class OpenWrite(file: String) extends Files[HandleW]
case class ReadLine(h: HandleR) extends Files[Option[String]]
case class WriteLine(h: HandleW, line: String) extends Files[Unit]

trait HandleR
trait HandleW
```

The only problem is that we now need to write a monolithic loop:

```
def loop(f: HandleR, c: HandleW): Free[Files, Unit] = for {
  line <- Suspend { ReadLine(f) }
  _ <- line match {
    case None => IO.unit(())
    case Some(s) => Suspend {
                     WriteLine(fahrenheitToCelsius(s.toDouble))
                   } flatMap (_ => loop(f, c))
  }
} yield b

def convertFiles = for {
  f <- Suspend(OpenRead("fahrenheit.txt"))
  c <- Suspend(OpenWrite("celsius.txt"))
  _ <- loop(f,c)
} yield ()
```

There's nothing inherently wrong with writing a monolithic loop like this, but it's not composable. Suppose we decide later that we'd like to compute a five-element moving average of the temperatures. Modifying our `loop` function to do this would be somewhat painful. Compare that to the equivalent change we might make to `List`-based code, where we could define a `movingAvg` function and just stick it before or after our conversion to Celsius:

```
def movingAvg(n: Int)(l: List[Double]): List[Double]

cs = movingAvg(5)(lines.map(s => fahrenheitToCelsius(s.toDouble))).
    map(_.toString)
```

Even `movingAvg` could be composed from smaller pieces—we could build it using a generic combinator, `windowed`:

```
def windowed[A](n: Int, l: List[A])(f: A => B)(m: Monoid[B]): List[B]
```

The point is that programming with a composable abstraction like `List` is much nicer than programming directly with the primitive I/O operations. Lists aren't really special in this regard—they're just one instance of a composable API that's pleasant to use. And we shouldn't have to give up all the nice compositionality that we've come to expect from FP just to write programs that make use of efficient, streaming I/O.[19] Luckily we don't have to. As we'll see in chapter 15, we get to build whatever abstractions we

---

[19] One might ask if we could just have various `Files` operations return the `Stream` type we defined in chapter 5. This is called *lazy I/O*, and it's problematic for several reasons we'll discuss in chapter 15.

want for creating computations that perform I/O. If we like the metaphor of lists or streams, we can design a list-like API for expressing I/O computations. If we discover some other composable abstraction, we can find a way of using that instead. Functional programming gives us that flexibility.

13.8 Summary

This chapter introduced a simple model for handling external effects and I/O in a purely functional way. We began with a discussion of factoring effects and demonstrated how effects can be moved to the outer layers of a program. We generalized this to an IO data type that lets us describe interactions with the outside world without resorting to side effects.

We discovered that monads in Scala suffer from a stack overflow problem, and we solved it in a general way using the technique of *trampolining*. This led us to the even more general idea of *free monads*, which we employed to write a very capable IO monad with an interpreter that used non-blocking asynchronous I/O internally.

The IO monad is not the final word in writing effectful programs. It's important because it represents a kind of lowest common denominator when interacting with the external world. But in practice, we want to use IO directly as little as possible because IO programs tend to be monolithic and have limited reuse. In chapter 15, we'll discuss how to build nicer, more composable, more reusable abstractions using essentially the same technique that we used here.

Before getting to that, we'll apply what we've learned so far to fill in the other missing piece of the puzzle: *local effects*. At various places throughout this book, we've made use of local mutation rather casually, with the assumption that these effects weren't *observable*. In the next chapter, we'll explore what this means in more detail, see more examples of using local effects, and show how *effect scoping* can be enforced by the type system.

Local effects and mutable state

14

In the first chapter of this book, we introduced the concept of referential transparency, setting the premise for purely functional programming. We declared that pure functions can't mutate data in place or interact with the external world. In chapter 13, we learned that this isn't exactly true. We *can* write purely functional and compositional programs that describe interactions with the outside world. These programs are unaware that they can be interpreted with an evaluator that has an effect on the world.

In this chapter we'll develop a more mature concept of referential transparency. We'll consider the idea that effects can occur *locally* inside an expression, and that we can guarantee that no other part of the larger program can observe these effects occurring.

We'll also introduce the idea that expressions can be referentially transparent *with regard to* some programs and not others.

14.1 Purely functional mutable state

Up until this point, you may have had the impression that in purely functional programming, you're not allowed to use mutable state. But if we look carefully, there's nothing about the definitions of referential transparency and purity that disallows mutation of *local* state. Let's refer to our definitions from chapter 1:

> **Definition of referential transparency and purity**
> An expression e is referentially transparent if for all programs p all occurrences of e in p can be replaced by the result of evaluating e without affecting the meaning of p.
>
> A function f is pure if the expression f(x) is referentially transparent for all referentially transparent x.

By that definition, the following function is pure, even though it uses a `while` loop, an updatable `var`, and a mutable array.

Listing 14.1 In-place `quicksort` with a mutable array

```
def quicksort(xs: List[Int]): List[Int] = if (xs.isEmpty) xs else {
  val arr = xs.toArray
  def swap(x: Int, y: Int) = {          ←─────────  Swaps two elements in an array
    val tmp = arr(x)
    arr(x) = arr(y)
    arr(y) = tmp
  }
  def partition(n: Int, r: Int, pivot: Int) = {  ←─┐  Partitions a portion of the
    val pivotVal = arr(pivot)                        │  array into elements less
    swap(pivot, r)                                   │  than and greater than
    var j = n                                        │  pivot, respectively
    for (i <- n until r) if (arr(i) < pivotVal) {
      swap(i, j)
      j += 1
    }
    swap(j, r)
    j
  }
  def qs(n: Int, r: Int): Unit = if (n < r) {  ←────┐  Sorts a portion of
    val pi = partition(n, r, n + (n - r) / 2)        │  the array in place
    qs(n, pi - 1)
    qs(pi + 1, r)
  }
  qs(0, arr.length - 1)
  arr.toList
}
```

The `quicksort` function sorts a list by turning it into a mutable array, sorting the array in place using the well-known quicksort algorithm, and then turning the array back into a list. It's not possible for any caller to know that the individual subexpressions inside the body of `quicksort` aren't referentially transparent or that the local methods `swap`, `partition`, and `qs` aren't pure, because at no point does any code outside the `quicksort` function hold a reference to the mutable array. Since all of the mutation is locally scoped, the overall function is pure. That is, for any referentially transparent expression `xs` of type `List[Int]`, the expression `quicksort(xs)` is also referentially transparent.

Local effects

A mutation that happens inside a function is not a side effect if nothing outside the function refers to the mutated object.

Some algorithms, like quicksort, need to mutate data in place in order to work correctly or efficiently. Fortunately for us, we can always safely mutate data that's created locally. Any function can use side-effecting components internally and still present a pure external interface to its callers, and we should feel no shame taking advantage of this in our own programs. We may prefer purely functional components in our implementations for other reasons—they're easier to get right, can be assembled more easily from other pure functions, and so on—but in principle there's nothing wrong with building a pure function using local side effects in the implementation.

14.2   A data type to enforce scoping of side effects

The preceding section makes it clear that pure functions may have side effects with respect to data that's *locally scoped*. The quicksort function may mutate the array because it allocated that array, it's locally scoped, and it's not possible for any outside code to observe the mutation. If, on the other hand, quicksort somehow mutated its input list directly (as is common in mutable collection APIs), that side effect would be observable to all callers of quicksort.

There's nothing wrong with doing this sort of loose reasoning to determine the scoping of side effects, but it's sometimes desirable to *enforce* effect scoping using Scala's type system. The constituent parts of quicksort would have direct side effects if used on their own, and with the types we're using, we get no help from the compiler in controlling the scope of these side effects. Nor are we alerted if we accidentally leak side effects or mutable state to a broader scope than intended. In this section, we'll develop a data type that uses Scala's type system to enforce scoping of mutations.[1]

Note that we could just work in IO, but that's really not appropriate for local mutable state. If quicksort returned IO[List[Int]], then it would be an IO action that's perfectly safe to run and would have no side effects, which isn't the case in general for arbitrary IO actions. We want to be able to distinguish between effects that are safe to run (like locally mutable state) and external effects like I/O. So a new data type is in order.

14.2.1   A little language for scoped mutation

The most natural approach is to make a little language for talking about mutable state. Writing and reading a state is something we can already do with the State[S,A] monad, which you'll recall is just a function of type S => (A, S) that takes an input state and produces a result and an output state. But when we're talking about mutating the state *in place*, we're not really passing it from one action to the next. What we'll pass instead is a kind of token marked with the type S. A function called with the token then has the authority to mutate data that's tagged with the same type S.

This new data type will employ Scala's type system to gain two static guarantees. We want our code to *not compile* if it violates these invariants:

---

[1]   There's a cost in terms of efficiency and notational convenience, so think of this as another technique you have at your disposal, not something that must be employed every time you make use of local mutation.

- If we hold a reference to a mutable object, then nothing can observe us mutating it.
- A mutable object can never be observed outside of the scope in which it was created.

We relied on the first invariant for our implementation of quicksort—we mutated an array, but since no one else had a reference to that array, the mutation wasn't observable outside our function definition. The second invariant is more subtle; it's saying that we won't leak references to any mutable state as long as that mutable state remains in scope. This invariant is important for some use cases; see the sidebar.

Another use case for typed scoping of mutation

Imagine writing a file I/O library. At the lowest level, the underlying OS file read operation might fill up a mutable buffer of type Array[Byte], reusing the same array on every read instead of allocating a new buffer each time. In the interest of efficiency, it might be nice if the I/O library could simply return a "read-only" view of type Seq[Byte] that's backed by this array, rather than defensively copying the bytes to a fresh data structure. But this isn't quite safe—the caller may keep around this (supposedly) immutable sequence, and when we overwrite the underlying array on the next read, that caller will observe the data changing out from under it! To make the recycling of buffers safe, we need to restrict the scope of the Seq[Byte] view we give to callers and make sure that callers can't retain references (directly or indirectly) to these mutable buffers when we begin the next read operation that clobbers the underlying Array[Byte]. See the chapter notes for chapter 15 for more discussion of this sort of use case.

We'll call this new local-effects monad ST, which could stand for *state thread*, *state transition*, *state token*, or *state tag*. It's different from the State monad in that its run method is protected, but otherwise its structure is exactly the same.

Listing 14.2 Our new ST data type

```
sealed trait ST[S,A] { self =>
  protected def run(s: S): (A,S)
  def map[B](f: A => B): ST[S,B] = new ST[S,B] {
    def run(s: S) = {
      val (a, s1) = self.run(s)
      (f(a), s1)
    }
  }
  def flatMap[B](f: A => ST[S,B]): ST[S,B] = new ST[S,B] {
    def run(s: S) = {
      val (a, s1) = self.run(s)
      f(a).run(s1)
    }
  }
}
```

```
object ST {
  def apply[S,A](a: => A) = {
    lazy val memo = a          ←——    Cache the value in
    new ST[S,A] {                      case run is called
      def run(s: S) = (memo, s)        more than once.
    }
  }
}
```

The run method is protected because an S represents the ability to *mutate* state, and we don't want the mutation to escape. So how do we then run an ST action, giving it an initial state? These are really two questions. We'll start by answering the question of how we specify the initial state.

It's not necessary that you understand every detail of the implementation of ST. What matters is the idea that we can use the type system to constrain the scope of mutable state.

14.2.2 *An algebra of mutable references*

Our first example of an application for the ST monad is a little language for talking about mutable references. This takes the form of a combinator library with some primitives. The language for talking about mutable memory cells should have these primitive commands:

- Allocate a new mutable cell
- Write to a mutable cell
- Read from a mutable cell

The data structure we'll use for mutable references is just a wrapper around a protected var:

```
sealed trait STRef[S,A] {
  protected var cell: A
  def read: ST[S,A] = ST(cell)
  def write(a: A): ST[S,Unit] = new ST[S,Unit] {
    def run(s: S) = {
      cell = a
      ((), s)
    }
  }
}

object STRef {
  def apply[S,A](a: A): ST[S, STRef[S,A]] = ST(new STRef[S,A] {
    var cell = a
  })
}
```

The methods on STRef to read and write the cell are pure, since they just return ST actions. Note that the type S is *not* the type of the cell that's being mutated, and we never actually use the value of type S. Nevertheless, in order to call apply and actually run one of these ST actions, we do need to have a value of type S. That value therefore serves as a kind of token—an authorization to mutate or access the cell—but it serves no other purpose.

The `STRef` trait is sealed, and the only way to construct an instance is by calling the `apply` method on the `STRef` companion object. The `STRef` is constructed with an initial value for the cell, of type `A`. But what's returned is not a naked `STRef`, but an `ST[S, STRef[S,A]]` action that constructs the `STRef` when run and given the token of type `S`. It's important to note that the `ST` action and the `STRef` that it creates are tagged with the *same* `S` type.

At this point, let's try writing a trivial `ST` program. It's awkward right now because we have to choose a type `S` arbitrarily. Here, we arbitrarily choose `Nothing`:

```
for {
  r1 <- STRef[Nothing,Int](1)
  r2 <- STRef[Nothing,Int](1)
  x  <- r1.read
  y  <- r2.read
  _  <- r1.write(y+1)
  _  <- r2.write(x+1)
  a  <- r1.read
  b  <- r2.read
} yield (a,b)
```

This little program allocates two mutable `Int` cells, swaps their contents, adds one to both, and then reads their new values. But we can't yet *run* this program because run is still protected (and we could never actually pass it a value of type `Nothing` anyway). Let's work on that.

14.2.3 *Running mutable state actions*

By now you may have figured out the plot with the `ST` monad. The plan is to use `ST` to build up a computation that, when run, allocates some local mutable state, proceeds to mutate it to accomplish some task, and then discards the mutable state. The whole computation is referentially transparent because all the mutable state is private and locally scoped. But we want to be able to *guarantee* that. For example, an `STRef` contains a mutable var, and we want Scala's type system to guarantee that we can never extract an `STRef` out of an `ST` action. That would violate the invariant that the mutable reference is local to the `ST` action, breaking referential transparency in the process.

So how do we safely run `ST` actions? First we must differentiate between actions that are safe to run and ones that aren't. Spot the difference between these types:

- `ST[S, STRef[S, Int]]` (not safe to run)
- `ST[S, Int]` (completely safe to run)

The former is an `ST` action that returns a mutable reference. But the latter is different. A value of type `ST[S,Int]` is literally just an `Int`, even though computing the `Int` may involve some local mutable state. There's an exploitable difference between these two types. The `STRef` involves the type `S`, but `Int` doesn't.

We want to disallow running an action of type `ST[S, STRef[S,A]]` because that would expose the `STRef`. And in general we want to disallow running any `ST[S,T]` where T involves the type S. On the other hand, it's easy to see that it should always be safe to run an ST action that doesn't expose a mutable object. If we have such a pure action of a type like ST[S, Int], it should be safe to pass it an S to get the Int out of it. Furthermore, *we don't care what S actually is* in that case because we're going to throw it away. The action might as well be polymorphic in S.

In order to represent this, we'll introduce a new trait that represents ST actions that are safe to run—in other words, actions that are polymorphic in S:

```
trait RunnableST[A] {
  def apply[S]: ST[S,A]
}
```

This is similar to the idea behind the Translate trait from chapter 13. A value of type RunnableST[A] is a function that takes a *type* S and produces a *value* of type ST[S,A].

In the previous section, we arbitrarily chose Nothing as our S type. Let's instead wrap it in RunnableST making it polymorphic in S. Then we don't have to choose the type S at all. It will be supplied by whatever calls apply:

```
val p = new RunnableST[(Int, Int)] {
  def apply[S] = for {
    r1 <- STRef(1)
    r2 <- STRef(2)
    x  <- r1.read
    y  <- r2.read
    _  <- r1.write(y+1)
    _  <- r2.write(x+1)
    a  <- r1.read
    b  <- r2.read
  } yield (a,b)
}
```

We're now ready to write the runST function that will call apply on any polymorphic RunnableST by arbitrarily choosing a type for S. Since the RunnableST action is polymorphic in S, it's guaranteed to not make use of the value that gets passed in. So it's actually completely safe to pass (), the value of type Unit!

The runST function must go on the ST companion object. Since run is protected on the ST trait, it's accessible from the companion object but nowhere else:

```
object ST {
  def apply[S,A](a: => A) = {
    lazy val memo = a
    new ST[S,A] {
      def run(s: S) = (memo, s)
    }
  }
  def runST[A](st: RunnableST[A]): A =
    st.apply[Unit].run(())._1
}
```

We can now run our trivial program p from earlier:

```
scala> val p = new RunnableST[(Int, Int)] {
     |   def apply[S] = for {
     |     r1 <- STRef(1)
```

```
  |       r2 <- STRef(2)
  |       x  <- r1.read
  |       y  <- r2.read
  |       _  <- r1.write(y+1)
  |       _  <- r2.write(x+1)
  |       a  <- r1.read
  |       b  <- r2.read
  |     } yield (a,b)
  |   }
p: RunnableST[(Int, Int)] = $anon$1@e3a7d65

scala> val r = ST.runST(p)
r: (Int, Int) = (3,2)
```

The expression runST(p) uses mutable state internally, but it doesn't have any side effects. As far as any other expression is concerned, it's just a pair of integers like any other. It will always return the same pair of integers and it'll do nothing else.

But this isn't the most important part. Most importantly, we *cannot* run a program that tries to return a mutable reference. It's not possible to create a RunnableST that returns a naked STRef:

```
scala> new RunnableST[STRef[Nothing,Int]] {
  |     def apply[S] = STRef(1)
  |   }
<console>:17: error: type mismatch;
 found    : ST[S,STRef[S,Int]]
 required: ST[S,STRef[Nothing,Int]]
               def apply[S] = STRef(1)
```

In this example, we arbitrarily chose Nothing just to illustrate the point. The point is that the type S is bound in the apply method, so when we say new RunnableST, that type isn't accessible.

Because an STRef is always tagged with the type S of the ST action that it lives in, it can never escape. And this is guaranteed by Scala's type system! As a corollary, the fact that you can't get an STRef out of an ST action guarantees that if you have an STRef, then you are inside of the ST action that created it, so it's always safe to mutate the reference.

A note on the wildcard type

It's possible to bypass the type system in runST by using the *wildcard type*. If we pass it a RunnableST[STRef[_, Int]], this will allow an STRef to escape:

```
scala> val ref = ST.runST(new RunnableST[STRef[_, Int]] {
  |     def apply[S] = for {
  |       r1 <- STRef(1)
  |     } yield r1
  |   })
ref: STRef[_, Int] = STRef$$anonfun$apply$1$$anon$6@20e88a41
```

(continued)

The wildcard type is an artifact of Scala's interoperability with Java's type system. Fortunately, when you have an `STRef[_,Int]`, using it will cause a type error:

```
scala> new RunnableST[Int] {
     |    def apply[R] = for { x <- ref.read } yield x }
 error   : type mismatch;
 found   : ST[_$1,Int]
 required: ST[R,Int]
               def apply[R] = for { x <- ref.read } yield x }
                                    ^
```

This type error is caused by the fact that the wildcard type in `ref` represents some concrete type that only `ref` knows about. In this case it's the `S` type that was bound in the `apply` method of the `RunnableST` where it was created. Scala is unable to prove that this is the same type as `R`. Therefore, even though it's possible to abuse the wildcard type to get the naked `STRef` out, this is still safe since we can't use it to mutate or access the state.

14.2.4 Mutable arrays

Mutable references on their own aren't all that useful. Mutable arrays are a much more compelling use case for the `ST` monad. In this section, we'll define an algebra for manipulating mutable arrays in the `ST` monad and then write an in-place `quicksort` algorithm compositionally. We'll need primitive combinators to allocate, read, and write mutable arrays.

Listing 14.3   An array class for our `ST` monad

Scala requires an implicit Manifest for constructing arrays. →

```
sealed abstract class STArray[S,A](implicit manifest: Manifest[A]) {
  protected def value: Array[A]
  def size: ST[S,Int] = ST(value.size)

  def write(i: Int, a: A): ST[S,Unit] = new ST[S,Unit] {    ←  Write a value at the
    def run(s: S) = {                                           given index of the array.
      value(i) = a
      ((), s)
    }
  }
                                                           Read the value at the
                                                           given index of the array.
  def read(i: Int): ST[S,A] = ST(value(i))    ←

  def freeze: ST[S,List[A]] = ST(value.toList)    ←   Turn the array into an
}                                                       immutable list.

object STArray {
  def apply[S,A:Manifest](sz: Int, v: A): ST[S, STArray[S,A]] =    ←
    new STArray[S,A] {
      lazy val value = Array.fill(sz)(v)           Construct an array of the given
    }                                              size filled with the value v.
}
```

Note that Scala can't create arrays for every type A. It requires that a `Manifest[A]` exists in implicit scope. Scala's standard library provides manifests for most types that you would in practice want to put in an array.

Just like with `STRef`, we always return an `STArray` packaged in an `ST` action with a corresponding `S` type, and any manipulation of the array (even reading it) is an `ST` action tagged with the same type `S`. It's therefore impossible to observe a naked `STArray` outside of the `ST` monad (except by code in the Scala source file in which the `STArray` data type itself is declared).

Using these primitives, we can write more complex functions on arrays.

EXERCISE 14.1

Add a combinator on `STArray` to fill the array from a `Map` where each key in the map represents an index into the array, and the value under that key is written to the array at that index. For example, `xs.fill(Map(0->"a", 2->"b"))` should write the value `"a"` at index 0 in the array `xs` and `"b"` at index 2. Use the existing combinators to write your implementation.

```scala
def fill(xs: Map[Int,A]): ST[S,Unit]
```

Not everything can be done efficiently using these existing combinators. For example, the Scala library already has an efficient way of turning a list into an array. Let's make that primitive as well:

```scala
def fromList[S,A:Manifest](xs: List[A]): ST[S, STArray[S,A]] =
  ST(new STArray[S,A] {
    lazy val value = xs.toArray
  })
```

14.2.5 *A purely functional in-place quicksort*

The components for `quicksort` are now easy to write in `ST`—for example, the `swap` function that swaps two elements of the array:

```scala
def swap[S](i: Int, j: Int): ST[S,Unit] = for {
  x <- read(i)
  y <- read(j)
  _ <- write(i, y)
  _ <- write(j, x)
} yield ()
```

EXERCISE 14.2

Write the purely functional versions of `partition` and `qs`.

```
def partition[S](arr: STArray[S,Int],
                 n: Int, r: Int, pivot: Int): ST[S,Int]
def qs[S](a: STArray[S,Int], n: Int, r: Int): ST[S,Unit]
```

With those components written, `quicksort` can now be assembled out of them in the ST monad:

```
def quicksort(xs: List[Int]): List[Int] =
  if (xs.isEmpty) xs else ST.runST(new RunnableST[List[Int]] {
    def apply[S] = for {
      arr     <- STArray.fromList(xs)
      size    <- arr.size
      _       <- qs(arr, 0, size - 1)
      sorted  <- arr.freeze
    } yield sorted
  })
```

As you can see, the ST monad allows us to write pure functions that nevertheless mutate the data they receive. Scala's type system ensures that we don't combine things in an unsafe way.

EXERCISE 14.3

Give the same treatment to `scala.collection.mutable.HashMap` as we've given here to references and arrays. Come up with a minimal set of primitive combinators for creating and manipulating hash maps.

14.3 *Purity is contextual*

In the preceding section, we talked about effects that aren't observable because they're entirely local to some scope. A program can't observe mutation of data unless it holds a reference to that data.

But there are other effects that may be non-observable, depending on who's looking. As a simple example, let's take a kind of side effect that occurs all the time in ordinary Scala programs, even ones that we'd usually consider purely functional:

```
scala> case class Foo(s: String)

scala> val b = Foo("hello") == Foo("hello")
b: Boolean = true

scala> val c = Foo("hello") eq Foo("hello")
c: Boolean = false
```

Here `Foo("hello")` looks pretty innocent. We could be forgiven if we assumed that it was a completely referentially transparent expression. But each time it appears, it produces a *different* `Foo` in a certain sense. If we test two appearances of `Foo("hello")` for equality using the `==` function, we get `true` as we'd expect. But testing for *reference equality* (a notion inherited from the Java language) with `eq`, we get `false`. The two appearances of `Foo("hello")` aren't references to the "same object" if we look under the hood.

Note that if we evaluate `Foo("hello")` and store the result as `x`, then substitute `x` to get the expression `x eq x`, it has a different result:

```
scala> val x = Foo("hello")
x: Foo = Foo(hello)

scala> val d = x eq x
d: Boolean = true
```

Therefore, by our original definition of referential transparency, *every data constructor in Scala has a side effect*. The effect is that a new and unique object is created in memory, and the data constructor returns a reference to that new object.

For most programs, this makes no difference, because most programs don't check for reference equality. It's only the `eq` method that allows our programs to observe this side effect occurring. We could therefore say that it's not a side effect at all in the context of the vast majority of programs.

Our definition of referential transparency doesn't take this into account. Referential transparency is *with regard to* some context and our definition doesn't establish this context.

A more general definition of referential transparency

An expression `e` is referentially transparent with regard to a program `p` if every occurrence of `e` in `p` can be replaced by the result of evaluating `e` without affecting the meaning of `p`.

This definition is only slightly modified to reflect the fact that not all programs observe the same effects. We say that an effect of `e` is *non-observable* by `p` if it doesn't affect the referential transparency of `e` with regard to `p`. For instance, most programs can't observe the side effect of calling a constructor, because they don't make use of `eq`.

This definition is still somewhat vague. What is meant by "evaluating"? And what's the standard by which we determine whether the meaning of two programs is the same?

In Scala, there's a kind of standard answer to this first question. We'll take evaluation to mean *reduction to some normal form*. Since Scala is a strictly evaluated language, we can force the evaluation of an expression `e` to normal form in Scala by assigning it to a `val`:

```
val v = e
```

And referential transparency of `e` with regard to a program `p` means that we can rewrite `p`, replacing every appearance of `e` with `v` without changing the meaning of our program.

But what do we mean by "changing the meaning of our program"? Just what *is* the meaning of a program? This is a somewhat philosophical question, and there are various ways of answering it that we won't explore in detail here.[2] But the general point is that when we talk about referential transparency, it's always with regard to some *context*. The context determines what sort of programs we're interested in, and also how we assign meaning to our programs. Establishing this context is a choice; we need to decide what aspects of a program participate in that program's meaning.

Let's explore this subtlety a bit further.

14.3.1 *What counts as a side effect?*

Earlier, we talked about how the eq method is able to *observe* the side effect of object creation. Let's look more closely at this idea of observable behavior and program meaning. It requires that we delimit what we consider observable and what we don't. Take, for example, this method that has a definite side effect:

```
def timesTwo(x: Int) = {
  if (x < 0) println("Got a negative number")
  x * 2
}
```

If we replace timesTwo(1) with 2 in our program, we don't have the same program in every respect. It may compute the same result, but we can say that the meaning of the program has changed. But this isn't true for all programs that call timesTwo, nor for all notions of program equivalence.

We need to decide up front whether changes in standard output are something we care to observe—whether it's part of the changes in behavior that *matter* in our context. In this case, it's exceedingly unlikely that any other part of the program will be able to observe that println side effect occurring inside timesTwo.

Of course, timesTwo has a *hidden dependency* on the I/O subsystem. It requires access to the standard output stream. But as we've seen, most programs that we'd consider purely functional also require access to some of the underlying machinery of Scala's environment, like being able to construct objects in memory and discard them. At the end of the day, we have to decide for ourselves which effects are important enough to track. We could use the IO monad to track println calls, but maybe we don't want to bother. If we're just using the console to do some temporary debug logging, it seems like a waste of time to track that. But if the program's correct behavior depends in some way on what it prints to the console (like if it's a UNIX command line utility), then we definitely want to track it.

This brings us to an essential point: tracking effects is a *choice* we make as programmers. It's a value judgement, and there are trade-offs associated with how we choose. We can take it as far as we want. But as with the context of referential transparency, in Scala there's a kind of standard choice. For example, it would be completely valid and

---

[2] See the chapter notes for links to further reading.

possible to track memory allocations in the type system if that really mattered to us. But in Scala we have the benefit of automatic memory management, so the cost of explicit tracking is usually higher than the benefit.

The policy we should adopt is to *track those effects that program correctness depends on.* If a program is fundamentally about reading and writing files, then file I/O should be tracked in the type system to the extent feasible. If a program relies on object reference equality, it would be nice to know that statically as well. Static type information lets us know what kinds of effects are involved, and thereby lets us make educated decisions about whether they matter to us in a given context.

The ST type in this chapter and the IO monad in the previous chapter should have given you a taste for what it's like to track effects in the type system. But this isn't the end of the road. You're limited only by your imagination and the expressiveness of Scala's types.

14.4 Summary

In this chapter, we discussed two different implications of referential transparency.

We saw that we can get away with mutating data that never escapes a local scope. At first blush it may seem that mutating state can't be compatible with pure functions. But as we've seen, we can write components that have a pure interface and mutate local state behind the scenes, and we can use Scala's type system to guarantee purity.

We also discussed that what counts as a side effect is actually a choice made by the programmer or language designer. When we talk about functions being pure, we should have already chosen a context that establishes what it means for two things to be equal, what it means to execute a program, and which effects we care to take into account when assigning meaning to our program.

Stream processing and incremental I/O

We said in the introduction to part 4 that functional programming is a *complete* paradigm. Every imaginable program can be expressed functionally, including programs that interact with the external world. But it would be disappointing if the IO type were the only way to construct such programs. IO and ST work by simply embedding an imperative programming language into the purely functional subset of Scala. While programming within the IO monad, we have to reason about our programs much like we would in ordinary imperative programming.

We can do better. In this chapter, we'll show how to recover the high-level compositional style developed in parts 1–3 of this book, even for programs that interact with the outside world. The design space in this area is enormous, and our goal here is not to explore it completely, but just to convey ideas and give a sense of what's possible.

15.1 Problems with imperative I/O: an example

We'll start by considering a simple concrete usage scenario that we'll use to highlight some of the problems with imperative I/O embedded in the IO monad. Our first easy challenge in this chapter is to write a program that checks whether the number of lines in a file is greater than 40,000.

This is a deliberately simple task that illustrates the essence of the problem that our library is intended to solve. We could certainly accomplish this task with ordinary imperative code, inside the IO monad. Let's look at that first.

Listing 15.1 Counting line numbers in imperative style

```
def linesGt40k(filename: String): IO[Boolean] = IO {
  val src = io.Source.fromFile(filename)          ←——         scala.io.Source has
  try {                                                       convenience functions for reading
    var count = 0                                             from external sources like files.
    val lines: Iterator[String] = src.getLines    ←——
    while (count <= 40000 && lines.hasNext) {                 Obtain a stateful
      lines.next         ←——                                 Iterator from
      count += 1                                              the Source.
    }                             Has the side effect of
    count > 40000                 advancing to the next
  }                               element.
  finally src.close
}
```

We can then *run* this IO action with unsafePerformIO(linesGt40k("lines.txt")), where unsafePerformIO is a side-effecting method that takes IO[A], returning A and actually performing the desired effects (see section 13.6.1).

Although this code uses low-level primitives like a while loop, a mutable Iterator, and a var, there are some *good* things about it. First, it's *incremental*—the entire file isn't loaded into memory up front. Instead, lines are fetched from the file only when needed. If we didn't buffer the input, we could keep as little as a single line of the file in memory at a time. It also terminates early, as soon as the answer is known.

There are some bad things about this code, too. For one, we have to remember to close the file when we're done. This might seem obvious, but if we forget to do this, or (more commonly) if we close the file outside of a finally block and an exception occurs first, the file will remain open.[1] This is called a *resource leak*. A file handle is an example of a scarce resource—the operating system can only have a limited number of files open at any given time. If this task were part of a larger program—say we were scanning an entire directory recursively, building up a list of all files with more than 40,000 lines—our larger program could easily fail because too many files were left open.

We want to write programs that are *resource-safe*—they should close file handles as soon as they're no longer needed (whether because of normal termination or an exception), and they shouldn't attempt to read from a closed file. Likewise for other resources like network sockets, database connections, and so on. Using IO directly can be problematic because it means our programs are entirely responsible for ensuring their own resource safety, and we get no help from the compiler in making sure that they do this. It would be nice if our library would ensure that programs are resource-safe by construction.

But even aside from the problems with resource safety, there's something unsatisfying about this code. It entangles the high-level algorithm with low-level concerns about iteration and file access. Of course we have to obtain the elements from some

---

[1] The JVM will actually close an InputStream (which is what backs a scala.io.Source) when it's garbage collected, but there's no way to guarantee this will occur in a timely manner, or at all! This is especially true in generational garbage collectors that perform "full" collections infrequently.

resource, handle any errors that occur, and close the resource when we're done, but our program isn't *about* any of those things. It's about counting elements and returning a value as soon as we hit 40,000. And that happens *between* all of those I/O actions. Intertwining the algorithm and the I/O concerns is not just ugly—it's a barrier to composition, and our code will be difficult to extend later. To see this, consider a few variations of the original scenario:

- Check whether the number of *nonempty* lines in the file exceeds 40,000.
- Find a line index before 40,000 where the first letters of consecutive lines spell out `"abracadabra"`.

For the first case, we could imagine passing a `String => Boolean` into our `linesGt40k` function. But for the second case, we'd need to modify our loop to keep track of some further state. Besides being uglier, the resulting code will likely be tricky to get right. In general, writing efficient code in the `IO` monad generally means writing monolithic loops, and monolithic loops are not composable.

Let's compare this to the case where we have a `Stream[String]` for the lines being analyzed:

```
lines.zipWithIndex.exists(_._2 + 1 >= 40000)
```

Much nicer! With a `Stream`, we get to assemble our program from preexisting combinators, `zipWithIndex` and `exists`. If we want to consider only nonempty lines, we can easily use `filter`:

```
lines.filter(!_.trim.isEmpty).zipWithIndex.exists(_._2 + 1 >= 40000)
```

And for the second scenario, we can use the `indexOfSlice` function defined on `Stream`,[2] in conjunction with `take` (to terminate the search after 40,000 lines) and `map` (to pull out the first character of each line):

```
lines.filter(!_.trim.isEmpty).
      take(40000).
      map(_.head).
      indexOfSlice("abracadabra".toList)
```

We want to write something like the preceding when reading from an actual file. The problem is that we don't have a `Stream[String]`; we have a file from which we can read. We could cheat by writing a function `lines` that returns an `IO[Stream[String]]`:

```
def lines(filename: String): IO[Stream[String]] = IO {
  val src = io.Source.fromFile(filename)
  src.getLines.toStream append { src.close; Stream.empty }
}
```

This is called *lazy I/O*. We're cheating because the `Stream[String]` inside the `IO` monad isn't actually a pure value. As elements of the stream are forced, it'll execute

---

[2]   If the argument to `indexOfSlice` doesn't exist as a subsequence of the input, it returns -1. See the API docs for details, or experiment with this function in the REPL.

side effects of reading from the file, and only if we examine the entire stream and reach its end will we close the file. Although lazy I/O is appealing in that it lets us recover the compositional style to some extent, it's problematic for several reasons:

- It isn't resource-safe. The resource (in this case, a file) will be released only if we traverse to the end of the stream. But we'll frequently want to terminate traversal early (here, `exists` will stop traversing the `Stream` as soon as it finds a match) and we certainly don't want to leak resources every time we do this.
- Nothing stops us from traversing that same `Stream` again, after the file has been closed. This will result in one of two things, depending on whether the `Stream` *memoizes* (caches) its elements once they're forced. If they're memoized, we'll see excessive memory usage since all of the elements will be retained in memory. If they're not memoized, traversing the stream again will cause a read from a closed file handle.
- Since forcing elements of the stream has I/O side effects, two threads traversing a `Stream` at the same time can result in unpredictable behavior.
- In more realistic scenarios, we won't necessarily have full knowledge of what's happening with the `Stream[String]`. It could be passed to some function we don't control, which might store it in a data structure for a long period of time before ever examining it. Proper usage now requires some out-of-band knowledge: we can't just manipulate this `Stream[String]` like a typical pure value— we have to know something about its origin. This is bad for composition, where we shouldn't have to know anything about a value other than its type.

15.2 Simple stream transducers

Our first step toward recovering the high-level style we're accustomed to from `Stream` and `List` while doing I/O is to introduce the notion of *stream transducers* or *stream processors*. A stream transducer specifies a transformation from one stream to another. We're using the term *stream* quite generally here to refer to a sequence, possibly lazily generated or supplied by an external source. This could be a stream of lines from a file, a stream of HTTP requests, a stream of mouse click positions, or anything else. Let's consider a simple data type, `Process`, that lets us express stream transformations.[3]

Listing 15.2 The `Process` data type

```
sealed trait Process[I,O]

case class Emit[I,O](
    head: O,
    tail: Process[I,O] = Halt[I,O]())
  extends Process[I,O]
```

We use a default argument so that we can say `Emit(xs)` as shorthand for `Emit(xs, Halt())`.

---

[3] We've chosen to omit variance annotations in this chapter for simplicity, but it's possible to write this as `Process[-I,+O]`. We're also omitting some trampolining that would prevent stack overflows in certain circumstances. See the chapter notes for discussion of more robust representations.

```
case class Await[I,O](
    recv: Option[I] => Process[I,O])
  extends Process[I,O]

case class Halt[I,O]() extends Process[I,O]
```

A `Process[I,O]` can be used to transform a stream containing `I` values to a stream of `O` values. But `Process[I,O]` isn't a typical function `Stream[I] => Stream[O]`, which could consume the input stream and construct the output stream. Instead, we have a state machine that must be driven forward with a *driver*, a function that simultaneously consumes both our `Process` and the input stream. A `Process` can be in one of three states, each of which signals something to the driver:

- `Emit(head,tail)` indicates to the driver that the `head` value should be emitted to the output stream, and the machine should then be transitioned to the `tail` state.
- `Await(recv)` requests a value from the input stream. The driver should pass the next available value to the `recv` function, or `None` if the input has no more elements.
- `Halt` indicates to the driver that no more elements should be read from the input or emitted to the output.

Let's look at a sample driver that will actually interpret these requests. Here's one that transforms a `Stream`. We can implement this as a method on `Process`:

```
def apply(s: Stream[I]): Stream[O] = this match {
  case Halt() => Stream()
  case Await(recv) => s match {
    case h #:: t => recv(Some(h))(t)
    case xs => recv(None)(xs)          ←——————— Stream is empty.
  }
  case Emit(h,t) => h #:: t(s)
}
```

Thus, given `p: Process[I,O]` and `in: Stream[I]`, the expression `p(in)` produces a `Stream[O]`. What's interesting is that `Process` is agnostic to how it's fed input. We've written a driver that feeds a `Process` from a `Stream`, but we could also write a driver that feeds a `Process` from a file. We'll get to writing such a driver a bit later, but first let's look at how we can construct a `Process`, and try things out in the REPL.

15.2.1 *Creating processes*

We can convert any function `f: I => O` to a `Process[I,O]`. We just `Await` and then `Emit` the value received, transformed by f:

```
def liftOne[I,O](f: I => O): Process[I,O] =
  Await {
    case Some(i) => Emit(f(i))
    case None => Halt()
  }
```

Let's try this out in the REPL:

```
scala> val p = liftOne((x: Int) => x * 2)
p: Process[Int,Int] = Await(<function1>)

scala> val xs = p(Stream(1,2,3)).toList
xs: List[Int] = List(2)
```

As we can see, this `Process` just waits for one element, emits it, and then stops. To transform a whole stream with a function, we do this repeatedly in a loop, alternating between awaiting and emitting. We can write a combinator for this, `repeat`, as a method on `Process`:

```
def repeat: Process[I,O] = {
  def go(p: Process[I,O]): Process[I,O] = p match {
    case Halt() => go(this)                    ←——————————— Restart the process if
    case Await(recv) => Await {                               it halts on its own.
      case None => recv(None)        ←———————
      case i => go(recv(i))                      Don't repeat if
    }                                            terminated from source.
    case Emit(h, t) => Emit(h, go(t))
  }
  go(this)
}
```

This combinator replaces the `Halt` constructor of the `Process` with a recursive step, repeating the same process forever.

We can now lift any function to a `Process` that maps over a `Stream`:

```
def lift[I,O](f: I => O): Process[I,O] = liftOne(f).repeat
```

Since the `repeat` combinator recurses forever and `Emit` is strict in its arguments, we have to be careful not to use it with a `Process` that never waits! For example, we can't just say `Emit(1).repeat` to get an infinite stream that keeps emitting 1. Remember, `Process` is a stream *transducer*, so if we want to do something like that, we need to transduce one infinite stream to another:

```
scala> val units = Stream.continually(())
units: scala.collection.immutable.Stream[Unit] = Stream((), ?)

scala> val ones = lift((_:Unit) => 1)(units)
ones: Stream[Int] = Stream(1, ?)
```

We can do more than map the elements of a stream from one type to another—we can also insert or remove elements. Here's a `Process` that filters out elements that don't match the predicate p:

```
def filter[I](p: I => Boolean): Process[I,I] =
  Await[I,I] {
    case Some(i) if p(i) => emit(i)
    case _ => Halt()
  }.repeat
```

We simply await some input and, if it matches the predicate, emit it to the output. The call to repeat makes sure that the Process keeps going until the input stream is exhausted. Let's see how this plays out in the REPL:

```
scala> val even = filter((x: Int) => x % 2 == 0)
even: Process[Int,Int] = Await(<function1>)

scala> val evens = even(Stream(1,2,3,4)).toList
evens: List[Int] = List(2, 4)
```

Let's look at another example of a Process, sum, which keeps emitting a running total of the values seen so far:

```
def sum: Process[Double,Double] = {
  def go(acc: Double): Process[Double,Double] =
    Await {
      case Some(d) => Emit(d+acc, go(d+acc))
      case None => Halt()
    }
  go(0.0)
}
```

This kind of definition follows a common pattern in defining a Process—we use an inner function that tracks the current state, which in this case is the total so far.

Here's an example of using sum in the REPL:

```
scala> val s = sum(Stream(1.0, 2.0, 3.0, 4.0)).toList
s: List[Double] = List(1.0, 3.0, 6.0, 10.0)
```

Let's write some more Process combinators to help you get accustomed to this style of programming. Try to work through implementations of at least some of these exercises until you get the hang of it.

■ **EXERCISE 15.1**

Implement take, which halts the Process after it encounters the given number of elements, and drop, which ignores the given number of arguments and then emits the rest. Also implement takeWhile and dropWhile, that take and drop elements as long as the given predicate remains true.

```
def take[I](n: Int): Process[I,I]

def drop[I](n: Int): Process[I,I]

def takeWhile[I](f: I => Boolean): Process[I,I]

def dropWhile[I](f: I => Boolean): Process[I,I]
```

■ **EXERCISE 15.2**

Implement count. It should emit the number of elements seen so far. For instance, count(Stream("a", "b", "c")) should yield Stream(1, 2, 3) (or Stream(0, 1, 2, 3), your choice).

```
def count[I]: Process[I,Int]
```

■ **EXERCISE 15.3**

Implement mean. It should emit a running average of the values seen so far.

```
def mean: Process[Double,Double]
```

Just as we've seen many times throughout this book, when we notice common patterns when defining a series of functions, we can factor these patterns out into generic combinators. The functions sum, count and mean all share a common pattern. Each has a single piece of state, has a state transition function that updates this state in response to input, and produces a single output. We can generalize this to a combinator, loop:

```
def loop[S,I,O](z: S)(f: (I,S) => (O,S)): Process[I,O] =
  Await((i: I) => f(i,z) match {
    case (o,s2) => emit(o, loop(s2)(f))
  })
```

□ **EXERCISE 15.4**

Write sum and count in terms of loop.

15.2.2 *Composing and appending processes*

We can build up more complex stream transformations by *composing* Process values. Given two Process values f and g, we can feed the output of f to the input of g. We'll name this operation |> (pronounced *pipe* or *compose*) and implement it as a function on Process.[4] It has the nice property that f |> g *fuses* the transformations done by f and g. As soon as values are emitted by f, they're transformed by g.

---

[4] This operation might remind you of function composition, which feeds the (single) output of a function as the (single) input to another function. Both Process and Function1 are instances of a wider abstraction called a *category*. See the chapter notes for details.

Hard: Implement |> as a method on Process. Let the types guide your implementation.

```
def |>[O2](p2: Process[O,O2]): Process[I,O2]
```

We can now write expressions like filter(_ % 2 == 0) |> lift(_ + 1) to filter and map in a single transformation. We'll sometimes call a sequence of transformations like this a *pipeline.*

Since we have Process composition, and we can lift any function into a Process, we can easily implement map to transform the output of a Process with a function:

```
def map[O2](f: O => O2): Process[I,O2] = this |> lift(f)
```

This means that the type constructor Process[I,_] is a functor. If we ignore the input side I for a moment, we can just think of a Process[I,O] as a sequence of O values. This implementation of map is then analogous to mapping over a Stream or a List.

In fact, most of the operations defined for ordinary sequences are defined for Process as well. We can, for example, *append* one process to another. Given two processes x and y, the expression x ++ y is a process that will run x to completion and then run y on whatever input remains after x has halted. For the implementation, we simply replace the Halt of x with y (much like how ++ on List replaces the Nil terminating the first list with the second list):

```
def ++(p: => Process[I,O]): Process[I,O] = this match {
  case Halt() => p
  case Emit(h, t) => Emit(h, t ++ p)
  case Await(recv) => Await(recv andThen (_ ++ p))
}
```

With the help of ++ on Process, we can define flatMap:

```
def flatMap[O2](f: O => Process[I,O2]): Process[I,O2] = this match {
  case Halt() => Halt()
  case Emit(h, t) => f(h) ++ t.flatMap(f)
  case Await(recv) => Await(recv andThen (_ flatMap f))
}
```

The obvious question is then whether Process[I,_] forms a monad. It turns out that it does! To write the Monad instance, we have to partially apply the I parameter of Process—a trick we've used before:

```
def monad[I]: Monad[({ type f[x] = Process[I,x]})#f] =
  new Monad[({ type f[x] = Process[I,x]})#f] {
    def unit[O](o: => O): Process[I,O] = Emit(o)
```

```
def flatMap[O,O2](p: Process[I,O])(
                  f: O => Process[I,O2]): Process[I,O2] =
    p flatMap f
}
```

The unit function just emits the argument and then halts, similar to unit for the List monad.

This Monad instance is the same idea as the Monad for List. What makes Process more interesting than just List is that it can accept *input*. And it can transform that input through mapping, filtering, folding, grouping, and so on. It turns out that Process can express almost any stream transformation, all the while remaining agnostic to how exactly it's obtaining its input or what should happen with its output.

EXERCISE 15.6

Implement zipWithIndex. It emits a running count of values emitted along with each value; for example, Process("a","b").zipWithIndex yields Process(("a",0), ("b",1)).

EXERCISE 15.7

Hard: Come up with a generic combinator that lets you express mean in terms of sum and count. Define this combinator and implement mean in terms of it.

EXERCISE 15.8

Implement exists. There are multiple ways to implement it, given that exists(_ % 2 == 0)(Stream(1,3,5,6,7)) could produce Stream(true) (halting, and only yielding the final result), Stream(false,false,false,true) (halting, and yielding all intermediate results), or Stream(false,false,false,true,true) (*not* halting, and yielding all the intermediate results). Note that because |> fuses, there's no penalty to implementing the "trimming" of this last form with a separate combinator.

```
def exists[I](f: I => Boolean): Process[I,Boolean]
```

We can now express the core stream transducer for our line-counting problem as count |> exists(_ > 40000). Of course, it's easy to attach filters and other transformations to our pipeline.

15.2.3 Processing files

Our original problem of answering whether a file has more than 40,000 elements is now easy to solve. But so far we've just been transforming pure streams. Luckily, we can just as easily use a file to drive a Process. And instead of generating a Stream as the result, we can accumulate what the Process emits similar to what foldLeft does on List.

Listing 15.3   Using `Process` with files instead of streams

```
def processFile[A,B](f: java.io.File,
                     p: Process[String, A],
                     z: B)(g: (B, A) => B): IO[B] = IO {
  @annotation.tailrec
  def go(ss: Iterator[String], cur: Process[String, A], acc: B): B =
    cur match {
      case Halt() => acc
      case Await(recv) =>
        val next = if (ss.hasNext) recv(Some(ss.next))
                   else recv(None)
        go(ss, next, acc)
      case Emit(h, t) => go(ss, t, g(acc, h))
    }
  val s = io.Source.fromFile(f)
  try go(s.getLines, p, z)
  finally s.close
}
```

We can now solve the original problem with the following:

```
processFile(f, count |> exists(_ > 40000), false)(_ || _)
```

EXERCISE 15.9 ⸺⸺⸺⸺⸺⸺⸺⸺⸺⸺⸺⸺⸺⸺⸺⸺⸺⸺⸺⸺⸺⸺⸺

Write a program that reads degrees Fahrenheit as Double values from a file, one value per line, sends each value through a process to convert it to degrees Fahrenheit, and writes the result to another file. Your program should ignore blank lines in the input file, as well as lines that start with the # character. You can use the function toCelsius.

```
def toCelsius(fahrenheit: Double): Double =
  (5.0 / 9.0) * (fahrenheit - 32.0)
```

15.3   *An extensible process type*

Our existing Process type implicitly assumes an *environment* or *context* containing a single stream of values. Furthermore, the *protocol* for communicating with the driver is also fixed. A Process can only issue three instructions to the driver—Halt, Emit, and

Await—and there's no way to extend this protocol short of defining a completely new type. In order to make Process extensible, we'll parameterize on the protocol used for issuing requests of the driver. This works in much the same way as the Free type we covered in chapter 13.

Listing 15.4 An extensible `Process` type

```
trait Process[F[_],O]

object Process {
  case class Await[F[_],A,O](
    req: F[A],
    recv: Either[Throwable, A] => Process[F,O])
  extends Process[F,O]


  case class Emit[F[_],O](
    head: O,
    tail: Process[F,O]) extends Process[F,O]


  case class Halt[F[_],O](err: Throwable) extends Process[F,O]


  case object End extends Exception
  case object Kill extends Exception
}
```

The recv function now takes an Either so we can handle errors.

Halt due to err, which could be an actual error or End indicating normal termination.

An Exception that indicates normal termination. This allows us to use Scala's exception mechanism for control flow.

An Exception that indicates forceful termination. We'll see how this is used later.

Unlike Free[F,A], a Process[F,O] represents a *stream* of O values (O for output) produced by (possibly) making external requests using the protocol F via Await. The F parameter serves the same role here in Await as the F parameter used for Suspend in Free from chapter 13.

The important difference between Free and Process is that a Process can request to Emit values multiple times, whereas Free always contains one answer in its final Return. And instead of terminating with Return, the Process terminates with Halt.

To ensure resource safety when writing processes that close over some resource like a file handle or database connection, the recv function of Await takes an Either[Throwable,A]. This lets recv decide what should be done if there's an error while running the request req.[5] We'll adopt the convention that the End exception indicates that there's no more input, and Kill indicates the process is being forcibly terminated and should clean up any resources it's using.[6]

---

[5] The recv function should be trampolined to avoid stack overflows by returning a TailRec[Process[F,O]], but we've omitted this detail here for simplicity.

[6] There are some design decisions here—we're using exceptions, End and Kill, for control flow, but we could certainly choose to indicate normal termination with Option, say with Halt[F[_],O](err: Option[Throwable]).

The `Halt` constructor picks up a *reason* for termination in the form of a `Throwable`. The reason may be `End`, indicating normal termination due to exhausted input; `Kill`, indicating forcible termination; or some other error (note that `Exception` is a subtype of `Throwable`).

This new `Process` type is more general than the previous `Process`, which we'll refer to from now on as a "single-input `Process`" or a "`Process1`", and we can represent a single-input `Process` as a special instance of this generalized `Process` type. We'll see how this works in section 15.3.3.

First, note that a number of operations are defined for `Process` *regardless* of the choice of F. We can still define ++ (append), `map`, and `filter` for `Process`, and the definitions are almost identical to before. Here's ++ (see chapter code for other functions, including `repeat`, `map`, and `filter`), which we define in terms of a more general function, `onHalt`.

> **Listing 15.5   The `onHalt` and ++ functions**

```
def onHalt(f: Throwable => Process[F,O]): Process[F,O] = this match {
  case Halt(e) => Try(f(e))
  case Emit(h, t) => Emit(h, t.onHalt(f))
  case Await(req,recv) => Await(req, recv andThen (_.onHalt(f)))
}
def ++(p: => Process[F,O]): Process[F,O] =
  this.onHalt {
    case End => p
    case err => Halt(err)
  }
```

Uses the helper function `Try`.

Consult p only on normal termination.

Otherwise, keep the current error.

A call to `p.onHalt(f)` replaces the e inside the `Halt(e)` at the end of p with `f(e)`, allowing us to extend a process with further logic and giving us access to the reason for termination. The definition uses the helper function `Try` with a capital T, which safely evaluates a `Process`, catching any exceptions and converting them to `Halt` (see the following code). This is important for resource safety. In general, our goal is to catch and deal with all exceptions, rather than placing that burden on users of our library. Luckily, there are just a few key combinators that can generate exceptions. As long as we ensure these combinators are exception-safe, we'll be able to guarantee the resource safety of all programs that use `Process`. The ++ function is defined in terms of `onHalt`—so long as the first `Process` terminates normally, we continue with the second process; otherwise, we re-raise the error.

Here's the helper function `Try`:

```
def Try[F[_],O](p: => Process[F,O]): Process[F,O] =
  try p
  catch { case e: Throwable => Halt(e) }
```

We'll also introduce the helper function `await`, which is a curried version of the `Await` constructor for better type inference:

```
def await[F[_],A,O](
    req: F[A])(
    recv: Either[Throwable,A] => Process[F,O]): Process[F,O] =
  Await(req, recv)
```

Again, using ++, we define `flatMap`. This is another combinator where we must take care to ensure exception safety—we don't know for sure whether `f` will throw an exception, so we wrap calls to `f` in `Try` once again. Other than that, the definition looks very similar to what we wrote before:

```
def flatMap[O2](f: O => Process[F,O2]): Process[F,O2] =
  this match {
    case Halt(err) => Halt(err)
    case Emit(o, t) => Try(f(o)) ++ t.flatMap(f)
    case Await(req,recv) =>
      Await(req, recv andThen (_ flatMap f))
  }
```

Let's see what else we can express with this new `Process` type. The `F` parameter gives us a lot of flexibility.

15.3.1 Sources

Before, we had to write a separate function to drive a process forward while reading from a file. Now, we can represent an effectful source directly using a `Process[IO,O]`.[7]

To see how `Process[IO,O]` is indeed a source of `O` values, consider what the `Await` constructor looks like when we substitute `IO` for `F`:

```
case class Await[A,O](
  req: IO[A],
  recv: Either[Throwable, A] => Process[IO,O]
) extends Process[IO,O]
```

Thus, any requests of the "external" world can be satisfied just by running or flatMap-ping into the `IO` action `req`. If this action returns an `A` successfully, we invoke the `recv` function with this result, or a `Throwable` if `req` throws one. Either way, the `recv` function can fall back to another process or clean up any resources as appropriate. Here's a simple interpreter of an I/O `Process` that collects all the values emitted.

Listing 15.6 The `runLog` function

```
def runLog[O](src: Process[IO,O]): IO[IndexedSeq[O]] = IO {
  val E = java.util.concurrent.Executors.newFixedThreadPool(4)
  @annotation.tailrec
  def go(cur: Process[IO,O], acc: IndexedSeq[O]): IndexedSeq[O] =
    cur match {
      case Emit(h,t) => go(t, acc :+ h)
      case Halt(End) => acc
      case Halt(err) => throw err
      case Await(req,recv) =>
```

---

[7] There are some issues with making this representation resource-safe that we'll discuss shortly.

```
          val next =
            try recv(Right(unsafePerformIO(req)(E)))
            catch { case err: Throwable => recv(Left(err)) }
          go(next, acc)
      }
    try go(src, IndexedSeq())
    finally E.shutdown
}
```

An example usage of this is to enumerate all the lines in a file:

```
import java.io.{BufferedReader,FileReader}
val p: Process[IO, String] =
  await(IO(new BufferedReader(new FileReader("lines.txt")))) {
    case Right(b) =>
      lazy val next: Process[IO,String] = await(IO(b.readLine)) {
        case Left(e) => await(IO(b.close))(_ => Halt(e))
        case Right(line) =>
          if (line eq null) Halt(End)
          else Emit(line, next)
      }
      next
    case Left(e) => Halt(e)
  }
```

Handle forcible termination or termination due to an error.

The `readLine` function on `BufferedReader` returns `null` when it reaches the end of file.

Then we can use `runLog(p)` to get all the lines in the file `lines.txt` as an `IO[IndexedSeq[String]]`.

Note that we're making sure that the file is closed regardless of how the process terminates. In section 15.3.2, we'll discuss how to ensure that all such processes close the resources they use (they're *resource-safe*), and discover a few generic combinators for ensuring resource safety.

EXERCISE 15.10

The `runLog` function can be defined more generally for any `Monad` in which it's possible to catch and raise exceptions (for instance, the `Task` type mentioned in chapter 13, which adds this capability to the `IO` type). Define this more general version of `runLog`. Note that this interpreter can't be tail-recursive, and relies on the underlying monad for stack safety.

```
trait Process[F[_],O] {
  def runLog(implicit F: MonadCatch[F]): F[IndexedSeq[O]]
  ...
}

trait MonadCatch[F[_]] extends Monad[F] {
  def attempt[A](a: F[A]): F[Either[Throwable,A]]
  def fail[A](t: Throwable): F[A]
}
```

15.3.2 *Ensuring resource safety*

`Process[IO,O]` can be used for talking to external resources like files and database connections, but we must take care to ensure resource safety—we want all file handles to be closed, database connections released, and so on, even (especially!) if exceptions occur. Let's look at what we need to make this happen. We already have most of the machinery in place. The `Await` constructor's `recv` argument can handle errors, choosing to clean up if necessary. And we're catching exceptions in `flatMap` and other relevant combinators so we can ensure that we gracefully pass them to `recv`. All we have to do is make sure that the `recv` function actually calls the necessary cleanup code.

To make the discussion concrete, suppose we have `lines: Process[IO,String]` representing the lines of some large file. This is a *source* or *producer*, and it implicitly references a resource (a file handle) that we want to ensure is closed regardless of how this producer is consumed.

When should we close this file handle? At the very end of our program? No, ideally we'd close the file once we know we're done reading from `lines`. We're certainly done if we reach the last line of the file—at that point there are no more values to produce and it's safe to close the file. So this gives us our first simple rule to follow: *A producer should free any underlying resources as soon as it knows it has no further values to produce, whether due to normal exhaustion or an exception.*

This isn't sufficient though, because the *consumer* of a process may itself decide to terminate consumption early. Consider `runLog { lines("names.txt") |> take(5) }`. The `take(5)` process will halt early after only five elements have been received, possibly before the file has been exhausted. In this case, we want to make sure before halting that any necessary resource freeing is run before the overall process completes. Note that `runLog` can't be responsible for this, since `runLog` has no idea that the `Process` it's interpreting is internally composed of two other `Process` values, one of which requires finalization.

Thus, we have our second simple rule to follow: *Any process d that consumes values from another process p must ensure that cleanup actions of p are run before d halts.*

This sounds rather error prone, but luckily we get to deal with this concern in just a single place, the `|>` combinator. We'll show how that works in section 15.3.3, when we show how to encode single-input processes using our general `Process` type.

So to summarize, a process `p` may terminate due to the following:

- Producer exhaustion, signaled by `End`, when the underlying source has no further values to emit
- Forcible termination, signaled by `Kill`, due to the consumer of `p` indicating it's finished consuming, possibly before the producer `p` is exhausted
- Abnormal termination due to some `e: Throwable` in either the producer or consumer

And no matter the cause, we want to close the underlying resource(s) in each case.

Now that we have our guidelines, how do we actually implement this? We need to make sure the `recv` function in the `Await` constructor always runs the "current" set of cleanup actions when it receives a `Left`. Let's introduce a new combinator, `onComplete`, which lets us append logic to a `Process` that will be run regardless of how the first `Process` terminates. The definition is similar to `++`, with one twist:

```
def onComplete(p: => Process[F,O]): Process[F,O] =    ←    Like ++, but always
  this.onHalt {                                             runs p, even if this
    case End => p.asFinalizer          ←——————— Helper function    halts with an error.
    case err => p.asFinalizer ++ Halt(err)
  }
```

The `p` process is always run when `this` halts, but we take care to re-raise any errors that occur (rather than swallowing them) after running the cleanup action. The `asFinalizer` method converts a "normal" `Process` to one that will invoke itself when given `Kill`. The definition is subtle, but we use this to ensure that in `p1.onComplete(p2)`, `p2` is always run, even if the consumer of the stream wishes to terminate early:

```
def asFinalizer: Process[F,O] = this match {
  case Emit(h, t) => Emit(h, t.asFinalizer)
  case Halt(e) => Halt(e)
  case Await(req,recv) => await(req) {
    case Left(Kill) => this.asFinalizer
    case x => recv(x)
  }
}
```

Putting all this together, we can use the `onComplete` combinator to create a resource-safe `Process[IO,O]` backed by the lines of a file. We define it in terms of the more general combinator, `resource`:

```
def resource[R,O](acquire: IO[R])(
                  use: R => Process[IO,O])(
                  release: R => Process[IO,O]): Process[IO,O] =
  await[IO,R,O](acquire)(r => use(r).onComplete(release(r)))
```

■ **EXERCISE 15.11**

This idiom of using `await` to "evaluate" the result of some `IO` action isn't specific to `IO`. Implement the generic combinator `eval` to promote some `F[A]` to a `Process` that emits only the result of that `F[A]`. Also implement `eval_`, which promotes an `F[A]` to a `Process`, emitting no values. Note that implementing these functions doesn't require knowing anything about `F`.

```
def eval[F[_],A](a: F[A]): Process[F,A]

def eval_[F[_],A,B](a: F[A]): Process[F,B]
```

And now here is `lines`:

```
def lines(filename: String): Process[IO,String] =
  resource
    { IO(io.Source.fromFile(filename)) }
    { src =>
        lazy val iter = src.getLines // a stateful iterator
        def step = if (iter.hasNext) Some(iter.next) else None
        lazy val lines: Process[IO,String] = eval(IO(step)).flatMap {
          case None => Halt(End)
          case Some(line) => Emit(line, lines)
        }
        lines
    }
    { src => eval_ { IO(src.close) } }
```

The `resource` combinator, using `onComplete`, ensures that our underlying resource is freed regardless of how the process is terminated. The only thing we need to ensure is that `|>` and other consumers of `lines` gracefully terminate it when they're finished consuming. We'll address this next, when we redefine single-input processes and implement the `|>` combinator for our generalized `Process` type.

15.3.3 *Single-input processes*

We now have nice, resource-safe sources, but we don't yet have any way to apply transformations to them. Fortunately, our `Process` type can also represent the single-input processes we introduced earlier in this chapter. To represent `Process1[I,O]`, we craft an appropriate `F` that only allows the `Process` to make requests for elements of type `I`. Let's look at how this works—the encoding is unusual in Scala, but there's nothing fundamentally new here:

```
case class Is[I]() {
  sealed trait f[X]
  val Get = new f[I] {}
}
```

It's strange to define the trait `f` inside of `Is`. Let's unpack what's going on. Note that `f` takes one parameter, `X`, but we have just one instance, `Get`, which fixes `X` to be the `I` in the outer `Is[I]`. Therefore, the type `Is[I]#f`[8] can only ever be a request for a value of type `I`! Given the type `Is[I]#f[A]`, Scala will complain with a type error unless the type A *is* the type `I`. Now that we have all this, we can define `Process1` as just a type alias:

```
type Process1[I,O] = Process[Is[I]#f, O]
```

To see what's going on, it helps to substitute the definition of `Is[I]#f` into a call to `Await`:

```
case class Await[A,O](
  req: Is[I]#f[A], recv: Either[Throwable,A] => Process[Is[I]#f,O]
) extends Process[Is[I]#f,R]
```

---

[8] Note on syntax: recall that if x is a type, x#foo references the type foo defined inside x.

From the definition of Is[I]#f, we can see that req can only be Get: f[I], the only value of this type. Therefore, I and A must be the same type, so recv must accept an I as its argument, which means that Await can only be used to request I values. This is important to understand—if this explanation didn't make sense, try working through these definitions on paper, substituting the type definitions.

Our Process1 alias supports all the same operations as our old single-input Process. Let's look at a couple. We first introduce a few helper functions to improve type inference when calling the Process constructors.

Listing 15.7   Type inference helper functions

```
def await1[I,O](
    recv: I => Process1[I,O],
    fallback: Process1[I,O] = halt1[I,O]): Process1[I, O] =
  Await(Get[I], (e: Either[Throwable,I]) => e match {
    case Left(End) => fallback
    case Left(err) => Halt(err)
    case Right(i) => Try(recv(i))
  })

def emit1[I,O](h: O, tl: Process1[I,O] = halt1[I,O]): Process1[I,O] =
  emit(h, tl)

def halt1[I,O]: Process1[I,O] = Halt[Is[I]#f, O](End)
```

Using these, our definitions of combinators like lift and filter look almost identical to before, except they return a Process1:

```
def lift[I,O](f: I => O): Process1[I,O] =
  await1[I,O](i => emit(f(i))) repeat

def filter[I](f: I => Boolean): Process1[I,I] =
  await1[I,I](i => if (f(i)) emit(i) else halt1) repeat
```

Let's look at process composition next. The implementation looks similar to before, but we make sure to run the latest cleanup action of the left process before the right process halts:

If this has halted, do the appropriate cleanup.

Before halting, gracefully terminate this, using ++ to preserve the first error, if any occurred.

```
def |>[O2](p2: Process1[O,O2]): Process[F,O2] = {
  p2 match {
    case Halt(e) => this.kill onHalt { Halt(e) ++ Halt(e2) }
    case Emit(h, t) => Emit(h, this |> t)
    case Await(req,recv) => this match {
      case Halt(err) => Halt(err) |> recv(Left(err))
      case Emit(h,t) => t |> Try(recv(Right(h)))
      case Await(req0,recv0) => await(req0)(recv0 andThen (_ |> p2))
    }
  }
}
def pipe[O2](p2: Process1[O,O2]): Process[F,O2] =
  this |> p2
```

We use a helper function, `kill`—it feeds the `Kill` exception to the outermost `Await` of a `Process` but ignores any of its remaining output.

Listing 15.8 `kill` helper function

```
@annotation.tailrec
final def kill[O2]: Process[F,O2] = this match {
  case Await(req,recv) => recv(Left(Kill)).drain.onHalt {
    case Kill => Halt(End)          ←
    case e => Halt(e)                     We convert the Kill
  }                                       exception back to
  case Halt(e) => Halt(e)                 normal termination.
  case Emit(h, t) => t.kill
}

final def drain[O2]: Process[F,O2] = this match {
  case Halt(e) => Halt(e)
  case Emit(h, t) => t.drain
  case Await(req,recv) => Await(req, recv andThen (_.drain))
}
```

Note that `|>` is defined for any `Process[F,O]` type, so this operation works for transforming a `Process1` value, an effectful `Process[IO,O]`, and the two-input `Process` type we'll discuss next.

With `|>`, we can add convenience functions on `Process` for attaching various `Process1` transformations to the output. For instance, here's `filter`, defined for any `Process[F,O]`:

```
def filter(f: O => Boolean): Process[F,O] =
  this |> Process.filter(f)
```

We can add similar convenience functions for `take`, `takeWhile`, and so on. See the chapter code for more examples.

15.3.4 *Multiple input streams*

Imagine if we wanted to "zip" together two files full of temperatures in degrees Fahrenheit, `f1.txt` and `f2.txt`, add corresponding temperatures together, convert the result to Celsius, apply a five-element moving average, and output the results one at a time to `celsius.txt`.

We can address these sorts of scenarios with our general `Process` type. Much like effectful sources and `Process1` were just specific instances of our general `Process` type, a `Tee`, which combines two input streams in some way,[9] can also be expressed as a `Process`. Once again, we simply craft an appropriate choice of `F`:

```
case class T[I,I2]() {
  sealed trait f[X] { def get: Either[I => X, I2 => X] }
  val L = new f[I] { def get = Left(identity) }
```

---

[9] The name *Tee* comes from the letter *T*, which approximates a diagram merging two inputs (the top of the T) into a single output.

```
    val R = new f[I2] { def get = Right(identity) }
}
def L[I,I2] = T[I,I2]().L
def R[I,I2] = T[I,I2]().R
```

This looks similar to our `Is` type from earlier, except that we now have two possible values, `L` and `R`, and we get an `Either[I => X, I2 => X]` to distinguish between the two types of requests during pattern matching.[10] With `T`, we can now define a type alias, `Tee`, for processes that accept two different types of inputs:

```
type Tee[I,I2,O] = Process[T[I,I2]#f, O]
```

Once again, we define a few convenience functions for building these particular types of `Process`.

Listing 15.9 Convenience functions for each input in a `Tee`

```
def haltT[I,I2,O]: Tee[I,I2,O] =
  Halt[T[I,I2]#f,O](End)

def awaitL[I,I2,O](
    recv: I => Tee[I,I2,O],
    fallback: => Tee[I,I2,O] = haltT[I,I2,O]): Tee[I,I2,O] =
  await[T[I,I2]#f,I,O](L) {
    case Left(End) => fallback
    case Left(err) => Halt(err)
    case Right(a) => Try(recv(a))
  }

def awaitR[I,I2,O](
    recv: I2 => Tee[I,I2,O],
    fallback: => Tee[I,I2,O] = haltT[I,I2,O]): Tee[I,I2,O] =
  await[T[I,I2]#f,I2,O](R) {
    case Left(End) => fallback
    case Left(err) => Halt(err)
    case Right(a) => Try(recv(a))
  }

def emitT[I,I2,O](h: O, tl: Tee[I,I2,O] = haltT[I,I2,O]): Tee[I,I2,O] =
  emit(h, tl)
```

Let's define some `Tee` combinators. Zipping is a special case of `Tee`—we read from the left, then the right (or vice versa), and then emit the pair. Note that we get to be explicit about the order we read from the inputs, a capability that can be important when a `Tee` is talking to streams with external effects:[11]

---

[10] The functions `I => X` and `I2 => X` inside the `Either` are a simple form of *equality witness*, which is just a *value* that provides evidence that one type is equal to another.

[11] We may also wish to be *inexplicit* about the order of the effects, allowing the driver to choose nondeterministically and allowing for the possibility that the driver will execute both effects concurrently. See the chapter notes for some additional discussion.

```
def zipWith[I,I2,O](f: (I,I2) => O): Tee[I,I2,O] =
  awaitL[I,I2,O](i =>
  awaitR          (i2 => emitT(f(i,i2)))) repeat

def zip[I,I2]: Tee[I,I2,(I,I2)] = zipWith((_,_))
```

This transducer will halt as soon as either input is exhausted, just like the zip function on List. There are lots of other Tee combinators we could write. Nothing requires that we read values from each input in lockstep. We could read from one input until some condition is met and then switch to the other; read 5 values from the left and then 10 values from the right; read a value from the left and then use it to determine how many values to read from the right, and so on.

We'll typically want to feed a Tee by connecting it to two processes. We can define a function on Process that combines *two* processes using a Tee. It's analogous to |> and works similarly. This function works for any Process type.

Listing 15.10 The tee function

Emit any leading values and then recurse.

We check whether the request is for the left or right side.

There are values available, so feed them to the Tee.

It's a request from the right Process, and we get a witness that recv takes an O2. Otherwise, this case is exactly analogous.

If t halts, gracefully kill off both inputs.

It's a request from the left Process, and we get a witness that recv takes an O.

The Tee is requesting input from the left, which is halted, so halt.

No values are currently available, so wait for a value, and then continue with the tee operation.

```
def tee[O2,O3](p2: Process[F,O2])(t: Tee[O,O2,O3]): Process[F,O3] =
  t match {
    case Halt(e) => this.kill onComplete p2.kill onComplete Halt(e)
    case Emit(h,t) => Emit(h, (this tee p2)(t))
    case Await(side, recv) => side.get match {
      case Left(isO) => this match {
        case Halt(e) => p2.kill onComplete Halt(e)
        case Emit(o,ot) => (ot tee p2)(Try(recv(Right(o))))
        case Await(reqL, recvL) =>
          await(reqL)(recvL andThen (this2 => this2.tee(p2)(t)))
      }
      case Right(isO2) => p2 match {
        case Halt(e) => this.kill onComplete Halt(e)
        case Emit(o2,ot) => (this tee ot)(Try(recv(Right(o2))))
        case Await(reqR, recvR) =>
          await(reqR)(recvR andThen (p3 => this.tee(p3)(t)))
      }
    }
  }
```

15.3.5   *Sinks*

How do we perform output using our `Process` type? We'll often want to send the output of a `Process[IO,O]` to some *sink* (perhaps sending a `Process[IO,String]` to an output file). Somewhat surprisingly, we can represent a sink as a process that *emits functions*:

```
type Sink[F[_],O] = Process[F[_], O => Process[F,Unit]]
```

This makes a certain kind of sense. A `Sink[F[_], O]` provides a sequence of functions to call with the input type `O`. The function returns `Process[F,Unit]`. Let's look at a `Sink` that writes strings to a file:

```
def fileW(file: String, append: Boolean = false): Sink[IO,String] =
  resource[FileWriter, String => Process[IO,Unit]]
    { IO { new FileWriter(file, append) }}
    { w => constant { (s: String) => eval[IO,Unit](IO(w.write(s))) }}
    { w => eval_(IO(w.close)) }

def constant[A](a: A): Process[IO,A] =      ⟵——————— The infinite, constant stream
  eval[IO,A](IO(a)).repeat
```

That was easy. And notice what *isn't* included—there's no exception handling code here—the combinators we're using guarantee that the `FileWriter` will be closed if exceptions occur or when whatever is feeding the `Sink` signals it's done.

We can use `tee` to implement a combinator `to`, a method on `Process` which pipes its output to a `Sink`:

```
def to[O2](sink: Sink[F,O]): Process[F,Unit] =
  join { (this zipWith sink)((o,f) => f(o)) }
```

■ **EXERCISE 15.12**

The definition of `to` uses a new combinator, `join`, defined for any `Process`, which concatenates a nested `Process`. Implement `join` using existing primitives. This combinator should be quite familiar to you from previous chapters.

```
def join[F[_],O](p: Process[F, Process[F,O]]): Process[F,O]
```

Using `to`, we can now write programs like the following:

```
val converter: Process[IO,Unit] =
  lines("fahrenheit.txt").
  filter(!_.startsWith("#")).
  map(line => fahrenheitToCelsius(line.toDouble).toString).
  pipe(intersperse("\n")).
  to(fileW("celsius.txt")).
  drain
```

This uses the helper function `drain`, which just ignores all output of a `Process`:

```
final def drain[O2]: Process[F,O2] = this match {
  case Halt(e) => Halt(e)
  case Emit(h, t) => t.drain
  case Await(req,recv) => Await(req, recv andThen (_.drain))
}
```

When run via `runLog`, `converter` will open the input file and the output file and incrementally transform the input stream, ignoring commented lines.

15.3.6 *Effectful channels*

We can generalize `to` to allow responses other than `Unit`. The implementation is identical! It turns out that the operation just has a more general type than we gave it. Let's call the more general operation `through`:

```
def through[O2](p2: Process[F, O => Process[F,O2]]): Process[F,O2] =
  join { (this zipWith p2)((o,f) => f(o)) }
```

Let's introduce a type alias for this pattern:

```
type Channel[F[_],I,O] = Process[F, I => Process[F,O]]
```

`Channel` is useful when a pure pipeline must execute some I/O action as one of its stages. A typical example might be an application that needs to execute database queries. It would be nice if our database queries could return a `Process[IO,Row]`, where `Row` is some representation of a database row. This would allow the program to process the result set of a query using all the fancy stream transducers we've built up so far.

Here's a signature for a simple query executor, which uses `Map[String,Any]` as the (untyped) row representation (see the chapter code for the implementation):

```
import java.sql.{Connection, PreparedStatement, ResultSet}

def query(conn: IO[Connection]):
    Channel[IO, Connection => PreparedStatement, Map[String,Any]]
```

We could certainly write a `Channel[PreparedStatement, Source[Map[String,Any]]]`, so why don't we? Because we don't want code that uses our `Channel` to have to worry about how to obtain a `Connection` (which is needed to build a `PreparedStatement`). That dependency is managed entirely by the `Channel` itself, which also takes care of closing the connection when it's finished executing queries.

15.3.7 *Dynamic resource allocation*

Realistic programs may need to allocate resources dynamically, while transforming some input stream. For example, we may encounter scenarios like the following:

- *Dynamic resource allocation*—Read a file, `fahrenheits.txt`, containing a list of filenames. Concatenate these files into a single logical stream, convert this stream to Celsius, and output the joined stream to `celsius.txt`.

- *Multi-sink output*—Similar to dynamic resource allocation, but rather than producing a single output file, produce an output file for each input file in `fahrenheits.txt`. Name the output file by appending `.celsius` onto the input file name.

Can these capabilities be incorporated into our definition of `Process` in a way that preserves resource safety? Yes, they can! We actually already have the power to do these things, using the `flatMap` combinator that we've already defined for an arbitrary `Process` type.

For instance, `flatMap` plus our existing combinators let us write this first scenario as follows:

```
val convertAll: Process[IO,Unit] = (for {
  out <- fileW("celsius.txt").once        ←——  Trim the stream to, at
  file <- lines("fahrenheits.txt")              most, a single element;
  _ <- lines(file).                             see chapter code.
      map(line => fahrenheitToCelsius(line.toDouble)).
      flatMap(celsius => out(celsius.toString)).
} yield ()) drain
```

This code is completely resource-safe—all file handles will be closed automatically by the runner as soon as they're finished, even in the presence of exceptions. Any exceptions encountered will be thrown to the `runLog` function when invoked.

We can write to multiple files just by switching the order of the calls to `flatMap`:

```
val convertMultisink: Process[IO,Unit] = (for {
  file <- lines("fahrenheits.txt")
  _ <- lines(file).
      map(line => fahrenheitToCelsius(line.toDouble)).
      map(_ toString).
      to(fileW(file + ".celsius"))
} yield ()) drain
```

And of course, we can attach transformations, mapping, filtering, and so on at any point in the process:

```
val convertMultisink2: Process[IO,Unit] = (for {
  file <- lines("fahrenheits.txt")
  _ <- lines(file).
      filter(!_.startsWith("#")).
      map(line => fahrenheitToCelsius(line.toDouble)).
      filter(_ > 0). // ignore below zero temperatures
      map(_ toString).
      to(fileW(file + ".celsius"))
} yield ()) drain
```

There are additional examples using this library in the chapter code.

15.4 Applications

The ideas presented in this chapter are widely applicable. A surprising number of programs can be cast in terms of stream processing—once you're aware of the abstraction, you begin seeing it everywhere. Let's look at some domains where it's applicable:

- *File I/O*—We've already demonstrated how to use stream processing for file I/O. Although we've focused on line-by-line reading and writing for the examples here, we can also use the library for processing binary files.

- *Message processing, state machines, and actors*—Large systems are often organized as a system of loosely coupled components that communicate via message passing. These systems are often expressed in terms of *actors*, which communicate via explicit message sends and receives. We can express components in these architectures as stream processors. This lets us describe extremely complex state machines and behaviors using a high-level, compositional API.

- *Servers, web applications*—A web application can be thought of as converting a stream of HTTP requests to a stream of HTTP responses.

- *UI programming*—We can view individual UI events such as mouse clicks as streams, and the UI as one large network of stream processors determining how the UI responds to user interaction.

- *Big data, distributed systems*—Stream-processing libraries can be *distributed* and *parallelized* for processing large amounts of data. The key insight here is that the nodes of a stream-processing network need not all live on the same machine.

If you're curious to learn more about these applications (and others), see the chapter notes for additional discussion and links to further reading. The chapter notes and code also discuss some extensions to the `Process` type we discussed here, including the introduction of *nondeterministic choice*, which allows for concurrent evaluation in the execution of a `Process`.

15.5 Summary

We began this book with a simple premise: that we assemble our programs using only pure functions. From this sole premise and its consequences, we were led to explore a completely new approach to programming that's both coherent and principled. In this final chapter, we constructed a library for stream processing and incremental I/O, demonstrating that we can retain the compositional style developed throughout this book even for programs that interact with the outside world. Our story, of how to use FP to architect programs both large and small, is now complete.

FP is a deep subject, and we've only scratched the surface. By now you should have everything you need to continue the journey on your own, to make functional programming a part of your own work. Though good design is always difficult, expressing your code functionally will become effortless over time. As you apply FP to more problems, you'll discover new patterns and more powerful abstractions.

Enjoy the journey, keep learning, and good luck!

index